AFTER WAR

AFTER WAR

*The Political Economy of
Exporting Democracy*

Christopher J. Coyne

STANFORD ECONOMICS AND FINANCE
An Imprint of Stanford University Press
Stanford, California

Stanford University Press
Stanford, California

Library of Congress Cataloging-in-Publication Data

Coyne, Christopher J.
  The political economy of exporting democracy / Christopher J. Coyne.
    p. cm.
  Includes bibliographical references and index.
  ISBN-13: 978-0-8047-5439-2 (cloth : alk. paper)
  ISBN-13: 978-0-8047-5440-8 (pbk. : alk. paper)
  1. Postwar reconstruction—Economic aspects. 2. Imperialism—Economic aspects. 3. Democracy—United States—Economic aspects. 4. United States—Military policy—Economic aspects. 5. United States—Foreign economic relations. I. Title.
  HB195.C697 2007
  338.91—dc22
                              2007019280

Typeset by Bruce Lundquist in 10/14 Minion

For my parents

Contents

Acknowledgments

I N UNDERTAKING the research and writing of this book, I have bene-
fited from useful discussion and comments from Scott Beaulier, Tony
Carilli, Emily Chamlee-Wright, Greg Dempster, Jack Goldstone, David Hen-
derson, Jeff Hummel, Justin Isaacs, Claire Morgan, Ben Powell, Frederic Sautet,
Jeremy Schwartz, Russ Sobel, Virgil Storr, Ed Stringham, and Richard Wagner.
I would also like to thank Alan Harvey, Martha Cooley, Margo Beth Crouppen,
Sarah Ives, and Jared Smith at Stanford University Press for their assistance.

Parts of this book were presented at the Economics Seminar Series at
West Virginia University; the Workshop in Applied Political Economy at San
Jose State University; The Mercatus Center at George Mason University; The
Workshop in Philosophy, Politics and Economics at George Mason Univer-
sity; The Colloquium on Market Institutions & Economic Processes at New
York University; and the conference "Mr. Jefferson Goes to the Middle East" at
Grove City College. I am grateful to the participants for their comments and
suggestions.

I owe special thanks to Peter Leeson for providing useful discussion and
detailed comments throughout the preparation of this manuscript. I am grateful to Tyler Cowen for initially encouraging me to pursue this line of research
as well as for his comments and suggestions. My greatest thanks go to Peter
Boettke, who has been a source of encouragement, discussion, comments, and
suggestions from the inception of this project. Finally, I am grateful to my
wife, Sara, for her constant support throughout.

The Mercatus Center at George Mason University provided a post-doctoral fellowship including financial support and office space during the summer of 2006, when a large part of this book was written. I would like to especially thank Brian Hooks and Claire Morgan for organizing my visit. Financial support for this research from Hampden-Sydney College is also acknowledged.

1 Can Liberal Democracy
Be Exported at Gunpoint?

"We are led, by events and common sense, to one conclusion: The survival of liberty in our land increasingly depends on the success of liberty in other lands. The best hope for peace in our world is the expansion of freedom in all the world."

"[I]t is the policy of the United States to seek and support the growth of democratic movements and institutions in every nation and culture, with the ultimate goal of ending tyranny in our world."

—*George W. Bush, Inaugural Address, January 20, 2005*[1]

O N FEBRUARY 15, 1898, the battleship *USS Maine* exploded and sank in the port of Havana, Cuba. This event occurred at the same time that support was increasing among Americans for military intervention in Cuba. Civil violence between Spanish occupiers and Cuban rebels seeking independence was ongoing within the Spanish colony, and public opinion in the United States concerning this situation was largely shaped by the spread of often exaggerated stories in the major newspapers detailing the inhumane treatment of Cubans by the Spanish.[2] Debate continues to this day about the cause of the explosion on the *USS Maine*, but the papers at the time claimed it was an act of sabotage by the Spanish. In fact, with such headlines as "Remember the *Maine!*" serving as rallying cries for those in favor of intervention, U.S. public opinion supporting military action reached an all-time high.

With public opinion behind him, President William McKinley asked Congress on April 11, 1898 for the authority to send troops to Cuba to end the civil unrest. In addition to the reported inhumane treatment of Cubans, however, McKinley's greater, and unspoken, concern was the protection of American economic interests.[3] Eight days later, Congress passed a joint resolution proclaiming Cuba to be "free and independent" and calling for a complete Spanish withdrawal.

The resolution also authorized the president to use as much force as necessary in achieving this goal. The Teller Amendment to the resolution indicated that it was not the intentions of the United States to control Cuba and made clear that, once the U.S. military defeated the Spanish occupiers, Cubans would be granted their freedom. On April 25, Congress officially declared a state of war between the United States and Spain.

In a series of battles with the Spanish naval fleet, the United States quickly gained control of the waterways around Cuba, preventing Spanish ground troops from receiving additional supplies and support, and within a month, Cuba was securely under U.S. control. The signing of the Treaty of Paris in December 1898 marked the official end of the war. Per the terms of the treaty, Spain relinquished Puerto Rico and Guam to the United States while sovereignty of the Philippines was transferred to the United States for $20 million. In addition, Spain ceded its claim to Cuba, but as per the Teller Amendment, the United States did not assume permanent control.

Despite the fact that it never assumed official sovereignty over Cuba, however, the U.S. military continued its occupation through 1902, serving as the active government. During the occupation, the United States built infrastructure, including public sanitation, an education system, and a postal service. In 1900, a constitution was drafted and municipal elections were held. Under U.S. pressure, a series of amendments were attached to the constitution that simultaneously allowed the United States the ability to influence Cuban policy while disengaging from daily operations of the country in order to comply with the letter of the Teller Amendment if not its spirit.

One such amendment to the constitution, the Platt Amendment, provided the conditions for the withdrawal of U.S. troops from Cuba. The amendment also granted the United States control of Guantánamo Bay, a naval base, which somewhat infamously, or perhaps notoriously, it continues to utilize to this day. It also restricted Cuba from transferring land to any nation other than the United States. Finally, the amendment provided rules regarding Cuba's ability to float foreign debt and enter into treaties with non-U.S. countries. Perhaps most important, the Platt Amendment specified that the United States could intervene in Cuban affairs whenever the U.S. government deemed it appropriate. With the adoption of the constitution, U.S. troops were withdrawn in 1902, and Tomás Estrada Palma, a strong supporter of the initial U.S. intervention and of U.S. policy regarding Cuba in general, became Cuba's first president on May 20 of that year.[4]

The American occupation of Cuba was important for several reasons. As highlighted above, it was the catalyst for Cuba's independence from Spain, but more important from a U.S. foreign policy perspective, the occupation marked one of the first U.S. attempts to shape political, economic, and social outcomes via military intervention and occupation. The experience in Cuba marked the beginning of a trend of intervention and occupation that has continued into the twenty-first century with the occupation of Iraq and Afghanistan.

The United States would utilize the stipulations of the Platt Amendment twice more over the twenty-year period following the initial occupation. In 1906, the United States again occupied Cuba to surpress civil insurgency. President Estrada Palma's reelection was met with violent opposition from the Liberals (the National Liberals and the Republic Liberals), and the U.S. occupation, which lasted until 1909, focused on restoring order and establishing a new democratic government in the wake of Estrada Palma's eventual resignation. Yet another U.S. occupation of Cuba occurred from 1917 to 1922 due to an uprising inspired by the Russian Revolution. The U.S. military was charged with ending the uprising and protecting U.S. property and interests.

If the goal of this series of U.S. occupations in Cuba was to plant the seeds of a sustaining liberal democratic government that would ultimately become a long-term ally of the United States, one must obviously consider it a failure. Since the end of the last U.S. occupation in 1922, Cuba has had several short-lived governments followed by the emergence of two oppressive dictatorships, those of Fulgencio Batista (1940–1959) and Fidel Castro (1959–present).

Over two decades after the United States exited Cuba for the final time, at the conclusion of World War II, the United States engaged in the most ambitious effort in its history of democratizing war-torn countries with the occupation and reconstruction of West Germany and Japan. In both cases, the outcome was drastically different than that in Cuba. In both West Germany and Japan, military occupiers were able to successfully transform war-torn countries into liberal democracies that have survived to this day.

In May of 1945, Germany surrendered unconditionally to the Allied forces. Leaders from the Allied countries had gathered in a series of conferences both before and after Germany's surrender to determine a common occupation policy. The main tenets of this policy were that Germany would be partitioned and each Allied power would control a zone, Nazism would be abolished, the country would be democratized, war criminals would be punished, and reparations would be paid. The United States would carry out the reconstruction of its Western zone from 1945–1955.

The physical infrastructure, economy, and morale of the German people had been devastated by the war. During the occupation of its zone, the United States disbanded the government and assumed control of the provision of public goods at the municipal and local level and managed administrative and budgetary functions. Despite the destruction of the country, economic recovery occurred relatively quickly. Although there were many economic ups and downs, annual economic indicators showed double-digit growth in the GDP of West Germany from 1947 to 1952.[5] Historians and policymakers continue to debate the factors that contributed to this recovery. Some attribute it to the aid delivered under the Marshall Plan, and others emphasize the currency and fiscal reforms of Ludwig Erhard as the catalyst of the recovery.[6] Whatever one concludes on this issue, few would disagree that the reconstruction effort was able to transform West Germany into a liberal democracy. This is not to indicate that the reconstruction process did not suffer any setbacks. The process was far from smooth, both within each zone and also across zones. Progress occurred at different rates and on different margins, but overall, if the standard against which the reconstruction of West Germany is judged is the sustainability of the reconstructed orders, it must be deemed a success.

Although the specifics of the U.S. experience in Japan were clearly different, the outcome was very similar to that of West Germany. Following the use of nuclear bombs on Hiroshima and Nagasaki, Japanese officials surrendered unconditionally in September 1945. As with Germany, Japan's infrastructure, economy, and morale had been severely damaged during the war. The terms of Japan's surrender had been determined by the United States, the United Kingdom, and China at the Potsdam Conference in July of 1945. In addition to unconditional surrender, the Potsdam Declaration required the purging of certain government officials, as well as the democratization of Japan; military disarmament; and the establishment of freedom of thought, speech, and religion.

Despite the fact that several countries agreed to the terms of surrender at Potsdam, the Supreme Commander for the Allied Powers, U.S. General Douglas MacArthur, directed the occupation unilaterally. He decided basic policies and utilized his position of power to implement them. The unilateral power of the United States in Japan during this period is evidenced by the fact that no other Allied nation challenged U.S. authority during the reconstruction process.[7] MacArthur orchestrated sweeping and drastic changes throughout Japanese society, including within the government and civil administration, the economy, civil society, the education system, and the military. In the process, MacArthur achieved icon-like status among the Japanese populace.[8] A new constitution was drafted over a relatively short period of time and went into effect in May 1947. According to the guidelines of the constitution, the emperor lost all military and political power and became a figurehead of the state. As with Germany, there were many bumps in the road, but most observers would agree that occupiers had established a sustainable liberal democracy by the time they exited Japan in April 1952.

The successful cases of Japan and West Germany have lasting importance. Not only do they exist in contrast to the failures in Cuba, these cases laid the groundwork for the perception that the United States had the ability to successfully export liberal democracy at gunpoint. Indeed, the United States undertook several subsequent efforts to export liberal democracy during the Cold War, including to Vietnam, Cambodia, and the Dominican Republic. Although these attempts largely failed, efforts to establish liberal democracy abroad continue to this day.

In October 2001, the United States began military operations in Afghanistan in response to the September 11, 2001, attacks on the World Trade Center and the Pentagon. The aim of the operation was to eliminate the Taliban government and the al-Qaeda organization. Military operations were swift and effective. With the assistance of the Northern Alliance, the United States gained control of Kabul, the capital city of Afghanistan.[9] In December 2001, representatives from the United States and the Northern Alliance as well as expatriate Afghan leaders met in Bonn, Germany. The result of the conference, the Bonn Agreement, outlined a roadmap and timetable for bringing peace, stability, and democracy to Afghanistan. In January 2004, Afghanistan's constitutional *Loya Jirga* approved a new constitution.

In March 2003, while U.S. forces were still attempting to reconstruct Afghanistan along the guidelines put forth in the Bonn Agreement, the United States began a military operation in Iraq. The specific aim of the operation was to overthrow the regime of Saddam Hussein and replace it with a liberal democracy. The hope was, or seemed to be, that establishing democracy in Iraq would have positive spillover effects for the rest of the Middle East. The 2003 operation, much like the earlier U.S. military operation in Iraq in January 1991, went smoothly and met little resistance. The United States, with superior military technology and leadership, was able to topple the comparatively poorly trained and ill-equipped Iraqi army quickly. The result was the collapse of the Hussein regime. President Bush publicly declared on April 16, 2003, that Iraq had been "liberated."[10]

As of this writing, the situations in Afghanistan and Iraq continue to unfold. It is too early to determine with certainty whether these reconstructions will achieve their desired end of creating sustaining liberal democracies. However, while the initial military operations in both countries were successful, the aftermath has been a different story. In both cases, the existing governing regimes were easily toppled, but subsequent reconstruction efforts have been met with strong resistance.[11] Dispersed pockets of insurgents located throughout each country characterize the nature of the resistance—there is no longer a central enemy that can be confronted head-on. Moreover, costs—both monetary and human—have substantially exceeded initial predictions. Further, public opinion in the United States seems to be turning against prolonging the occupations, and support is increasing for withdrawal sooner rather than later.[12] It may take several years, or even decades, before the outcomes of these efforts can be judged as successes or failures, but at least in the short term the likelihood of success is not looking good compared to what happened after World War II in West Germany and Japan.

These brief narratives are not meant to do justice to the complexities of the cases discussed. Instead, the purpose is to highlight the long and varied history of U.S. attempts to utilize military forces to occupy and reconstruct countries along liberal democratic lines. It is interesting to note that early failures in Cuba did not prevent the United States from further military intervention before and after World War II, and certainly West Germany and Japan are clear cases of successful reconstruction. However, the failure of a series of reconstruction efforts between the 1960s and the 1990s, coupled with the current difficulties in Afghanistan and Iraq, seems to call America's ability to export liberal democracy via military occupation into question.

Given the ongoing struggle in both Afghanistan and Iraq and the growing discontent among the U.S. electorate, we should expect the issues associated with reconstruction to remain at center stage for the foreseeable future. In August 2004, a new office—the Office of the Coordinator for Reconstruction and Stabilization—was created within the State Department to oversee U.S.-led reconstruction efforts. If the present paradigm is maintained in spite of the widely publicized logistical issues and changing public sentiment, we can safely assume that U.S. involvement in such efforts will only increase.

The effort to win the "war on terror" has been a driving force behind the emphasis on spreading democracy via military occupation. In this context, the underlying logic is that the spread of democracy will greatly reduce, if not eradicate, the terrorist threat. It is widely recognized that the major threat to the United States is no longer a few powerful countries, as during the Cold War, but instead the threat posed by countries lacking a strong and effective central government.[13] Reconstruction efforts attempt to remedy this situation by establishing the foundations of sustaining liberal democratic institutions.

Moreover, there is also an increasing call in the academic literature for the United States to embrace its role as an empire. A key advocate of this position, Niall Ferguson, contends that America should utilize its relative position of power in the world to impose liberal political and economic institutions in weak and failed states.[14] These efforts, Ferguson contends, should not be constrained by the "light footprint" approach to occupation, but instead should establish colonial administrations, when necessary, to achieve the desired ends. I will return to this "brute force" theory later, but for now, the key point is that there is good reason to believe that U.S. involvement in reconstruction efforts will continue beyond Afghanistan and Iraq.

Given the long history of U.S. reconstruction efforts, coupled with what is sure to be the continued relevance of the issue in the future, a central question comes to the forefront: Is military occupation and reconstruction an effective means for exporting liberal democracy? The purpose of this book is to answer that question. Looking at the historical record, and as noted in this chapter thus far, one observes some clear cases of success, such as the post–World War II reconstructions of Japan and West Germany, but the historical record also includes a large number of clear failures. I seek to contribute to our understanding of these drastically different outcomes. Specifically, my goal is to understand the precise mechanisms and contexts that contribute to or prevent success.

To pursue this line of inquiry, I will ask some fundamental questions about how economics can explain the logic of continued conflict as well as efforts by external parties to resolve those conflicts by establishing cooperation grounded in liberal democratic institutions. Why does conflict persist? What mechanisms facilitate, or impede, the transformation of conflict to cooperation? What constraints do occupiers face in the reconstruction process? Can occupiers cause more harm than good? Are there alternatives to reconstruction that can generate institutional and social change toward liberal institutions? Finding answers to these questions is critical to understanding the viability of reconstruction as an effective means of exporting liberal democracy.

I contend that the tools of economics can shed light on these questions by illuminating the ability of foreign powers to construct sustaining liberal democracies in weak, failed, and conflict-torn states. Economics can also offer insight into the process of social change. Sustainable social change requires a shift in underlying preferences. This shift can be influenced through brute force or through voluntary acceptance. I contend that the latter is more effective in generating liberal democracy. I further argue that a key mechanism for generating sustainable change is a commitment to free trade, not only in goods and services, but also in cultural products, ideas, and institutions. Unfortunately, throughout the history of U.S. foreign policy, including the recent occupations of Afghanistan and Iraq, emphasis has been placed on military occupation and reconstruction while inadequate attention has been paid to the alternative of exporting liberal values, ideas, and institutions through non-intervention, trade, and exchange.

What's Economics Got to Do with It?

For the most part, research regarding the fundamental questions stated in the previous section has been limited to the disciplines of history, political science, and public policy, and my primary aim is to contribute to this existing literature by employing the tools of economics. Reconstruction was a popular topic among some prominent twentieth-century economists, including Walter Heller, John Maynard Keynes, Ludwig von Mises, and Bertil Ohlin.[15] Nonetheless, few recent economists have turned their attention to this problem. To fill this gap, I seek to analyze the reconstruction process through an economic lens. I contend that doing so will contribute substantially to the ongoing debate regarding the ability of governments to effectively export sustainable liberal democracy via military occupation.

When one looks at the fundamental nature of the reconstruction process, it becomes evident that economic issues are of central importance. That is, postwar reconstruction requires the creation of political rules and can therefore be considered a problem in political economy. A central emphasis of political economy is "the reason of rules."[16] The underlying logic is that rules provide the parameters within which individuals can carry out private activities while simultaneously establishing the scope and strength of political institutions and the activities of political agents within those institutions.

Viewed from the perspective of political economy, the reconstruction process can be seen as an issue of incentive compatibility. Occupiers must establish the "rules of the game" but also ensure that institutions are in place that provide incentives for the populace of the reconstructed country to follow those rules once occupiers exit. As the economist Avner Greif emphasizes, institutions are patterns of behavior that persist because they provide incentives that lead people to behave in ways that reproduce those same patterns over time.[17] The economic view of successful reconstruction thus entails finding and establishing a set of incentives that make people prefer continuing within a liberal democratic order as compared to any available alternatives. Economic analysis can assist in understanding if the formal and informal rules and institutions of the reconstruction "game" provide such incentives.

A discussion and analysis of reconstruction must draw on knowledge from a wide range of disciplines. As an economist, I perhaps lack the insights a historian, political scientist, or regional expert might provide given their purviews. However, the tools of economics have not been used to examine the basic nature of the problems faced in reconstruction. A lack of theoretical understanding of the challenges involved in reconstruction has led to bad policy and repeated failures in efforts to reconstruct weak, failed, and conflict-torn states; hence this book.

To illuminate this last point, consider the growing literature that criticizes the current efforts in Iraq for a lack of foresight, planning, and execution.[18] The analysis provided here can assist in understanding not only the current situation in Iraq but also the limitations of future efforts to construct liberal democracies via military occupation. Applying the economic way of thinking to the topic of reconstruction will yield insights that are of interest not only to academics in a wide range of disciplines but also to policymakers as well.

What Does Reconstruction Entail?

For purposes of clarification, I should specify the terminology and assumptions that serve as the foundation for the analysis that follows. I define *reconstruction* as the rebuilding of both formal and informal institutions.[19] More specifically, the reconstruction process involves the restoration of physical infrastructure and facilities; minimal social services; and structural reform in the political, economic, social, and security sectors.

The terms *reconstruction, state building, nation building,* and *peacekeeping* are often used interchangeably. For my purpose, however, these terms capture overlapping but essentially different activities. Reconstruction requires rebuilding, and in some cases building from scratch, both formal and informal institutions in order to achieve fundamental political, economic, and social change. State building and nation building can be seen as a subset of reconstruction and involve transferring governance capabilities. Likewise, peacekeeping can be seen as a subset of reconstruction that involves stabilizing a conflict-torn society.

When I use the term *reconstruction,* I am referring to the process in its entirety, from the initial occupation through the exit of occupying forces, as well as the wide array of activities that occupiers undertake in the political, economic, and social arenas. The reconstruction process includes nation building, state building, and peacekeeping, but it also goes beyond these activities as well. It is possible for foreign governments to undertake nation building or peacekeeping missions without engaging in a broader reconstruction effort. For example, the operation in Somalia in the mid-1990s started as a humanitarian peacekeeping mission and only later became a broader effort at reconstruction.

Post-conflict reconstruction efforts can be categorized depending on the nature of the conflict that precedes the reconstruction. Categories would include civil wars or humanitarian efforts (for example, as in Somalia and Kosovo), the perceived threat of future conflict (as in Afghanistan and Iraq), or international wars (as in Germany and Japan). Within these various categories of conflict, one can further classify the role of the occupying power. At one extreme is long-term colonization and at the other extreme is liberation—and there is a range of possibilities in between.

Part of classifying the role of the occupying power involves clarifying the means used to achieve the desired ends. On the one extreme in this regard is the "brute force" approach, which emphasizes the complete domination of the post-conflict country using whatever force is necessary to impose liberal democratic institutions. At the other extreme is the "light footprint" approach, which places heavy emphasis on the involvement of local indigenous actors coupled with as little international presence as possible. Under the light-footprint approach, the role of international forces tends to be limited to peacekeeping-oriented operations, such as maintaining general order and stability. This does not mean that international forces are restrained from intervening in specific affairs as deemed necessary, but rather that such "hands-on" interventions are viewed as a last resort. These categorical distinctions will influence the issues involved in the reconstruction process and will be considered throughout the analysis.

I define ultimate success in the reconstruction process as the achievement of a self-sustaining liberal democratic, economic, and social order that does not rely on external monetary or military support.[20] A successful reconstruction does not require fully mature or "consolidated" institutions, but it does require that the seeds for such institutions be planted. In other words, several years after the exit of occupiers, we should observe movement toward a consolidated liberal democracy.

I take this goal as the given end of reconstruction efforts, meaning that I do not consider *whether* the end goal is itself good or bad. In the context of U.S. politics, the view that sustainable liberal democracy is critical to peace can be traced back to at least Woodrow Wilson, the twenty-eighth president of the United States, who sought to make "the world safe for democracy."[21] Historically, military occupation and reconstruction have been the means used to achieve this desired state of affairs.

Ultimate success does not necessarily mean military forces have entirely left the postwar country, however. For instance, the United States still has troops stationed in Japan and Germany. The main characteristic of a successful effort is the official end of the reconstruction by the occupiers, coupled with the sustainability of reconstructed political, economic, and social orders in the absence of military interventions or monetary support. For instance, neither Germany nor Japan would collapse if the United States withdrew existing forces currently stationed in those countries. If, in fact, a reconstructed country's institutions would unravel once troops exited or monetary or humanitarian aid ended, the reconstruction is deemed to have failed to achieve its goal.

Throughout the analysis I will be careful to use the term *liberal democracy.* As Fareed Zakaria has emphasized, "democracy" is often confused with "liberal democracy."[22] Democracy deals with the method of selecting government officials, while liberal democracy deals with the goals of government: the protection of individual rights, the rule of law, and so on. In the absence of constitutional liberalism, democracy will not necessarily yield the desired results as defined by U.S. foreign policy objectives. The election of Hitler in Germany or the elections in Iran, considered by most to be a corrupt sham, provide but two illustrations of the point that democracy in itself is not enough to obtain the desired outcome of liberal democracy.

Although politicians and policymakers often state the end goal of reconstruction efforts as "spreading democracy," what they implicitly mean is the establishment of liberal democratic institutions along Western lines—if not in specific design then at least based upon Western principles. This difference is more than semantics. Compared to establishing a lasting liberal democracy, holding elections is relatively easy. During U.S.-led occupations, elections have been held in Haiti, Bosnia, and Kosovo. However, it remains far from clear that these countries could be classified as self-sustaining liberal democracies.

The means available to occupiers to achieve the goal of sustainable liberal democracy include an array of resources that consist of physical assets as well as knowledge and information about the specific country and reconstruction in general. The use of these means is constrained by other factors, such as culture and historical experiences in the country being reconstructed and domestic and international public opinion. Along these lines, I will also pay careful attention to the important distinction between *controllable* and *uncontrollable* variables. Controllable variables include those factors that occupying forces can vary as they choose: troop levels, monetary aid, timing of elections, and so on. Uncontrollable variables are those factors that cannot be varied at will by occupiers. Examples would include the beliefs and norms of the individuals in the country being reconstructed, or the pressure of domestic and international opinion to follow a certain course of action.

Although I recognize their critical importance, I will not address the normative issues associated with military intervention and occupation. Instead, I will argue purely as an economist and limit my discussion to empirical questions. My focus on the positive aspect of reconstruction is not intended to downplay the importance of ethical issues. Instead, the normative aspects of the reconstruction issue are beyond the scope of what I address in this inquiry.[23]

My starting point in this argument is that reconstruction efforts have taken place in the past and are currently under way in Afghanistan and Iraq. In addition, on the basis of the indications provided by policymakers and the realities of the world, I assume that further attempts at reconstruction will take place in the future. Given the historical reality and the assumption about future efforts, I will focus on understanding what economics can contribute to our understanding of whether military occupation and reconstruction are effective means for achieving the desired ends of spreading liberal democracy to conflict-torn, weak, and failed states.

Is Military Occupation the Means to Liberal Democracy? A First Take

The narratives that began this chapter provided some insight into the U.S. experience with occupation and reconstruction. Now that we have established what reconstruction entails, as well as the end goal of reconstruction efforts, it makes sense to take a closer look at the historical record of U.S.-led reconstruction efforts. Doing so will provide some initial insight into the question of whether military occupation is an effective means for generating sustainable liberal democracy.

To see if a general pattern exists regarding the success and sustainability of U.S.-led reconstruction efforts, I will utilize the well-known Polity IV Index.[24] The Polity IV Index ranks the political institutions of a country on a twenty-one-point scale of institutionalized democracy. A combined "Polity Score" is then calculated by subtracting the Autocracy (0 to 10) score from the Democracy (0 to 10) score. The resulting scale ranges from +10 (fully democratic) to −10 (fully autocratic). This index is especially useful because data are provided for most countries from the 1800s through 2003.

The categories of democracy and autocracy incorporate several key dimensions. Institutionalized democracy, as defined by the authors of Polity IV, consists of three key elements: (1) the presence of institutions and procedures through which citizens can express their preferences, (2) the presence of institutionalized constraints on the executive, and (3) the guarantee of civil liberties for all citizens in both their daily lives and political participation. The authors define autocracy by a specific set of characteristics as well. Autocracies "suppress competitive political participation. Their chief executives are chosen in a regularized process of selection within the political elite, and once in office they exercise power with few institutional constraints."[25]

To provide some concrete examples of what these scores mean in terms of actual governments, Iraq under the Hussein regime had a Polity Score of −9 in 2002, while Afghanistan scored a −7 under the Taliban in 2000. As of 2003, Egypt scored a −6, Syria a −9, and Saudi Arabia a −10. In contrast, as of 2003, all of the members of the G-8 had a Polity Score of +10 except for France, which scored a +9, and Russia, which scored a +7.

A key question in this inquiry concerns which Polity Score to use as a benchmark for a successful reconstruction. The Polity Project has considered a score of +7 or more as necessary for a country to be a mature and "internally coherent democracy."[26] This same benchmark has been employed in several studies focusing on democratic peace.[27]

To be as charitable as possible, however, I will employ a substantially lower score of +4. To put this score in context, as of 2003, Iran, which President Bush declared to be a member of the "Axis of Evil," was a +3. By employing a +4 score as a benchmark, I am essentially asking, "Were U.S.-led reconstruction efforts able to generate a political regime slightly better than present-day Iran?"

Timing is yet another issue in making a judgment regarding the success of a reconstruction process. If the end goal of reconstruction efforts is to establish a self-sustaining liberal democracy, one must consider the status of these countries well after occupying forces exit the country. In some cases, as in postwar Japan and West Germany, liberal democracy might occur relatively quickly, but in other instances, reconstruction efforts might plant the seeds of liberal democracy that only blossom several years down the line. Likewise, a country might appear to be a liberal democracy when occupiers initially exit the country only to unravel soon thereafter. What is important in our consideration here, and I would argue, on the largest of scales, is whether reconstructed liberal democratic institutions are sustainable over the long run.

There is debate among political scientists regarding the time frame of when a democracy becomes established or "consolidated." The suggested time frame ranges anywhere from ten to twenty-five years.[28] Recognizing that there is not a consensus on this issue, I will consider the Polity Score for U.S.-led reconstruction efforts in five-year intervals: five, ten, fifteen, and twenty years after the exit of occupying troops. In other words, I want to understand if these countries had a political regime that scored at least a +4 in five-year increments after the official and final exit of U.S. occupiers. The results are summarized in Table 1.1.[29]

For those entries in italics, there is no data available from the Polity Index for the country or time period in question. Nevertheless, I have attempted to fill in data as much as possible using supplemental metrics and common sense about the situations of the countries in question. For instance, most would agree that given the current developments in Somalia, it does not have the necessary score at the end of 2005—ten years after the exit of U.S. occupiers—to consider it a success. Similar reasoning applies to Haiti, which the United States exited in 1996. As of 2006, Haiti remains in a state of utter disarray. It is the poorest country in the Western hemisphere, with approximately 80 percent of the population living in abject poverty. United Nations peacekeepers are a central means of security for the country. The presidential election in February 2006 was characterized by accusations of corruption, fraud, and vote manipulation.[30] Likewise, instability continues to plague Lebanon because of such issues as the constant threat of assassination of the country's leaders and ongoing tensions with neighboring Israel and Syria. In contrast, Panama had relatively stable

TABLE 1.1 2003 Polity IV scores: U.S. military occupations, 20th and 21st centuries

Country	Occupation period	Democracy after . . . ?			
		5 years	10 years	15 years	20 years
Cuba	1898–1902	No	No	No	No
Philippines	1898–1946	Yes	Yes	Yes	Yes
Panama	1903–1936	No	No	No	Yes
Cuba	1906–1909	No	No	No	No
Nicaragua	1909–1910	No	No	No	No
Nicaragua	1912–1925	No	No	No	No
Mexico	1914–1917	No	No	No	No
Haiti	1915–1934	No	No	No	No
Cuba	1917–1922	No	No	No	No
Dominican Republic	1916–1924	No	No	No	No
Nicaragua	1926–1933	No	No	No	No
Italy	1943–1945	Yes	Yes	Yes	Yes
South Korea	1945–1948	No	No	No	No
Japan	1945–1952	Yes	Yes	Yes	Yes
Austria	1945–1955	Yes	Yes	Yes	Yes
West Germany	1945–1955	Yes	Yes	Yes	Yes
Lebanon	1958	No	No	Yes	No
South Vietnam	1964–1973	No	No	No	No
Dominican Republic	1965–1966	No	No	Yes	Yes
Cambodia	1970–1973	No	No	No	No
Lebanon	1982–1984	No	No	No	*No*
Grenada	1983	*Yes*	*Yes*	*Yes*	*Yes*
Panama	1989	Yes	Yes	*Yes*	—
Somalia	1993–1995	No	*No*	—	—
Haiti	1994–1996	No	*No*	—	—
Bosnia-Herzegovina	1996–2002	—	—	—	—
Kosovo	1999–present	—	—	—	—
Afghanistan	2001–present	—	—	—	—
Iraq	2003–present	—	—	—	—

political institutions through 2004, fifteen years after the exit of U.S. occupiers. Presidential elections between three competing parties were held in 2004. Public protests against government are generally tolerated, and civil and political rights are, for the most part, protected. Given this, I assume its Polity Score will either stay consistent or increase for the better once the index is updated.

Unfortunately, Grenada is absent from the Polity IV Index altogether. To categorize its performance, I use the Freedom House's *Freedom in the World* report.[31] Freedom House is an independent nongovernmental organization that focuses on understanding and analyzing worldwide trends of democracy and individual and political freedoms. The organization's well-known *Freedom in the World* report is an annual comparative study of individual and political rights at the global level. According to this report, Grenada has consistently fallen into the category of "free."[32] As such, I consider it to be a case of success. The relevant time increments have not yet passed for Bosnia, Afghanistan, or Iraq; and the final political status of Kosovo has yet to be determined, so it cannot be considered an independent state for scoring purposes.

What do the data indicate regarding the effectiveness of reconstruction as a means of achieving liberal democracy? In short, the historical record indicates that efforts to export liberal democracy at gunpoint are more likely to fail than succeed. Of the twenty-five reconstruction efforts, where five years have passed since the end of occupation, seven have achieved the stated benchmark, resulting in a 28 percent success rate. The rate of success stays the same for those cases where ten years have passed. For those efforts where at least fifteen years have passed, nine out of twenty-three have achieved the benchmark for success, resulting in a 39 percent success rate. Finally, of the twenty-two reconstruction efforts where twenty years have passed since the exit of occupiers, eight have reached the benchmark, resulting in a 36 percent success rate.

Note that this says nothing about the magnitude of the United States's impact in the outcomes of these countries. For instance, the Dominican Republic reached the relevant benchmark fifteen years after the exit of U.S. occupiers. However, it is difficult to judge the influence of the U.S. occupation fifteen years earlier on this outcome. In other words, it is unclear what the magnitude of the U.S. intervention actually was on the trajectory of this country. Similarly, Lebanon reached the benchmark fifteen years after the exit of U.S. occupiers in 1958. However, the country's political institutions unraveled only two years later and again fell below the benchmark. Nonetheless, considering U.S.-led reconstruction efforts in this manner sheds some light on the general pattern of success and failure. The general pattern indicates that attempts to spread liberal democracy via military occupation will fail more often than they will work.

Of those cases in Table 1.1 that failed to achieve a score of +4, have reconstruction efforts generated any positive change in the country's pre-occupation Polity Score? I assume no benchmark in this consideration but simply ask the question more specifically as follows: "Did the reconstruction effort have any positive impact on the country's pre-occupation Polity Score as measured five, ten, fifteen, or twenty years after the end of the occupation?" The results are summarized in Table 1.2.

Any positive increase in the score is recorded as a "Yes," while any score that stays constant or falls is recorded as a "No." As Table 1.2 indicates, in only five instances did a country where reconstruction failed to achieve a +4 score experience *any* increase in its Polity Score from the pre-occupation level. In

TABLE 1.2 Impact of reconstruction on Polity Score for countries where reconstruction failed

Country	Occupation period	Did Polity Score improve after . . . ?			
		5 years	10 years	15 years	20 years
Cuba	1898–1902	—	—	—	—
Panama	1903–1936	No	No	Yes	Yes
Cuba	1906–1909	No	No	No	No
Nicaragua	1909–1910	Yes	Yes	Yes	Yes
Nicaragua	1912–1925	No	No·	No	No
Mexico	1914–1917	No	No	No	No
Haiti	1915–1934	Yes	Yes	No	No
Cuba	1917–1922	No	No	No	No
Dominican Republic	1916–1924	No	No	No	No
Nicaragua	1926–1933	No	No	No	No
South Korea	1945–1948	—	—	—	—
South Vietnam	1964–1973	No	No	No	No
Cambodia	1970–1973	Yes	No	Yes	Yes
Lebanon	1982–1984	No	No	No	*No*
Somalia	1993–1995	No	*No*	—	—
Haiti	1994–1996	Yes	*No*	—	—

Panama, the pre-occupation score was −3 and increased to −1 fifteen years later, in 1951, and to +4 twenty years later in 1956. Panama's score would fall to a −8 prior to the subsequent U.S. occupation in 1989. In Nicaragua, the Polity Score prior to the U.S. occupation in 1909 was −5 and improved to −3 after the exit of occupiers in 1910. Haiti saw an improvement from its pre-occupation score of −3 in 1914 to a score of 0 in 1938 and 1944, but this increase did not last, as a military coup occurred in 1946. Finally, Cambodia experienced an increase in its pre-occupation score of −9 in 1969 to a score of −7 in 1978, although this was not sustainable, as the country has been plagued by instability. Data for Cuba do not start until 1902, while the scoring for South Korea starts in 1948.

While fully recognizing that there is a wide array of factors contributing to the Polity Score of a country, a high-level review of the historical record of reconstruction efforts indicates that U.S. efforts have been either very successful or very unsuccessful. Where U.S.-led reconstruction efforts have been successful, they have generated consolidated liberal democracies. Japan, Austria, Italy, West Germany, and Panama, after the 1989 occupation, all have scores of +9 or above, which places them in the category of established and sustaining liberal democracies.

However, where these efforts have failed, they have either had no sustainable positive impact or have resulted in a lower score. Of the failures, Cuba is the closest to the benchmark of +4, scoring a +3 after the two latter U.S. occupations of the country. This is the same score Cuba possessed prior to these occupations, indicating that U.S. forces had no impact in either direction. However, as discussed in the opening narrative, the seeds of liberal democracy were not planted in Cuba, as evidenced by the Batista and Castro dictatorships. All of the other failures had negative scores or were considered in a state of transition or civil war for the relevant time increments.[33]

This exercise is meant to provide a first take, a basis for understanding whether military occupation is an effective means for achieving liberal democracy. Although there is no clear indication of what a "good" success rate might be, as noted earlier the United States has achieved a 28 percent success rate for reconstructions that ended at least ten years ago, a 39 percent success rate for those that ended at least fifteen years ago, and a 36 percent success rate for those that ended at least twenty years ago. In short, at the very least, the historical record shows more failures than successes and indicates that liberal democracy cannot be exported in a consistent manner at gunpoint. Admittedly, there are clear cases of success, but there are more clear cases of failure. Understanding these drastically different outcomes is the main aim of this book.

Overview of the Book

As stated previously, I analyze the issue of post-conflict reconstruction using the tools of economics, and in order to do so, I will draw on various economic fields, including Austrian Economics, Behavioral Economics, Constitutional Political Economy, New Institutional Economics, and Public Choice Economics. It is my view that each of these theoretical perspectives can offer us important insights that will contribute to answering the question driving this analysis. I do not assume any specialized knowledge of these fields on the part of the reader, but rather, I merely point out the synthesis of perspectives that the following analysis entails. Economics is a broad field of many complementary and contending perspectives, and this fact allows any economic investigator many tools with which to explore the issue at hand.

The methodology employed in this book is what has been called the "analytic narrative," which blends the analytical tools of economics with the narrative form of exposition common in historical research.[34] In other words, it combines the framework provided by economics with the emphasis on the context of historical occurrences. As such, this method provides a means of understanding past events and causal mechanisms that allow for the generation of policy implications for the present and future. For instance, the narrative approach allows for the exploration of strategic interaction and the impact of historical experiences on past and current reconstruction efforts.

This method is especially conducive to the analysis of reconstruction, which for a variety of reasons is a difficult topic to handle formally. There are some general databases, such as the aforementioned Polity IV Index, but the number of relevant and interacting variables in the reconstruction process is large and the actual variable set contains the histories of many different cultures for which no systematic database exists. As the political scientist Samuel Huntington has noted, there is no single factor, or set of factors, that "causes" democracy across countries and across time. Instead, democratization, or the lack thereof, in different countries is a result of differing causal combinations specific to the country.[35] Given this complexity, the analytic narrative method fits well with an analysis of reconstruction efforts generally in as much as attempts to establish liberal democracy have occurred in different countries at different times. Given these broad parameters, any approach will be relatively informal compared to that employed by my colleagues in most other fields of economics. Nevertheless, I feel that the importance of the topic and the potential contribution of the field of economics to our understanding of the reconstruction process militate in favor of study rather than neglect.

Chapter 2 provides a model to understand the reconstruction process, wherein I draw on some basic concepts from game theory in order to understand the reconstruction "game." I postulate that successful reconstructions are those in which occupiers are effectively able to transform situations of conflict into situations of coordination around a set of conjectures, beliefs, and expectations that support liberal democracy. The following two chapters then consider the mechanisms that contribute to, or prevent, the necessary transformation from conflict to cooperation. Chapter 3 focuses on the mechanisms that facilitate or prevent cooperation among the indigenous citizens of the country being reconstructed. Chapter 4 considers the mechanisms influencing the behavior of occupiers in their efforts to export liberal democracy.

After exploring the specifics of these mechanisms, I apply them to historical and current reconstruction efforts. I dedicate a chapter each to case studies for the following categories of reconstruction:

Successful reconstructions (as in Japan and West Germany)

Unsuccessful reconstructions (as in Somalia and Haiti)

Current reconstruction efforts (as in Afghanistan and Iraq)

The aim of these case studies is to illuminate how the framework and mechanisms developed in earlier chapters apply to historical and current reconstruction efforts. These case studies will also highlight the main implications of the analysis. I conclude by considering some competing alternatives to military occupation and reconstruction as means of generating sustainable liberal democracy. In doing so, I consider the strengths and weaknesses of each alternative.

Although my main focus is on past and current U.S.-led reconstruction efforts, the insights of this analysis, to be developed in the following chapters, can be generalized and applied to all reconstruction efforts across time and place. The results of this analysis will suggest four primary themes, or lessons to be learned, as described in the following text.

1. *Although policymakers and social scientists know what factors constitute a successful reconstruction, they know much less about how to bring about this end.*

We possess a firm understanding of what a successful reconstruction seeks to accomplish. For instance, we know that the rule of law; protection of individual, political, and property rights; and the smooth transfer of power between elected officials characterize a liberal democracy. Despite this understanding, however, much less is known about the appropriate steps to take to achieve this desired end. Stated differently, while we know *what* a successful reconstruction entails, we lack an understanding of *how* to bring about the desired end. Indeed, as the previous general analysis of U.S.-led reconstruction efforts has illustrated, liberal democracy via occupation has, more often than not, remained elusive. Thus, failure is not due to a lack of a clear end-goal, but instead, failure is due to the lack of knowledge of how to go about achieving the desired end. In other words, failure is due to the gap between the *know-what* and *know-how*.[36]

This uncertainty is evident in the ongoing debate among social scientists regarding the social and economic conditions that are conducive to a sustainable liberal democracy. Academics have long considered several factors, including a middle class and a certain level of economic development, ethnic homogeneity, historical experience with constitutions and liberal democracy, and a national identity, to be preconditions for a sustainable liberal democracy.[37] But recent research has called these previously assumed preconditions into question.

For instance, a recent cross-country study by Steven Fish and Robin Brooks finds, counter to prevailing wisdom, that social heterogeneity does not increase conflict or stifle democracy.[38] As Larry Diamond, a leading expert on democracy, has recently pointed out, scholars have spent decades attempting to understand the factors that contribute to stable democracies, but the wave of new democracies that arose between 1974 and 1994, a period wherein democracy spread to countries that lacked these conditions, "raised the prospect that democracy could emerge where the social scientists would least expect it."[39] On the one hand, this fact can be viewed as a positive, since it indicates that all countries have some democratic potential. On the other hand, however, this realization highlights the limited knowledge of scholars regarding the factors and causes of sustainable democracy. It is my contention that this latter realization should be reason for pause when considering reconstruction via military occupation as a policy option.[40]

Attempts to understand the various factors by comparing historical cases have yielded inconclusive results. For instance, a RAND study of several U.S.-led reconstructions attempts to generate "lessons learned" from these cases by focusing on several controllable variables. But in truth, when one looks across cases, it is unclear that there are any uniform lessons to be drawn. For instance, the number of troops per thousand inhabitants was significantly higher in Bosnia and Kosovo (18.6 and 20 per one thousand inhabitants respectively) as compared to Japan (5 per one thousand inhabitants). Along similar lines, Somalia had either the same number or more troops per thousand inhabitants than Japan over the first two and a half years of occupation and a drastically different outcome.

Likewise, it may appear that initial total monetary aid is an important controllable factor that contributes to ultimate success or failure, and indeed, total aggregate assistance during the first two years of occupation has varied greatly across historical reconstruction efforts, from $12 billion in Germany to approximately $5 billion in Bosnia, $4 billion in Japan, and slightly under $2 billion in Kosovo and Afghanistan. However, when adjusted for per capita assistance, one finds that Bosnia received approximately $1,400 per capita in aid, Kosovo received more than $800 per capita in aid, Germany received approximately $300 per capita in aid, and Japan less than $100 per capita in aid.[41]

When it comes down to it, policymakers and social scientists know what ultimate success entails. They also have an understanding of the array of factors that influence the reconstruction process. The level of military forces, foreign aid, the timing of elections, culture, historical experience, ethnic tensions, and the many other variables all matter for the ultimate outcome of reconstruction efforts. However, lacking is an understanding of *how* these controllable variables interact and influence each other as well as the "right" levels required for success on a consistent basis. In short, although the end goal is clear, the knowledge of how to employ various means to achieve this end is lacking. It is critical to keep this distinction in mind between the "know-what"—knowing what a successful reconstruction looks like—and the "know-how"—understanding how to bring about the desired end. It is only by recognizing this distinction that we can hope to understand why reconstruction efforts have failed to be consistently successful, and in some cases have caused more harm than good.

2. Uncontrollable variables serve as a constraint on controllable variables.
A key element of the economic way of thinking is the recognition of constraints. For instance, the amount of goods and services a consumer can purchase is constrained by his or her income and prices. In the context of reconstruction, key constraints are often neglected. Focus is often placed on the political and military leaders of the occupying forces as the main constraints.

One hears criticisms of these individuals for poor planning, too few troops, too little funding, lack of an exit strategy, and so on. If only these leaders would adjust their behavior either by shifting strategy or increasing monetary or physical resources, critics contend, the outcomes of reconstruction efforts would be drastically different. But focusing solely on political and military leaders as the key constraints overlooks the contextual constraints within the country being reconstructed.

In his analysis of Central and Eastern Europe, the economist Svetozar Pejovich concluded that the transition from communism to capitalism is not merely a technical issue.[42] In other words, the same expenditure of resources in different transition efforts will yield different outcomes. Similar reasoning applies to the case of reconstruction. Why is this the case? To borrow a phrase from Pejovich, "It's the culture, stupid."

Economists are often uncomfortable with the concept of "culture" because it is difficult to define let alone neatly quantify.[43] Indeed, there is no definition of culture that is universally accepted by social scientists. When I use the term *culture* in this analysis, I will follow those scholars who define the term as the informal rules that constrain human interaction.[44] From this viewpoint, a society's culture is the existing array of values, customs, traditions, belief systems, and other mores passed from one generation to the next. By this definition, culture is an "informal institution," which means that it is not formally mandated but coexists with formal institutions such as constitutions and written laws.

Acting within these formal and informal institutions are various individual actors and also organizations, which are groups of individuals joined for some common purpose.[45] Culture constrains the actions of individuals and the various organizational forms that individuals can achieve within a given set of formal institutions. In other words, the creation of a wide array of organizations—political groups (parties, councils, senates), economic bodies (families and firms), and social bodies (associations)—will be constrained by the existing endowment of culture. For instance, the economist Timur Kuran has analyzed how certain informal institutions in the Middle East have created "evolutionary bottlenecks" that serve as constraints on certain organizational forms.[46] Indeed, the limitations on certain organizational forms have been a main cause of economic stagnation in the region.

Culture is perhaps the greatest constraint on reconstruction efforts. Francis Fukuyama has argued that democratic consolidation must take place on four levels. Culture is the "deepest" level and therefore is "safely beyond the reach of institutional solutions, and hence of public policy."[47] In other words, controllable variables matter, but only up to a point. The same level of resources—monetary aid, troops, organization of elections, and so on—as was invested in West Germany and Japan in 1945 will generate a drastically different outcome in Afghanistan and Iraq in 2005. This is due to the fact that these countries have different endowments of culture—capital and knowledge that constrain the effectiveness of those resources.

The reader should note that this is not an argument for long-run cultural determinism. Indeed, research shows that all states possess some democratic potential.[48] Instead, culture can be seen as a short-term constraint on the process through which liberal democracy is established and evolves. Culture establishes the limits to the indigenous acceptance of policies implemented by occupiers at the time of the reconstruction, and formally reconstructed institutions require the existence of certain complementary institutions and capabilities to operate in the desired manner. Absent these complementary informal institutions, the same institutions transplanted in different societies will yield drastically different results. When the underlying culture and reconstruction efforts coincide, liberal orders will flourish, and absent this coincidence, the sustainability of reconstructed orders will be a constant struggle.[49] Continued force will be required where voluntary acceptance is absent. Given that the projected end of reconstruction is a self-sustaining liberal democracy, this is not a desirable state of affairs.

3. Reconstruction efforts suffer from a nirvana fallacy.

The term *nirvana fallacy* was first used by the economist Harold Demsetz to describe the comparison of real markets to ideal government institutions lacking imperfection.[50] Such a comparison leads to the conclusion that government intervention is required to overcome the failures of markets. Flawless government intervention is desirable when compared to imperfect market outcomes.

Demsetz argued that such comparisons were unrealistic, leading to faulty analyses and conclusions. The reality is that government also suffers from imperfections, and due to these imperfections, government actors may fail to allocate resources as effectively as even an imperfect market. In short, one cannot assume that "the grass is greener on the other side," that government intervention will yield a better outcome as compared to the situation that would exist in the absence of those interventions.

A similar fallacy often applies to reconstruction efforts. In the context of reconstruction, a nirvana fallacy occurs when it is assumed that, in the face of a weak, failed, or illiberal government, external occupiers can provide a better outcome relative to what would exist in the absence of those efforts. This is not to say that reconstruction efforts can never have beneficial effects, but neither can it be assumed that occupation will yield beneficial outcomes.

As subsequent chapters will make clear, occupiers face constraints not just within the country being reconstructed but also from their home country as well. For instance, the political decision-making process in the country carrying out the reconstruction will influence the overall effort. As will be discussed, the incentives created by the political system often lead political actors to produce policies that fail to align with the broader goals of the reconstruction effort.

Reconstruction efforts might not *merely* fail to achieve the desired end—there is also the real possibility that the efforts of foreign occupiers can cause more harm than good. Obviously, such harm is usually an unintended consequence, and as will be discussed further in subsequent chapters, these negative unintended consequences can occur along two key margins.

The first margin consists of unintended consequences that are *internal* to the country being reconstructed. In other words, the actions of occupiers may cause unintended harm within the country being reconstructed. One example of internal negative unintended consequences is the possibility that reconstruction efforts can distort the evolution of indigenous social structures and governance mechanisms. Perhaps the best example of this is the case of Somalia. To date, there have been seventeen failed foreign-led attempts—both by the United States and others—at national reconciliation in Somalia since the collapse of the Siad Barre regime in 1991. As will be discussed in more detail in Chapter 6, efforts to establish a central liberal democratic government have often *increased* conflict between various clans throughout the country instead of generating cooperation.

One can envision many other examples of negative internal unintended consequences as well. For instance, the United States supplied arms and financial support to Afghani rebels in the 1980s to fight Soviet forces. Some of those same weapons were used against U.S. forces during the invasion of Afghanistan in 2001. Clearly, the United States did not intend for the weapons to be used in this manner when they initially gave them to the rebels.

External unintended consequences can also result from reconstruction efforts. In other words, the actions of occupiers may generate "neighborhood effects" that cause harm to those outside the country being occupied. For instance, in a recent study, political scientists Edward Mansfield and Jack Snyder explore the claim that democracies are less likely to go to war. Their main finding is that, while it is true that consolidated democracies tend not to engage in conflict with one another, immature democracies making the transition from authoritarian regimes *do* tend to engage in conflict. What some may find more surprising is that the authors of this study find that immature democracies are *more* likely to engage in conflict and war than are authoritarian regimes. This is due to the fact that individuals vying for political positions in democratizing countries tend to appeal to hard-line nationalism in order to gain support, while separating themselves from both competitors within the country and foreigners as well.

To understand the implications of external unintended consequences, assume that the United States is successful in planting the seeds of democracy in Iraq. In such a case, political, economic, and social institutions would be fragile, as their full development would be far from complete. With a semi-democratized Iraq, one could envision an array of political competitors employing nationalism against neighboring countries to obtain positions of leadership and power. While these fragile institutions might provide minimal stability within Iraq, appeals to Iraqi nationalism might very well generate conflict between Iraq and its neighbors along the lines that Mansfield and Snyder outline. In such a situation, the United States might achieve the goal of bringing some semblance of stability to Iraq, but only at the cost of increasing the potential for conflict in the larger Middle East region.[51]

There are many other examples of external negative unintended consequences as well. For instance, some have argued that the current war in Iraq will generate a "blowback," whereby current reconstruction efforts will create the future generation of insurgents who will seek targets around the world.[52] As just discussed, in this case, efforts to bring stability to Iraq through reconstruction would generate negative consequences for other countries around the world.

To summarize this lesson to be learned, while the failure of endogenous institutions in countries with weak, failed, or illiberal governments may indeed be significant, the failures generated by foreign governments can be even greater. Interventions by foreign governments in these countries do not necessarily generate a preferable state of affairs in spite of the best intentions. While an effective and strong liberal government might be preferable to the current situation in such countries, often such an outcome is not a realistic option.

Further, unintended consequences resulting from foreign intervention may not just affect the country being reconstructed but may also inflict harm externally as well. This implies that a reconstruction that generates peaceful coordination on one margin may simultaneously increase conflict on other margins.

4. *Sustainable social change toward liberal democracy requires a shift in underlying preferences and opportunities.*

The economic way of thinking emphasizes that individuals have preferences and act within a set of constraints that place limits on their opportunities. A preference can refer to a predilection for certain goods or services or for a certain type of behavior. Preferences and a set of associated feasible opportunities are constrained by such things as cultural norms, mental capabilities, income, laws, and economic and political institutions. For instance, an individual has one set of opportunities within a context wherein individual and property rights are protected and a different set within a context wherein they are not, just as an individual who has never been exposed to a certain good cannot possibly have a strong preference for that product, because he or she is unaware of its existence.

Preferences and opportunities can change as the underlying factors and constraints change. For instance, individuals' preferences may change as they are introduced to new goods or services of which they were previously unaware. Likewise, an individual's opportunity to consume a certain good or service may change, perhaps through a change in income or a change in laws and political institutions that allows for the protection of individual and property rights. Likewise, changes in cultural norms may make previously unacceptable activities acceptable, which would increase the opportunities available to the individual.

Similar reasoning applies to specific behaviors in which individuals choose to engage. An individual's choice to engage in cooperation, civic activities, crime, terrorism, or insurgency is influenced by preferences and opportunities. Given that, sustainable social change requires either a shift in preferences or a shift in the opportunities facing members of society. If the aim is for members of a society to engage in activities that support liberal democracy, their preferences and opportunities must be such that they demand these behaviors. Individuals must possess the complementary informal institutions necessary for the operation of formally reconstructed institutions. Further, their preferences must include a commitment to the rule of law, individual and property rights, and markets—and they must have the opportunities to carry out this commitment.

Indeed, a key purpose of reconstruction efforts is to change the preferences and opportunities of the members of the country being reconstructed. Reconstruction efforts seek to foster preferences for freedom, democracy, the rule of law, markets, and tolerance. Likewise, these efforts seek to create a new set of opportunities that were not feasible prior to the occupation. These opportunities might include the ability to vote, open a business, worship in the church of one's choice, or utilize the legal system, among other possibilities.

The main implication is that successful social change requires a shift in underlying preferences and opportunities. The best way to bring these changes about remains an open question. Reconstruction efforts have been successful in changing the opportunity set that citizens face. For instance, overthrowing a political regime via military force has proved to be an achievable task, as evidenced by the recent efforts in Afghanistan and Iraq. Toppling a political regime clearly provides a new set of opportunities for citizens that were not previously available. The more difficult task for military occupiers has been to effectively shift the underlying preferences to support liberal democracies and Western-style institutions.

For instance, in the cases of Haiti, Somalia, Iraq, and Afghanistan, occupying forces have failed to coordinate citizens around reconstructed liberal institutions. In stark contrast, military occupation in these countries has produced a backlash that has contributed to increased violence and conflict. To reiterate, while formal rules can be changed quickly, they must be grounded in the informal everyday practices of a society in order to operate as desired. In the absence of complementary informal institutions, formally reconstructed institutions will be dysfunctional. Where these institutional complements are lacking, formal institutions will be ignored or fail to have the desired impact.

While policymakers and academics have typically focused on reconstruction efforts as a means of generating changes in preferences and opportunities, alternative mechanisms have been neglected. This is a mistake. It is my contention that political, economic, and social change that is imposed at the point of a gun is more likely to be met with resistance and is less likely to "stick" once occupiers exit the country. Among the key neglected mechanisms for fostering sustaining change is a commitment to non-intervention coupled with free trade and exchange, not just in physical goods and services but also in cultural products, ideas, beliefs, and institutions. Instead of employing illiberal means (occupation and coercion) to achieve liberal ends, the focus should shift to liberal means (non-intervention and free trade) to achieve liberal ends. As I will discuss, a commitment to non-intervention and free trade has a long tradition in the United States.

A commitment to non-intervention and free trade is one means of exercising what the political scientist Joseph Nye has called "soft power." The notion of soft power entails attracting and convincing others to shift their preferences in the desired manner.[53] This stands in contrast to "hard power," which relies on coercion to achieve the desired end. Free trade provides the potential to attract others to voluntarily adopt liberal values and institutions.

In addition to the widely recognized economic benefits, free trade produces cultural benefits by increasing the menu of choices available to all.[54] As Tyler Cowen, an economist, indicates, cross-cultural exchange allows different cultures to simultaneously maintain certain aspects of their unique identities while merging with others and becoming similar on other margins. Given that, free trade can be seen as a means of finding a common ground *between* cultures both within and across borders. A commitment to trade, coupled with non-intervention, provides the opportunity to exchange cultural practices and ideas and the potential for enemies to be transformed into trading partners. Along similar lines, free exchange allows for the imitation of both formal and informal institutions, as well as organizational structures within these institutions, across national borders, resulting in social change through peaceful interaction. Because of the potential for these positive outcomes, non-intervention and free trade deserve at least a fair hearing as a viable alternative to spreading liberal democracy via military occupation. Given the less-than-stellar record of the United States in spreading liberal democracy at gunpoint, such alternatives must be seriously considered.

2   From Conflict to Cooperation

T HE ECONOMIC WAY OF THINKING, which is grounded in a few core assumptions, provides a specific set of tools for understanding individual action and interaction. Economists assume that individuals act purposefully, meaning that they have specific goals that they seek to achieve. The opportunities to pursue these goals are constrained by a number of factors, including time, income, imperfect information, and informal and formal rules, including laws. Given their goals and constraints, individuals pursue their desired end using the best means known to them at the time of action. Further, actors adjust their behavior as their goals and constraints change.

Within this context, reconstruction efforts can be seen as an attempt to change the opportunities or constraints that individuals face. Liberal democratic institutions provide certain opportunities, such as voting and equal protection under the law, while simultaneously preventing other activities, such as violations of individual and property rights. A critical question, of course, is whether reconstruction efforts can successfully shift existing constraints to create opportunities for liberal political, economic, and social orders that sustain after the exit of occupiers. A closely related issue is whether or not the goals of people in the occupied country align with the broader aims of the reconstruction effort.

The economic way of thinking has been applied to a wide range of issues, among them crime, addiction, the family, politics and political decision making, the environment, education, religion, culture, and terrorism. Similarly, the economic way of thinking has been incorporated into other disciplines such as history (economic history), political science (public choice and political economy), law (law and economics), sociology (economic sociology), religion (economics of religion), and cultural studies (cultural economics). Along similar lines, the economic way of thinking can shed light on the reconstruction process, resulting in an "economics of reconstruction."

The core assumptions outlined above apply to the wide array of actors involved in the reconstruction process. Individuals in the country being reconstructed have specific goals and, given the constraints they face, try to achieve those goals in the best manner available. Both those citizens who cooperatively interact with occupying forces and those who engage in insurgency and terrorist acts have goals that they seek to achieve within the constraints they face. Likewise, occupiers have a set of goals they seek to obtain as well, which applies both to military forces "on the ground" and to politicians and policymakers directing the occupation from abroad. For instance, the U.S. military in general has a specific goal as regards their most recent occupations—bringing liberal democracy to Iraq and Afghanistan. However, individuals within the military also have specific goals or agendas—fame, power, maximizing their budgets, and so on—that may not necessarily mesh with the goal of the broader reconstruction effort. In similar fashion, individuals in the international community—the United Nations, neighboring countries to those being reconstructed, and so on—also pursue a specific set of goals given the array of constraints they face.

The pursuit of goals by this array of actors takes place simultaneously and amounts to a dynamic set of variables that influence the ultimate success or failure of the reconstruction effort. The extent to which the behaviors of those involved align with the broader aims of the reconstruction will contribute to the success of the effort. In contrast, the extent to which these behaviors clash with those of the reconstruction effort will contribute to its failure, as those involved in the reconstruction process will struggle to find a mutually satisfying and sustainable set of common goals and activities. That is, the challenge of reconstruction is to work with citizens' broader goals and find incentives such that their pursuit of those goals will produce behaviors that align with the desired liberal institutions.

To provide a concrete example of this last point, consider the major ethnic groups—the Arabs and Kurds—and religious groups—the Shi'a and Sunni Muslims—within Iraq. As will be discussed in subsequent chapters, each of these groups has a distinct agenda in the reconstruction of Iraq. The Kurds want to maintain their independence and autonomy, the Sunnis seek to maintain their position of power achieved during the Hussein era, while the Shi'a seek power in the new Iraq as well as retribution for repression under the former regime. Some aspects of these groups' agendas support U.S. efforts in Iraq to some degree even as other aspects work against those efforts. While the ultimate effect of these conflicting agendas on the larger reconstruction effort in Iraq will become evident only over time, the pursuit of conflicting goals poses a real and continued threat to the success of reconstruction. Similar reasoning can be extended to other reconstruction efforts as well.

Many have emphasized the importance of preexisting values and mores for the adoption of liberal democratic institutions. For instance, Alexis de Tocqueville contended that America's democracy rests primarily on the values and habits of its citizens and only secondarily on its institutions.[1] My focus on the role of incentives, and the assumption that all people respond to incentives, should not be read as neglecting the importance of values. Indeed, in subsequent chapters I will discuss the importance of existing values, norms, and belief systems as contributing factors to the success or failure of reconstruction efforts. My view is that while values may be crucial in constructing the right kinds of incentives, in order for institutions to change, people must find incentives and reinforcing consequences for acting in accord with those new institutions. Absent the proper incentives, these new institutions will fail regardless of the particular values of a society. It is within this context that economic analysis can contribute to our understanding of the reconstruction process.

A Framework for the Reconstruction Process

There is extensive precedent for the application of the economic way of thinking to the study of conflict and cooperation. In the *Strategy of Conflict,* Nobel Laureate Thomas Schelling focused on how the economic approach, and more specifically a game theoretic approach, could be used to illuminate the nature of conflict.[2] Along similar lines, Kenneth Boulding, in *Conflict and Defense,* utilized the tools of economics and game theory to analyze strategic interaction in situations of conflict.[3] The approaches and insights of these authors serve as the basis for the model developed here.[4] Game theory provides a means of considering strategic interaction between players, and as such, it provides a readily available means of considering the strategic interaction between the array of actors—all with their own goals and constraints—involved in reconstruction efforts. By drawing on some simple concepts from the theory of games, one is able to illuminate the nature of the reconstruction process.[5]

I start with the classic prisoner's dilemma game. In this well-known game, the two players are accomplices in a crime who have been captured by police. The police lack sufficient evidence to secure the maximum conviction unless at least one of the prisoners confesses. The police separate the suspects so that they cannot communicate and offer each suspect the opportunity to confess to the crime committed.

The prisoners are offered the following stipulations: If one chooses to confess while his accomplice remains silent, the police will reward the confession by dropping the charges against the individual who confesses. Further, his testimony will be used to convict the accomplice who remains silent and will guarantee the maximum sentence. If both prisoners confess, they will both be convicted using the testimony of the other and will receive a moderate sentence—a harsher sentence than in the absence of the confessions but less harsh than the maximum—as a reward for confessing. Finally, if both remain silent, they will be convicted and receive the minimum sentence because the lack of evidence precludes the maximum sentence. The payoff matrix in Figure 2.1 illustrates this situation.

In the figure, "Cooperate" refers to cooperation between the prisoners in remaining silent while "Defect" refers to confessing to the crime, or defecting

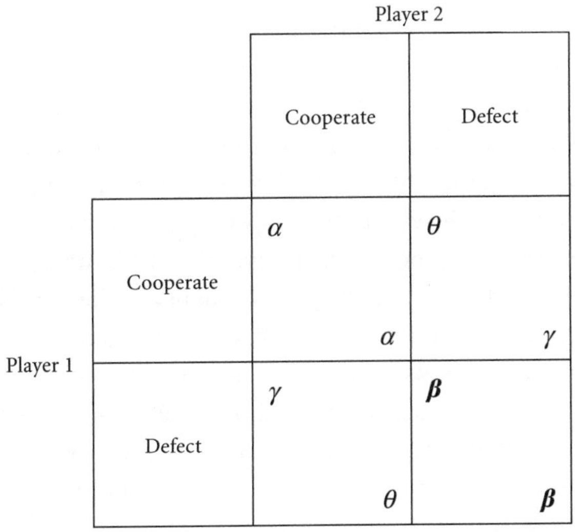

FIGURE 2.1 The Prisoner's Dilemma

from cooperation. The characters in each cell represent payoffs for each of the two players. The left-hand payoff indicates Player 1's payoff and the right-hand payoff represents Player 2's payoff. In this game $\gamma > \alpha > \beta > \theta$, and the Nash equilibrium of this game is the bolded lower right-hand cell: each player defects and both receive a moderate sentence.[6]

The logic behind this outcome is straightforward. Player 1, who chooses from the rows, will select row 2 ("Defect") regardless of his prediction of what Player 2, who chooses from the columns, will decide to do. This is due to the fact that the payoff possibilities associated with defection (γ and β) for Player 1 "dominate" the payoff possibilities associated with that received by choosing to cooperate (α and θ) no matter what Player 2 does. If Player 2 chooses to defect, Player 1 is better off defecting (β is preferable to θ). Likewise, if Player 2 chooses to cooperate, Player 1 is still better off defecting (γ is preferable to α). Similar reasoning applies to Player 2, who is better off choosing to defect no matter how he predicts Player 1 will choose to act. The final result is that both players choose to defect.

It is important to note that, as the payoffs indicate, the "Defect, Defect" outcome is suboptimal. Both players would be better off if they had both chosen to "Cooperate" with each other by remaining silent and receiving the minimum sentence. This scenario is illustrated in the upper-left cell, where each player would receive a payoff of α (which is greater than the β they each receive from defecting). However, unless there is some binding rule or convention that facilitates a commitment to cooperation, each player will individually choose to defect, leading to the suboptimal outcome in which both confess and receive a greater sentence than they would had they cooperated.

I extend the classic prisoner's dilemma game to illustrate the basic dilemma behind postwar reconstruction. The prisoner's dilemma captures the fundamental importance of incentives for cooperation with institutional change. Absent the incentive to coordinate around new institutions, many people will cooperate less than is socially optimal, hoping to reap personal gains, while others contribute to the public welfare in their stead. The existence of coordination-enhancing institutions, in contrast, can contribute to the creation of mutually reinforcing and binding rules that facilitate cooperation. In the presence of coordination-inducing mechanisms, people will have an incentive to cooperate and act in accord with reconstructed institutions, and such behavior will have reinforcing consequences.

The logic of the prisoner's dilemma has numerous institutional analogs in the postwar setting. Cooperating would consist of activities aimed at personal gains that align with the aims and goals of the reconstruction effort. Specifically, cooperating might include deciding not to loot or engage in terrorist acts, following the orders of the occupying power, committing to the bargaining process and delivering on agreements struck with rival groups, deciding to participate in civic groups working to foster liberal democracy, or respecting the rights of others. Likewise, defecting includes activities aimed mainly at obtaining personal enrichment, such as looting, corruption, breaking agreements, revenge, or even insurgency, that work to prevent successful reconstruction. In reality, many activities are too complex to be neatly categorized as "cooperation" or "defection." Nonetheless, the prisoner's dilemma provides a means of capturing the central predicament underlying attempts to export liberal democratic institutions to weak, failed, and conflict-torn countries.

I turn next to the "folk theorem," a well-known result in game theory.[7] The folk theorem suggests that a repeated prisoner's dilemma game can have a cooperative solution, provided that time horizons are sufficiently long. The logic here is straightforward. If individuals hold the appropriate conjectures and expectations, cooperation will be a dominant strategy. For instance, non-cooperators must expect to be punished, and for this to be enforced, non-punishers of non-cooperators must expect to be punished as well. If the appropriate conjectures exist, they will be mutually reinforcing and serve as a binding rule that enforces cooperation. Defecting will yield a current, or short-term, return but will be followed by many periods of punishment, with those punishment threats backed in turn by other threats of punishment. In essence, everyone is expecting a very long chain of consequences for any failure to either cooperate or punish. As an application, consider that dictatorships commonly use a perverted form of this logic to enforce compliance and support. Those who do not cooperate expect to be punished or tortured. Those who do not report non-cooperators can expect the same treatment, and so on.[8]

Of course, the folk theorem is not descriptive of reality, given that it typically cites highly complex trigger strategies, a specific rate of time preference, and long chains of punishment over time. Nonetheless, the folk theorem illustrates a fundamental fact about non-cooperative games: they can have significant cooperative elements, *provided* that individuals hold the right conjectures. A game of conflict can become much more like a game of cooperation if expectations and conjectures are sufficiently healthy and constructive. This simple relationship is at the core of the economic theory of reconstruction.

In other words, if individuals can coordinate efforts premised upon the appropriate conjectures, the prisoner's dilemma portrayed in Figure 2.1 can be transformed into a coordination game, as shown by Figure 2.2, in which players must choose between good and bad conjectures.

For simplicity, Figure 2.2 shows a basic two-person coordination game. In reality, the reconstruction situation is characterized by a multiperson coordination game involving the populace of the country being reconstructed. "Good Conjectures" refers to beliefs, opinions, and expectations that support activities that contribute to the development and sustainability of an extended liberal democratic order. By contrast, "Bad Conjectures" refers to a set of beliefs, opinions, and expectations generating behaviors that detract from the achievement of a liberal order. Japan and West Germany are examples of coordination around good conjectures while Stalin's reconstruction of East Germany is an example of coordination around bad conjectures.

In both cases, coordination took place, but the expectations of those involved differed greatly. In Japan and West Germany, "players" held a set of conjectures and expectations that enabled coordination around liberal institutions. Once in place, these institutions were self-sustaining. In East Germany, in contrast, players coordinated around Stalin's political order, but only at the threat of force. Many were able to get by, but only by submitting to Stalin's

		Player 2: Good Conjectures	Player 2: Bad Conjectures
Player 1	Good Conjectures	ϕ, ϕ	—
	Bad Conjectures	—	σ, σ

FIGURE 2.2 The Coordination Game

demands and rules. Reconstructed institutions in East Germany were not self-sustaining and required constant force and intervention.

As Figure 2.2 illustrates, coordination of effort premised upon good and constructive conjectures yields positive payoffs to both parties, as illustrated by the upper-left-corner payoff. It is also possible, however, that individuals may coordinate efforts premised upon destructive conjectures, which yield lower payoffs, as illustrated by the lower right corner. In this game, $\phi > \sigma$, and both players prefer the "good conjecture" equilibrium, in which they earn the higher payoff (ϕ, ϕ), to the "bad conjecture" equilibrium, in which they earn the lower payoff (σ, σ).

It is important to realize that there is no guarantee that the good conjecture equilibrium will be obtained. Large-scale coordination games characterized by network externalities are often a case of winner-take-all. A network external-ity occurs when the value of a product, service, standard, or norm increases as subsequent people adopt it. This logic can be applied to technology (for exam-ple, telephones and fax machines), technological standards (such as computer operating systems), and norms and laws (for example, the adoption of formal and informal rules and institutions). In a similar sense, conjectures and expec-tations in the reconstruction setting exhibit network externalities in that they increase in value as subsequent people adopt them. Individuals will want to adopt good conjectures only if people they interact with also adopt that same set of conjectures. Similarly, individuals will prefer to adopt bad conjectures if others do the same. Once a set of conjectures and expectations becomes the focal standard, subsequent players will want to adopt those same standards be-cause others already have.

The logic here is straightforward. One would not want to commit to lib-eral democracy and all that is associated with it if others are doing the oppo-site. Those who did not acquiesce to Stalin's demands often met with violent punishment or death. In this instance, adopting bad conjectures, despite the fact they were of inferior "quality" as compared to the good conjectures, was preferable because others had already accepted them as the standard. The prior adoption of the bad conjecture standard increased the value of that standard to subsequent choosers. Given this, a key part of understanding reconstruction is identifying the factors and mechanisms influencing the initial coordination around good or bad conjectures. If individuals initially coordinate around bad conjectures, this equilibrium will be self-enforcing. For instance, once Stalin's political and social systems were in place in East Germany, individuals could often do better by participating in the existing system rather than by choosing a different course of action. Of course, most individuals would have been better off under liberal institutions, but given the existing institutional environment, coordinating on bad conjectures was the best they could do.

For the sake of simplicity, the off-diagonals in Figure 2.2 are assigned a payoff of zero. However, this need not be the case. It is possible that a player who chooses to follow good conjectures may receive a negative payoff if the other player simultaneously chooses to follow bad conjectures.

To visualize the overall argument being put forth, imagine a reconstruction that has turned into a game of cooperation and coordination. In such a world, all individuals would be searching for cooperative solutions and a new and beneficial political order. For ultimate success, it will remain important for individuals to coordinate their expectations around the best equilibrium. Once in place, such an equilibrium would prove self-enforcing. No one would be tempted to respond with terrorist attacks, crime, or political subversion, and the overall task of reconstruction would be eased greatly. Within such a framework, a successful reconstruction entails the transformation of potential games of conflict into games of coordination premised upon good conjectures. The central issue is understanding the mechanisms that contribute to the transformation from conflict to coordination around good conjectures.

Admittedly, this model is a simplification of the reconstruction process, but it serves to highlight the underlying issues facing occupiers. In the face of widespread conflict or "defection," occupiers must create institutions approximating the folk theorem. If the rules of the reconstruction game can be defined in the appropriate manner, some scope exists for influencing whether interactions in social, economic, and political settings will be cooperative instead of noncooperative. Further, these coordinating-enhancing institutions must be sustainable once occupiers exit. If these institutions unravel upon the end of the occupation, coordination achieved during the reconstruction will erode and conflict will ensue.

It is important to note that the reconstruction process cannot be captured by any single game. Instead, one can envision a large number of overlapping games that include a variety of players over time. The framework developed above captures only the highest, or "meta-level," reconstruction game—establishing central liberal institutions such as a national government. However, within the overarching meta-level game, there are numerous nested mini-games that are simultaneously being played by the wide array of actors involved in the reconstruction process.

For instance, Figure 2.2 captures the interactions between different citizens of the occupied country. To the extent they can coordinate efforts based upon good conjectures, they will achieve a more stable and prosperous postwar outcome. The same game, however, can also characterize the relations between the citizens, or some subset thereof, and the occupying forces. If we assume that both the citizens and the occupiers would prefer that things go well and have at least a partial common understanding of what this might mean, the parties in each group still require favorable conjectures for a cooperative equilibrium to come about. If citizens expect all their problems to vanish immediately, and the occupiers expect regular terrorist attacks, relations are unlikely to be successful. One can envision a similar application of the framework to the wide array of relationships involving various combinations of citizens, occupiers, neighboring countries, and international organizations. Each actor involved in the reconstruction efforts—either directly or indirectly—will be part of a number of different and potentially overlapping games, all contributing to the overarching meta-level game, and hence, the success or failure of the reconstruction.

In reality, only rarely will games of conflict turn into games of pure coordination as illustrated in Figure 2.2. More commonly, individuals face decisions that include elements of both conflict and cooperation. For instance, if someone decides to lobby for liberal democracy, this will be viewed cooperatively by some of his or her allies but perhaps as a sign of betrayal by some of the person's other affiliations. Likewise, even when parties are cooperating to bargain over some outcome, there may be conflict over how to divide the surplus that results from cooperation.

As Larry Diamond has noted, one of the fundamental paradoxes of democracy is the underlying tension between conflict and consensus.[9] On the one hand, democracy involves political competition and hence some form of conflict. On the other hand, individuals must coordinate around boundaries that prevent the conflict from becoming too intense, which could lead to the unraveling and eventual demise of the democracy. One can think of social settings as lying along a spectrum, their position depending on the relevant elements of conflict and cooperation. The greater the cooperative elements in the relevant games, the easier it is to achieve desirable outcomes.

The Stylized Facts of Reconstruction

The framework developed here is consistent with several stylized facts about reconstructions.

  1. *Very rapid reconstruction is, in principle, possible.*
  The possibility of rapid and effective reconstruction is best illustrated by the cases of post–World War II Japan and West Germany. In both cases, external military forces established a liberal democratic order in a relatively short period of time. Further, they were able to coordinate the populace around good conjectures supporting the reconstruction effort. Rapid growth and democratization were under way once people knew to expect good outcomes. Physical capital, while always scarce, did not provide the relevant binding constraint.

  2. *Some countries seem never to reconstruct or even turn the corner.*
  Examples of countries that fall into this category include Haiti, Nicaragua, and Cambodia. These countries have been unable to exploit the technologies and beneficial institutions found in other parts of the world. Citizens in these countries have failed to coordinate their efforts to achieve good outcomes and remain stuck in a trap of underdevelopment, non-cooperative and destructive behavior, and unhealthy institutions. That is, their initial problems do not set self-correcting forces in motion and convergence is not observed.

  3. *Reconstructions will work either very well or not at all.*
  There is some tipping point regarding individuals and groups—spoilers, interest groups, and so on—engaged in conflict on one side and widespread coordination and cooperation on the other. Once this tipping point is reached, cooperative behavior becomes the dominant force and, despite the existence of some conflict, widespread cooperation becomes self-sustaining and self-extending.[10] When this occurs, reconstructed liberal orders become stable and no longer rely on external support in order to sustain. However, until this tipping point is reached, the forces of conflict will trump cooperation. Although elements of cooperation may exist, conflict will prevent the achievement of sustaining liberal institutions.

  This is evident when one looks at historical U.S.-led reconstruction efforts. A bimodal distribution can be observed consisting of clear cases of success, in which reconstruction efforts contributed to a consolidated democracy (Japan, West Germany, Austria) and clear cases of failure (Cuba, Nicaragua, Haiti,

Somalia). Returning to the Polity Scores considered in Chapter 1, we observe that almost all the successful cases of reconstruction generated scores above the minimum required to be considered a consolidated democracy. Likewise, as illustrated in Table 1.2, the cases in which reconstruction efforts failed, for the most part, did not generate any marked improvement in the political institutions of the countries in question. In short, there are clear successes, clear failures, and relatively few cases in between those extremes.

4. *Coordination is a necessary but not a sufficient condition for a successful reconstruction.*

A successful reconstruction is effectively able to transform situations of conflict into situations of coordination. However, while this transformation is necessary, it does not guarantee a successful outcome. Coordination can take place around both good and bad conjectures, opinions, and expectations, and each will generate very different outcomes. In other words, not only do occupiers need to transform situations of conflict into situations of coordination, they also need to solve the "coordination problem."

Japan and West Germany serve as two readily apparent examples of coordination around good conjectures. A variety of mechanisms allowed occupiers and citizens to overcome the coordination problem. In contrast, the case of Stalin's reconstruction of East Germany provides an example of coordination around bad conjectures. The Stalinist conquests of Eastern Europe led to fairly rapid political order, but people grew to expect a system of expropriation and ill-defined property rights. Coordination took place around perverse ends requiring continual interference on the part of the government to maintain the economic, political, and social orders—the mechanism through which the coordination problem was overcome was the widespread fear of coercive force.

The political scientists Russell Hardin, Edward Mansfield, and Jack Snyder have emphasized how mechanisms that generate coordination can contribute to, and intensify, conflict.[11] Hardin focuses on the use of ethnic identity as one such mechanism and cites Bosnia and Rwanda as two examples in which coordination resulted in conflict. In such instances, individuals coordinate with others along ethnic lines, and this coordination results in intergroup conflict between ethnicities.

In a similar fashion, Mansfield and Snyder provide statistical evidence to support the thesis that, in the process of consolidation, maturing democracies often face difficult transitions. Weak political institutions tend to exacerbate nationalism and national aggression, as political elites attempt to coordinate citizens around a set of conjectures in order to secure a position of power. In weak states, the focal points often established by elites do facilitate coordination, but these focal points often generate conflict either within or between states.

These studies support the contention that coordination is a necessary but not sufficient condition to achieve successful reconstruction. It is coordination around specific conjectures that generates a sustainable liberal democratic order.

The Paradox of Conflict

The aim of this analysis is to contribute to our understanding of why we observe cooperation in some reconstruction efforts and the persistence of conflict in others. The Coase theorem, formulated by Nobel Laureate Ronald Coase in 1960, can contribute to this goal. This theorem states that, with well-defined property rights and the absence of transaction costs, all allocations of property are equally efficient because interested parties will privately bargain to correct any existing inefficiencies.[12] An example will illuminate the theory.

In his seminal article, Coase presented an example involving a cattle-raiser's straying cattle that destroy a farmer's crops growing on the adjacent piece of property. The ability of the farmer to earn a living was negatively affected by the cattle-raiser's straying cattle. Prior to Coase's article, most economists believed that in such a situation, the government should intervene to either tax or altogether prevent the cattle from straying onto the neighboring property. One of Coase's key insights was that this standard view overlooked the fact that the problem was not one-sided, but rather, reciprocal in nature. Although the straying cattle clearly harm the farmer, preventing the cattle from grazing harms the cattle-raiser, whose livelihood is tied directly to the health of the cattle.

Assuming that there are two options under the law—either the farmer is responsible for keeping the straying cattle off his property or the cattle-raiser is responsible for keeping his cattle off the farmer's property—Coase pointed out that, despite the conflict, there was common ground for cooperation between the two parties. Namely, it was in the interest of both parties to achieve the better of the two outcomes. Coase pointed out that, if transaction costs were nonexistent, the two parties would negotiate a positive-sum agreement whereby both parties would benefit. This mutually beneficial outcome would occur, Coase indicated, no matter how property rights were assigned.

Consider a simple numerical illustration. Assume that the cost of the straying cattle to the farmer in the form of damaged crops is $200 a year. Further, assume that the cost of installing a fence for the farmer is $100 while the cost for the cattle-raiser is $150. In this case, the most efficient outcome is for the farmer to build the fence because he can avoid the $200 in annual damages for less than the cattle-raiser can. Now consider what happens under either of the two possible legal rules.

If the farmer is found to be responsible, he will consider his two options: he can either continue to incur $200 per year in crop damage or he can spend $100 to install a fence around his property. In this case, the farmer will choose to install the fence and will avoid $200 in damages by spending $100. The efficient outcome, the farmer installing the fence, is obtained.

Now consider what happens if the cattle-raiser is found to be responsible for preventing the cattle from straying onto the farmer's property. The cattle-raiser is aware that the farmer can install the fence for $50 less than it will cost him to install it. Given this, he will bargain with the farmer. He would be willing to pay the farmer the $100 that it will cost the farmer to install the fence plus part of the $50 surplus that he saves when the farmer installs the fence. Note that the economically efficient outcome is again achieved as the farmer ultimately installs the fence.

Coase originally penned his now famous theorem while analyzing the distribution of property rights over television and radio frequencies. However, the insights of the Coase theorem are equally applicable to any conflict.[13] The Coase theorem predicts that, given the assumptions of well-defined property rights and the absence of transaction costs, continued conflict should be an unlikely event. There are gains to be achieved by avoiding conflict and engaging in cooperative behavior through bargaining. It is in the interest of the individuals involved to peacefully reach a mutually beneficial agreement.

This is directly relevant to the reconstruction process. As the framework developed above indicates, a situation of conflict—illustrated by the prisoner's dilemma game in Figure 2.1—characterizes the basic dilemma behind postwar reconstruction. The parties involved will have the tendency to "defect," absent a binding rule or convention, instead of cooperatively contributing to the broader effort. If the assumptions of the theory hold, the Coase theorem predicts that this situation should not persist and instead parties should strike a mutually beneficial agreement. In such a case, all parties would be better off and would increase their standard of living as compared to life under continued conflict.

Of course, in reality one observes the persistence of conflict of various magnitudes across time and space. From divorce to pollution to violent conflicts, it would appear that the Coase theorem fails to describe the real world. This is mainly because the assumptions of the Coase theorem rarely, if ever, hold in practice. In other words, one often observes imperfect property rights and prohibitive transaction costs. While the Coase theorem is certainly an imperfect model of the world, it nevertheless serves as a useful framework for understanding the various factors that facilitate or constrain the predicted outcome of cooperation. In other words, within the context of occupation and reconstruction, it is important to understand the factors that contribute to, or prohibit, the transformation of situations of conflict into cooperation. What factors facilitate or prevent bargaining between parties toward a mutually beneficial agreement as predicted by the Coase theorem?

It is within this context that the next two chapters explore the various mechanisms at work in the reconstruction process. The underlying motivation can be stated in two ways, which can be viewed as two sides of the same coin. In terms of the framework developed in this chapter, we are seeking to understand mechanisms that approximate the folk theorem. In other words, we are looking for mechanisms that increase the payoff for individuals to perceive themselves as facing games of coordination rather than games of conflict. If these mechanisms exist, or if they can be established, games of conflict can be transformed into games of coordination. The central issue then becomes coordinating people around the "right" set of conjectures.

On the flip side of this coin, the subsequent chapters can be viewed in terms of the question regarding the Coase theorem. In short, we want to understand why the predicted outcome of the Coase theorem fails and conflict persists. Just as we seek to understand the mechanisms that facilitate the transformation from conflict to cooperation, we also want to understand the mechanisms that prevent the achievement of cooperation through mutually advantageous bargaining.[14]

3 Why Can't They All Get Along?

THE UNITED STATES did not suffer any conflict-related deaths during the post–World War II reconstructions of Japan and West Germany. Prior to the occupiers' arrival, however, such an outcome was not a foregone conclusion. In the case of West Germany, the United States feared that renegade guerilla forces consisting of members of the defeated German military would form to launch attacks against the occupiers throughout the country. But no violent resistance ever emerged.

Some have attributed the lack of resistance to the creation of a constabulary force by the occupiers.[1] The purpose of the force was to respond to civil unrest, gather intelligence, and train German police.[2] However, it is unclear that this was the reason for the widespread peace in the postwar period. The constabulary force was not actually established until about a year after the end of the war, and no serious unrest took place in the interim, indicating that German citizens had coordinated on a set of expectations and conjectures that supported peaceful interaction *prior* to the creation of the constabulary force.[3] The force may well have reinforced extant peaceful interaction, providing a mechanism for both control and dispute resolution within the already established framework of cooperation, but it is unclear that the constabulary force was the cause of that outcome.

Likewise, interactions between members of the populace and between the populace and occupiers were largely peaceful in Japan. As in West Germany, security issues were a major concern for occupiers in the immediate postwar period. Approximately 3.5 million Japanese troops were dispersed throughout the former empire, and it was far from certain that they would comply peacefully with the emperor's surrender command.[4] However, the Japanese citizens did in fact respond to the emperor's command of surrender as well as to the orders of General Douglas MacArthur, the Supreme Commander for the Allied Powers. This is not to say that there was not resistance or protest, however. For instance, a series of demonstrations in May 1946 protested the ineffectiveness of the food delivery system. The number of participants in the "Food May Day" demonstrations ranged from the low hundreds in some locations to several hundred thousand in others. Although there was some disorderly conduct during these protests, they were far from violent.[5]

Japanese citizens coordinated around a peaceful equilibrium, both with each other and with the occupiers, but it is difficult to attribute this widespread peace to the presence of military troops. Indeed, over the first two years of occupation, there were fewer troops per thousand citizens in Japan than there were during the occupations of West Germany, Kosovo, Bosnia, and Somalia—the first example experienced a like result but the rest experienced a worse outcome than in Japan.[6] Despite these relatively low troop levels, peace was sustained throughout the occupation and after.

A very different outcome resulted in the case of Somalia. In contrast to these aforementioned cases, in which military defeat and surrender had occurred prior to occupation, the United States entered Somalia amid conflict. Prior to military intervention by foreign governments, the situation in Somalia had escalated when various dissident factions throughout the country coordinated their efforts to overthrow the regime of Siad Barre. However, the cooperation between these factions did not continue after the collapse of the regime. One of the dissident groups created an interim government in the capital city of Mogadishu without consulting the other factions. A violent conflict between the interim government and a loose association of the other dissident groups ensued, which led to divided control of Mogadishu. The combination of civil war and a widespread drought and famine led to United Nations (UN) intervention in April of 1992.[7]

When it became evident that the original UN operation, which was charged with overseeing a cease-fire and delivering humanitarian aid, could not provide the necessary security, the scope of the mission was expanded. The UN Security Council authorized the deployment of a U.S.-led Unified Task Force in December 1992 with the goal of restoring peace and democratizing Somalia.

The expanded mission was immediately met with violent resistance from the various factions within the country.

In October 1993, an armed conflict between members of the U.S. operation and armed factions in Somalia resulted in more than a dozen American deaths and the withdrawal of U.S. troops soon thereafter. As depicted in the book and film *Black Hawk Down,* the situation in Somalia was characterized by widespread conflict between indigenous members of the Somali populace and occupiers. Military forces were unable to successfully change the trajectory of the country from conflict to coordination around liberal democratic ends. Although some humanitarian assistance was delivered, efforts were unable to generate sustaining change. To this day, the country remains without a centralized liberal democratic government.

In the case of Iraq, a dominant U.S. military easily toppled the autocratic regime of Saddam Hussein. However, a self-sustaining liberal democratic order has yet to be achieved, and insurgency has been strong from the outset of the occupation and continues seemingly unabated at the time of this writing. President Bush declared Iraq liberated on April 16, 2003, but from March 2003 (the start of major combat operations) through May 2007, the U.S. military has suffered over 3,400 total fatalities, with over 2,700 occurring during hostile incidents. Violent conflict has killed Iraqis as well—estimates of total civilian deaths since the start of the war range from 40,000 to 65,000. It is estimated that from June 2003 through May 2007 more than 6,800 Iraqi military and police, who are working to support the occupation, have been killed.[8] Kidnapping and assassinations of Iraqi citizens who support the U.S. occupation continue as do suicide bombing attacks and roadside bombs.[9] While no final conclusions can be reached regarding the long-term outcome of the reconstruction of Iraq, it is clear that three years after the country was officially declared liberated, a sustainable peace around liberal democratic institutions has not yet been realized.[10] Further, pessimism regarding the ultimate success of the effort is growing.

These narratives provide an interesting contrast. Why was there peaceful interaction in the reconstructions of West Germany and Japan while there is continued conflict and resistance in Somalia and Iraq? Why were parties in the former cases able to coordinate efforts based on peaceful interaction and good conjectures while those involved in the latter cases remain mired in a state of conflict? In other words, why did the populace "get along" in Japan and West Germany, and conversely, why can't the populace get along in Somalia and Iraq?

If the parties involved in the latter cases could coordinate on central, liberal democratic institutions, they would, in principle, be better off. Peaceful interaction would allow individuals to increase their standard of living as compared to their standard of living within a context of continued conflict. All parties could shift their resources away from conflict and instead allocate them to other productive and beneficial ends. Hence, the continuation of conflict would seem to fly in the face of common sense, and in the face of the outcomes predicted by the Coase theorem.

The fact that conflict continues in these venues serves to support the claim that although controllable factors such as troop levels, aid, and the timing of elections are important, they alone cannot account for the drastically different outcomes in the various attempts by the United States to export democracy. Thus, there must be other factors that explain the failure of parties to coordinate around liberal democratic outcomes in cases in which reconstruction efforts have failed to achieve the desired goal.

The most obvious reasons that the Coase theorem may fail to hold in the aforementioned cases are high transaction costs, a lack of well-defined property rights, or both. Recall that the Coase theorem states that when there are well-defined property rights *and* the absence of transaction costs, individuals will bargain to achieve a mutually beneficial outcome. If either of the two core assumptions fails to hold, however, the outcome predicted by the Coase theorem may not be realized.

Let us return to the prisoner's dilemma game illustrated in Figure 2.1. Remember, in the standard prisoner's dilemma game, the outcome that consists of both players "defecting" is suboptimal. Both parties would be better off if they could cooperate. However, without a binding rule or convention in place to promote cooperation, this superior outcome will not be achieved. In other words, if the transaction costs associated with establishing and enforcing a rule or convention are too high, the suboptimal outcome of defection will persist. Likewise, if property rights are not well-defined, and therefore parties cannot enter into a binding agreement, the cooperative outcome will not be obtained. This is due to the fact that, if agreements are not binding, there is nothing to stop one party from initially agreeing to cooperation only to defect and break the agreement in the future.

For instance, the Kuwaitis could not have offered Saddam Hussein a one-time payment to prevent the invasion of their country in August of 1990, for it is probable that Hussein would have accepted the payment only to carry out the invasion anyway. In short, an effective mechanism to enforce such a non-invasion-for-payment agreement was nonexistent. Given this fact, both transaction costs *and* property rights must be considered in the context of occupation and reconstruction. The existence of high transaction costs or poorly defined and enforced property rights within the context of a reconstruction effort may contribute to the failure to achieve cooperative outcomes and the persistence of conflict.

One should understand transaction costs to include the costs associated with bargaining and exchange. They involve finding a bargaining partner, striking a mutually beneficial agreement, and carrying out the stipulations of the agreement. In the context of reconstruction, transaction costs can take on various forms. For one, and perhaps most important, the relevant parties, factions, and leaders must be brought together to bargain toward a mutually beneficial agreement. Specifically, given the goal of establishing centralized liberal democratic political institutions, parties must be brought together to bargain on the exact form of a constitution and the resulting political, legal, economic, and social institutions. In theory, these "meta-institutions" will serve as the foundation of the reconstructed country.

However, simply bringing the relevant parties together to bargain does not guarantee a successful outcome. Once at the bargaining table, there are many other factors that contribute to the overall transaction costs. One specific factor is the total number of parties involved in the bargaining process. Obviously, it will be easier for fewer parties to find common ground than for a large number of parties, each with their own agenda. As the number of parties involved increases, so too does the cost of bargaining and the likelihood of reaching a mutually beneficial agreement. Likewise, the relative friendliness or hostility of the parties involved will also contribute to the overall transaction costs. The relevant parties may have past histories with one another that raise the cost of bargaining toward a peaceful compromise. For instance, if one party has repressed another in the past, hostilities may exist that prevent the achievement of an agreement in the current period.

Yet another potential factor influencing overall transaction costs is the willingness of parties to engage in "reasonable" behavior. In the context of reconstruction, reasonable behavior involves the willingness of individuals to make trade-offs and to compromise on certain issues in order to achieve a mutually beneficial agreement. Indeed, in some cases, parties may not want a liberal democracy and engage in unreasonable behavior to stall the bargaining process;

and in other cases, individuals may be unwilling to compromise regarding certain parts of their values or belief system to achieve an agreement.

For instance, individuals may be unwilling to relinquish their claim to certain lands that have religious significance, or they may demand that certain values and beliefs be included in the reconstructed country's constitution. In Afghanistan and Iraq, the issues of federalism, the role of Islam in politics, natural resource ownership, and the rights of women are but a few of the issues that may cause problems along these lines.[11] If parties refuse to make even marginal trade-offs and only want peace on their own terms, it will be extremely difficult to reach any kind of agreement.

The role of the occupiers can be viewed in the context of transaction costs and property rights as just discussed. In addition to seeking to maintain security and overseeing the reconstruction of infrastructure and political, economic, and social institutions, occupiers also seek to play the role of "mediator." In this role, occupiers seek to bring the relevant parties together to the bargaining table to facilitate a mutually beneficial agreement. Of course, those involved in the bargaining process must work within the overarching rules provided by the occupiers, and furthermore, occupiers typically stand ready to enforce any agreement reached, at least in the short run while they are present in the country. That is, there is an element of at least implied force on the part of the occupiers even in their role as moderator, which can mask the true outcome in the short term.

However, it is unclear to what degree occupiers can influence the transaction costs associated with the relevant parties striking a sustainable agreement. As the initial review in Chapter 1 of U.S.-led reconstruction efforts indicates, the United States has not been overly successful in its role as mediator. In those reconstruction efforts that have failed, the relevant parties have not struck sustainable bargains around good conjectures. Given this fact, it is important to understand the variables affecting transaction costs.

This chapter seeks to provide an answer to the question, "Why can't they get along?" To find an answer to this question, we will consider the mechanisms that facilitate or prohibit coordination in the reconstruction process. More specifically, we will consider some of the major factors, from the perspective of indigenous leaders and citizens, that contribute to the overall level of transaction costs associated with citizens striking a mutually beneficial and sustainable agreement. In other words, in the discussion that follows, an emphasis is placed on those factors specific to the country being reconstructed and how they influence interaction between indigenous citizens and between the citizens and occupiers. The aim is to gain insight into why citizens interact or fail to interact peacefully with each other and with the occupiers. By understanding the indigenous constraints facing occupiers, we will be better able to understand the poor record of the United States in exporting sustainable liberal democracy via military occupation.

The Art of Association[12]

In *Democracy in America,* the nineteenth-century French author Alexis de Tocqueville recorded his observations from his travels throughout America.[13] An outsider can often provide insight to the natives regarding issues and institutions they take for granted, and this is indeed the case with Tocqueville and U.S. policymakers. The United States has attempted to export Western-style liberal democracy via military occupation numerous times over the past century, but ironically, policymakers have neglected the factors that have allowed these institutions to sustain over the long run in their home country. As an outsider, Tocqueville was able to clearly recognize these factors and reported them in his writings. Judging from the most recent failures to export liberal democracy, it is obvious that modern-day policymakers and social scientists still have much to learn from an astute observer who wrote more than a century and a half ago.

While Tocqueville touched upon many subjects, one key area he addressed was how Americans interact with one another. He called this capacity for interaction the "art of association," and it was Tocqueville's contention that American citizens have a unique talent for engaging in this art.[14] What he was noting is that America had, and indeed has, a robust civil society that consists of an array of associations and social networks.[15] Tocqueville noted that these associations and networks were not the result of government design, legislation, or intervention, but instead, American civil society evolved through the ingenuity of self-reliant, entrepreneurial actors.

Within this context, Tocqueville introduced the concept of "self-interest rightly understood" to refer to the tendency for Americans to join together in voluntary associations and networks.[16] "Self-interest rightly understood" refers to actions undertaken by individuals to further the interests of the group, which in turn allow them to further their own private interests. Tocqueville noted that it is not the case in American society that individuals sacrifice their own self-interest for that of the larger community, but rather, that an individual realizes that his or her private interests are directly connected to the interests of the larger group and community. Thus, participation in associations and groups provides a positive contribution to the public good while simultaneously generating advantages for the individual. In short, private and public interests are not necessarily in conflict but are instead interconnected. To return to the framework in Chapter 2, the situation observed by Tocqueville is characterized by a coordination game, as illustrated in Figure 2.2, wherein interests are aligned instead of in conflict with one another as in the prisoner's dilemma situation.

According to Tocqueville, associations stand between the government, or the public sector, and the market, or the private sector. Associations allow individual members of a society to come together to solve common problems without relying on the government. Given this, civil society protects American society as a whole on the one hand from the extreme individualism of markets, and on the other hand, from arbitrary rule and the abuse of power by political actors. In short, associations create a shared identity that facilitates social interaction and allows individuals to cooperate to get things done.

Civil Society and Social Capital: Meaningful or Buzzwords?

Although Tocqueville's insights on the topic of civil society are widely recognized by social scientists, there is a lack of agreement on exactly *how* civil society matters for a liberal democracy.[17] For instance, there is continued debate regarding the specific nature of a civil society necessary to make it conducive to sustainable liberal democracy, including the magnitude of civil society required for such institutions. Despite this lack of consensus, Tocqueville's work on the role of associations as a critical element for sustainable liberal democracy contains critical insights for those working in the areas of democratic development and conflict resolution. Specifically, his civil society thesis—that the maintenance and sustainability of the political is directly dependent on the nonpolitical—has major implications for attempts by foreigners to establish liberal democratic institutions via military occupation. Indeed, as the situations in Afghanistan, Iraq, and Somalia would seem to clearly indicate, without the necessary art of association to serve as a foundation, central liberal democratic institutions will not be sustainable.

It is not the case that policymakers and social scientists have overlooked Tocqueville's civil society thesis. As mentioned, most realize (or at least they give lip-service to) the important role played by civil society in a sustainable liberal democracy. In fact, "civil society" has become a buzzword among policy-makers working in the development community over the past decade, and the degree to which the importance of civil society is currently valued can be measured by the increasing attention paid to the notion of "social capital" by both policymakers and academics.[18] Although there is no universally agreed upon definition of social capital, it is widely agreed that the concept encompasses the informal norms and values that lower transaction costs and facilitate interaction and coordination.

On the policy side, the World Bank has started a social capital initiative that emphasizes the importance of civil society in developing countries.[19] This initiative illustrates the current general trend on the part of international aid organizations to drastically increase their spending on programs to promote social capital and civil society in countries throughout the world.[20] As of 1995, international aid organizations spent, in total, over $4 billion on civil-society assistance programs, which accounts for over 8.5 percent of the total aid to developing countries.[21] The United States Agency for International Development (USAID) increased spending on civil society programs from $56.1 million in 1991 to $118.1 million in 1993, and the figure was $181.7 million in 1998.[22] This represents an increase of over 320 percent during the 1991–1998 period.

Likewise, scholars from across the social sciences are paying increasing attention to the nature and role of social capital in the functioning of society.[23] The focus on this concept began about a decade and a half ago in the academic literature, and attention to this topic shows no sign of abating. Although he was not the first to use the term *social capital*, the sociologist James Coleman is attributed with introducing the concept to the broader social science audience in his essay "Social Capital in the Creation of Human Capital."[24] According to Coleman, investing in relationships with others lowers the costs of interacting and transacting, and therefore represents a type of valuable capital. Since Coleman's essay appeared, scholars from across the social sciences have incorporated the concept into their models and research in various forms.[25] The result has been an increased focus on the role of relationships, networks, and informal norms in the functioning of society as well as on attempts to find formal measures for these variables.

Forgetting the "Art"
The great oversight of policymakers involved in reconstruction efforts, as well as the international development community in general, is to emphasize the importance of associations while neglecting the "art" involved in associating

in a manner conducive to liberal democracy. Success in this regard is not simply a matter of external support for the creation of voluntary associations.[26] While the creation of these associations may indeed strengthen existing social capital, the existence of associations at all presupposes the existence of a certain type of social capital that allows civil society to emerge in the first place. If these presupposed habits, skills, and knowledge are absent, the art of association necessary for Western-style institutions will be missing as well. Where conflict is the norm, conflict will tend to continue because the art of association necessary to transform the situation to one of coordination will be lacking.

Given its importance for liberal democracy, and the fact that policymakers and others give it so much attention, why has Tocqueville's insight regarding the *art* of association been neglected as a key constraint on the ability of foreigners to export such institutions? One possible explanation may be the fact that it is so difficult to formally measure and compare factors across cases and time. Indeed, attempts to provide various measures of social capital and civil society have yielded inconclusive and conflicting results.

Although policymakers and academics in a variety of fields understand what social capital and civil society entail, the various elements that compose these concepts cannot be aggregated into a single objective measure that would enable comparative analysis. While factors such as troop levels, monetary aid, and infrastructure projects can be neatly measured and tracked over time, gauging the endowment of the habits, skills, and knowledge necessary for the art of association cannot be easily quantified. This has not stopped academics and policymakers from attempting to find suitable proxies, but these efforts fail to capture the essence of Tocqueville's insight and have largely proved ineffective in informing policy decisions.

Implications for Reconstruction Efforts

Recognizing the general importance of the art of association for the functioning and sustainability of liberal democratic institutions has major implications for reconstruction efforts. As Tocqueville indicated, the art of association in America is a means of private governance whereby individuals can solve common problems. Associations are also a key check on the abuse of power by those in the political sphere. However, Tocqueville was careful to indicate that the art of association is a "habit" that is learned and developed. Mastering the art of association requires a certain set of skills and knowledge, and according to Tocqueville, Americans possess the necessary disposition to form effective associations. In other words, the habits necessary for the art of association are part of a society's cultural endowment, which encompasses the array of informal rules that in turn constrain interactions and the feasibility of various formal institutional and organizational arrangements.

The recognition that the existing endowment of a culture constrains the society's feasible set of formal institutions has a long tradition in the field of political economy.[27] John Stuart Mill explored the reason behind "the great rapidity with which countries recover from a state of devastation." Mill concluded that individuals "with the same skill and knowledge which they had before . . . have nearly all the requisites for their former amount of production."[28] Mill's insight is extremely relevant in the context of reconstruction.

Applied to modern reconstructions, Mill's insight indicates at least part of the reason efforts to reconstruct some countries were successful while efforts in others have failed. For example, different sets of knowledge and skills in pre-war Japan and Germany as compared to Haiti and Somalia are apparent factors in the success of the former and failure of the latter. As the political scientist Eva Bellin has concluded, the postwar endowments of Japan and Germany were conducive to the reconstruction efforts undertaken, facilitating the reconstruction process around cooperative ends. She concludes that, given their unique starting endowments, Japan and Germany cannot be used as a benchmark of occupiers' ability to export democracy in general.[29]

Similarly, F. A. Hayek, a Nobel Laureate economist, discussed the fundamental political principles that provide the foundation for a sustainable liberal political order. He highlighted the importance of past experiences and traditions, including the underlying beliefs and dispositions, "which in more fortunate countries have made constitutions work which did not explicitly state all that they presupposed, or which did not even exist in written form."[30] Hayek's point is that a constitution is a codification of the underlying beliefs, traditions, and habits of a society, and hence successful instruments of liberal democracies if those underlying elements were part of the cultural endowment in the first place. Stated the other way around, Western institutions presuppose a tacit understanding of certain core principles, and it could be argued that this understanding is a function of those core principles existing within the society implicitly prior to the reconstruction effort.

In the modern economics literature, the recognition of the importance of past experiences manifests itself in the concept of path dependency—the way in which institutions and beliefs developed in past periods constrain choices in the current period. In other words, past experiences will facilitate or constrain the transformation of situations of conflict into situations of coordination. Nobel Laureate economist Douglass North, who is a key contributor to the path dependency literature, has emphasized that formal rules and institutions are indeed important but must be complemented and reinforced by informal rules and institutions (conventions, beliefs, norms, and so on) in order to operate in the desired manner.[31]

In the case of failed reconstruction efforts, one institutional arrangement (here formal institutions such as associations and political and economic institutions) is not viable without its complement—informal institutions such as the habits, knowledge, and beliefs necessary for the appropriate art of association.[32] Together, the formal and informal institutions will operate effectively, but any disjuncture between the two will result in dysfunction.

North concludes that informal rules and institutions are the product of the "mental models" of the individuals involved. As such, informal institutions constrain the feasible set of organizational forms, and thus political, economic, and social associations and organizations that exist in the West may not be feasible in other parts of the world at some specific point in time. That is, the mental models will vary inevitably because different individuals are involved not only in general but also in kind. What constitutes an individual will be categorically different from culture to culture and society to society. North also emphasizes that social scientists lack a firm understanding of how informal norms evolve and develop, including how to influence the direction of mental models, and the resulting informal institutions, necessary to supplement and reinforce the desired formal institutions.[33] Once again, in the absence of these complementary informal institutions, formal institutions will not operate and evolve in the desired manner.

The key observation in this discussion is that countries being reconstructed have a preexisting endowment of culture—a certain set of informal skills, knowledge, and beliefs that either will empower them to effectively engage in the art of association necessary for liberal democracy or will limit their ability to do so. This existing endowment serves as a short-term constraint on the actions of occupiers. Attempting to transplant a formal institution is not the same thing as transplanting the entire social system that generated that institution in the first place. Absent the complementary institutions to serve as a foundation, reconstructed institutions will be dysfunctional, and situations of conflict will not be transformed into situations of coordination and cooperation.

The Dark Side of Social Capital

It is not just a case of the requisite knowledge existing or failing to exist within the culture under reconstruction. It is also possible that existing skills, knowledge, and habits stand in direct contrast to liberal democracy. Scholars have recently begun to pay attention to the "dark side" of social capital, which may include such things as the exclusion of outsiders or the pressure to conform to norms and values in order to remain part of a group.[34] For instance, social capital can lead to cooperation and reciprocation within a group, but it also necessarily excludes outsiders. Similarly, it is possible to have shared social capital within specific groups but conflict between groups. For example, terrorist organizations possess strong social capital between members of the organization. Often these organizations provide public goods such as education, religious services, healthcare, and welfare support for members.[35] However, the activities of these organizations are by definition destructive to an inclusive vision of society and to attempts by foreign governments to establish liberal democracy.

To illustrate this last point, consider that many of the same kinds of civic associations in terms of functionality that contribute to liberal democracy in the West—student organizations, political associations, charities, churches, and religious associations—often play a key role in supporting terrorism in the Middle East.[36] When such a situation exists, it is not the absence of associations, but rather the nature of the existing associations, that is the main issue. This reinforces the previous assertion that it is a challenge to effectively measure not just the magnitude but also the nature of civil society in any meaningful way. While a certain society may have many voluntary associations with much the same functionality as their counterparts in the West, these organizations may not be conducive to liberalism.

Although policymakers and social scientists have some understanding of *what* the concept of social capital entails, they have much less understanding of the exact nature of social capital conducive to liberal democracy, let alone *how* to shift existing social capital or create social capital anew. In addition to definitional issues, attempts to effectively quantify the "stock" of social capital have failed to effectively inform policy. Even if we are to put these issues aside, however, it is far from clear that policymakers can effectively create or manipulate social capital in the desired manner.

The fact that occupiers are constrained by a country's existing cultural endowment, in combination with the fact that policymakers and academics possess a poor understanding of how to manipulate this endowment in the desired manner when it does not already complement desired goals, indicates the following: Where tacit beliefs align with the formal constitution and rules of society, most individuals will already be following the rules, and the need for coercion to sustain the political, economic, and social orders will be minimal. In contrast, where there is a disconnect between tacit beliefs and formal rules and institutions, force will be required to substitute in cases in which informal complementary institutions are lacking. Given the ultimate goal of self-sustaining liberal institutions, this is not a desirable strategy. The key difficulty lies in gauging the nature and magnitude of the existing endowment, and our inability to adequately understand the cultural constraint should give pause to those considering engaging in occupation and reconstruction efforts.

Nested Games and the Meta-Game of Liberal Democracy[37]

One explanation for why parties involved in the reconstruction bargaining process fail to coordinate on the mutually beneficial outcome of a peaceful liberal democratic order is that what appears to be the optimal or "rational" course of action to outside observers may not be the best course of action from the standpoint of the parties actually involved in the bargaining process. In such a situation, the surplus that outside observers perceive to exist is, in reality, smaller than projected or nonexistent. Outside observers suffer from incomplete information and fail to observe the subtle nuances of the actual bargaining situation.

Consider the case of Iraq. From the standpoint of many outside the country, it seems obvious that a liberal democracy is a preferable state of affairs for Iraqi citizens. This is especially true when compared to life under the Hussein regime and the disorder and insurgency that has followed the defeat of that regime by U.S. military forces. Such a situation would allow Iraqi citizens to have their rights protected, participate politically, and interact peacefully. In economic terms, this outcome would result in specialization, widespread gains from trade, and increases in the overall standard of living. In terms of the framework developed in Chapter 2, many would be made better off by coordinating around "good conjectures" that support centralized, liberal democratic institutions.

However, focusing narrowly on the overarching reconstruction situation, or "meta-game," overlooks the fact that the various parties involved in the bargaining process are also playing numerous "mini-games" that compromise the larger meta-game. Let us return once again to the framework established in Chapter 2. The framework, consisting of the prisoner's dilemma and coordination games, serves not only to illuminate the overarching meta-level reconstruction game but also describes the numerous, overlapping mini-games present in the reconstruction setting. These mini-games might consist of intergroup interactions between individuals belonging to different groups, intragroup interactions between citizens within a group, or interactions between members of the various groups and occupiers.

The logic behind the nested-game framework is straightforward. While an actor's decision may appear suboptimal to outside observers, it is often the case that outside observers have an incomplete perspective that makes it appear as if the actors within the game are acting in a suboptimal manner.[38] In terms of the framework developed in Chapter 2, the players might have good reason to choose to "defect" or coordinate on "bad conjectures," even though to the outside observer it appears that cooperating is the obvious choice because of the higher payoff associated with that course of action. The problem is that, while the outside observer often focuses on the meta-game, the actors involved in the actual bargaining process are involved in a network of embedded or nested games.

This implies that reconstruction efforts will suffer when they focus on resolving the meta-level game of creating liberal institutions at the national level while neglecting, or placing secondary emphasis on, the nested games embedded within the meta-game. These nested games are the result of historical interactions and experiences that often occurred *prior* to the reconstruction effort, and in many cases, these nested games constrain the achievement of a solution to the general meta-game. Indeed, the nested games may be so complicated that the meta-game cannot be easily characterized let alone solved by occupying forces.

Return again to the current reconstruction of Iraq. In its role as mediator, the United States has undertaken major efforts to ensure that representatives from Iraq's major ethnic groups—the Arabs and Kurds—and religious groups—the Shi'a and Sunni Muslims—are at the bargaining table as the country's new constitution is drafted. Given the benefits of peaceful liberal democracy, it may appear to an outside observer that these parties will be able to strike a mutually beneficial agreement, but this conclusion overlooks the fact that these groups have a long history with one another that substantially raises the costs associated with bargaining. In other words, there are numerous nested games being played that make the meta-game extremely difficult to even describe adequately and perhaps impossible to solve in the short-term.

Given the deep divisions in the country, one could question whether Iraq is in fact a nation with a shared identity. Saddam Hussein was effectively able to solve the meta-game of establishing a central Iraqi government, but only through the continuous use of coercive force against various groups in society. To further understand these divisions, consider the following: while most of the Iraqi Kurds follow the religion of Sunni Islam, as do approximately one-fifth of the total Iraqi population, they possess their own unique cultural practices and use their own language; thus the Sunni Kurds have their own identity separate from the rest of the Sunnis in the country. Iraqi Kurds were violently repressed under the Hussein regime, but they experienced autonomy with the protection of the U.S. military following the end of the first Gulf War. Given this history, Kurds are skeptical of the Sunni minority, who controlled the country during the Hussein era, and are concerned about the possibility of losing their independence in the post-Hussein Iraq that is currently evolving.

Like the Kurds, the Arab Shi'a, who constitute approximately 60 percent of the Iraqi population, were violently victimized by the Sunni minority prior to the collapse of the Hussein government. In addition to violent repression, the Shi'a-dominated cities in Iraq, especially those in the southern region, suffered from a lack of investment and development under the Hussein regime. Again, this history between the Shi'a and Sunnis has created tensions that make coordination and bargaining between the two that much more difficult.[39]

These simultaneous games—the Sunni Kurds with the Shi'a Arabs, the Sunni Kurds with the Sunni Arabs, and the Shi'a Arabs with the Sunni Arabs—all make the larger meta-game that much more complex and raise the costs associated with successful bargaining.[40] Further complicating the meta-game, additional intragroup nested games are also taking place as individuals seek positions of power and to influence the direction of the country. Before the Iraqi meta-game can be solved in any meaningful way, coordination around cooperative ends must be achieved in the array of nested games that are currently being played, and the complexity of the situation makes the move, at least in the short term, appear to be utterly implausible.

The meta-game grows even more complex when the occupier's role as actor is factored into the overall picture. That is, in addition to various nested games between the groups within Iraq, these same groups are also engaged in a series of nested games with the occupiers. Although liberation and self-determination are among the stated motivations of the war and subsequent occupation of Iraq, occupiers have consistently intervened to influence the direction of the reconstruction. As a result of these actions, many Iraqi citizens view the American presence not as an exercise in liberation but as occupation for its own sake.[41]

A CNN/ *USA Today*/Gallup Poll of Iraqi citizens, conducted between March 22 and April 9, 2004, found that 71 percent of those polled viewed Coalition forces as occupiers, while only 19 percent viewed them as liberators.[42] Given this, many Iraqis have responded with resistance to attempts by occupiers to influence the outcome of the reconstruction. This course of action is summed up by an Iraqi tribal leader who told a reporter that the Americans should allow Iraqis to choose their own direction, or "we will keep resisting until we force them to leave the country."[43] The distrust of the United States is perhaps partially due to historical experiences with British colonizers as well as the United States's support of Israel, which adds yet another layer of complexity to the overall reconstruction game.

As an example, consider the following array of games involving the U.S. occupiers. As previously mentioned, the Sunni Kurds fear that a U.S.-mediated bargaining process will result in the loss of part of their independence and autonomy. Likewise, Sunni Arabs fear that the United States will punish them for their repression of the Shi'a Arabs and Sunni Kurds. In addition, Sunni Arabs are concerned by the prospect that they may lose much of the power that they possessed during the Hussein era. Finally, many Shi'a Arabs feel betrayed by the actions of the United States during the first Gulf War. From the viewpoint of many Shi'a, the United States did not provide them with support during their attempt to revolt and take power from the Hussein regime following U.S. military intervention. The revolt ultimately failed, and the Hussein regime maintained control of the country until the second Gulf War. As a result, the Shi'a further suffered under Hussein as punishment for the attempted revolt. Obviously, similar to the array of nested games between the indigenous groups in Iraqi society, the nested games between these groups and the U.S. occupiers significantly increase transaction costs and limit the occupiers' ability to be an effective mediator and contributes to the overall difficulty of achieving a cooperative solution in the Iraq meta-game.

All societies, democratic and non-democratic, developed and non-developed, are characterized by an array of nested games. However, in some societies there is an extant cooperative solution to these nested games that allows for a sustainable cooperative solution to the larger meta-game of coordinating on liberal democracy. By contrast, in other societies the nature of the nested games precludes the achievement of a cooperative solution to the meta-game of self-sustaining liberal institutions.

Political scientists recognize the importance of a national identity in the achievement of sustainable liberal democratic institutions. As the political scientist Eric Nordlinger indicates, it is more likely that a democratic political system will develop "when a national identity emerges first, followed by the institutionalization of the central government, and then the emergence of mass parties and mass electorate."[44] A national identity is shared across groups of individuals, and therefore requires some kind of solution to the larger meta-game. Conversely, however, where nested games preclude the development of a shared national identity, we should also expect the absence of a cooperative solution to the meta-game.

Nested Games and the Art of Association

A connection can be drawn between the recognition of the importance of nested games and the art of association discussed earlier. The art of association, as observed and reported by Tocqueville, allows individuals to find solutions to nested games and to in turn solve the larger meta-game. The art of association involves not just associations, however, but also the social networks that connect them. These cooperative solutions generated within associations and also *across* associations contribute to a shared identity that supports extended liberal democratic orders. Where the habits and disposition necessary for the required art of association are absent, cooperative solutions to the nested games that characterize a society will be missing as well. In such an instance, ties of trust and reciprocity between various individuals and between groups will be minimal to nonexistent, and conflict will be more likely than cooperation.

This fact has implications for changing the institutional trajectory of countries being reconstructed. Recall that social change toward sustainable liberal democracy requires that individuals conform to a set of "good conjectures," as illustrated in the coordination game in Figure 2.2. Through their actions, occupiers attempt to push the society in question toward the "good conjecture" equilibrium. Success in this endeavor requires the spread of liberal ideas, beliefs, values, and expectations that ultimately lead to the adoption or rejection of a new set of conjectures. The level of "connectivity" in a society will influence the costs associated with the spread of alternative sets of conjectures. The logic here is that, where connectivity and "bridging" ties exist, ideas will spread relatively quickly as compared to within a society that is fragmented.

Sociologists have developed diffusion theory to explain how ideas, innovations, or products spread through social networks and society.[45] Many of the studies employing diffusion theory have found that it only takes a small number of individuals, often referred to as "change agents," to adopt an idea, innovation, or product to make it acceptable to a large number of people. Change agents are focal individuals who have well-established reputations within their groups and in their social networks as first-movers. They are entrepreneurial in that they are alert to the benefits of adopting a new idea or activity and, in doing so, inform members of their social network about such new opportunities. Diffusion theory emphasizes the importance of the first mover for beginning the process of change and also that the magnitude of the transmission of an idea or innovation is constrained by the extent of available social networks.

Change agents are critical in the process of generating sustainable change toward good conjectures. They are able to interact in different social groups, facilitating cooperative outcomes to nested games. However, when a society lacks the art of association that allows for cross-group connectivity, social change will be more difficult and costly, and the diffusion of ideas will be limited. In fact, cooperative solutions to nested games may not be achievable, potentially preventing a solution to the larger meta-game. In contrast, when a society possesses the art of association that is conducive to widespread connectivity across individuals and groups, the process of solving nested games, and thus the larger reconstruction effort, stands a far better chance of success. There will be a greater likelihood of widely diffused knowledge around some shared expectations and a focal equilibrium. Some specific examples will clarify this assertion.

Consider for instance the case of Sheikh Muqtada al-Sadr, an anti-American Shi'a cleric in Iraq. Al-Sadr's followers look to him for guidance and leadership, and thus he can be viewed as a change agent who has the ability to start the diffusion process among his followers around either "good" or "bad" conjectures. Al-Sadr led an uprising in the city of Najaf in April 2004 that resulted in weeks of fighting between occupying troops and the insurgents who follow him. Moreover, precisely because he is recognized as a change agent, in the months following the initial drafting of the Iraqi constitution, opponents of the document courted al-Sadr in the hopes of convincing him to ask his followers to reject the proposed constitution.[46]

To the extent that al-Sadr supports and adopts the policies of U.S. occupying forces, he has the ability to diffuse "good conjectures" that will ease the overall reconstruction process. Conversely, to the extent that he resists the policies of the occupiers, he will contribute to the diffusion of ideas that run counter to the reconstruction. Ayatollah Ali al-Sistani, a well-respected Shi'a authority in Iraq, can be viewed in a similar light.[47]

Although al-Sadr and al-Sistani have dedicated followers who look to them for leadership, however, it is important to note that neither has widespread influence over Iraq as a whole, but instead over a specific religious group, the Shi'a. Even within the larger Shi'a group, al-Sadr and al-Sistani have different levels of influence, which further suggests the complexity of the nested games within the meta-game in Iraq—there are not only many groups within Iraq but many players within groups with varying degrees of influence as change agents. This also highlights the fact that Iraq currently lacks the art of association necessary for a shared national identity across all groups. We can contrast this situation with the case of Emperor Hirohito in Japan.

As will be discussed in detail in later chapters, the emperor played a key role as a change agent in the post–World War II reconstruction of Japan. In this role, the emperor served as a focal liaison between the occupying forces and the populace of Japan. As such, he served as a catalyst for the widespread diffusion of liberal ideas and contributed to the ultimate adoption of liberal institutions. This was especially important in convincing those Japanese citizens who were skeptical of U.S. efforts.[48] As will be demonstrated, a key reason that the emperor was effective in this role was because the larger Japanese meta-game was solved *prior* to the U.S. occupation. The emperor was a well-respected figure-head throughout Japanese society, and thus his participation in reconstruction reduced the cost of coordinating Japanese citizens around a set of good conjectures by legitimizing the occupier's message to Japanese citizens.

Implications for Reconstruction Efforts

Nested games are a critical consideration in understanding the factors involved in reconstructing weak, failed, and conflict-torn states. In many cases, these nested games constrain the achievement of a solution to the overarching meta-game. In other words, nested games may constrain the possibility of the far-reaching diffusion necessary to coordinate citizens around good conjectures. Viewing weak and failed states through the lens of the nested-game framework provides insight into why past reconstructions failed and conflict persisted. It also illuminates why there is good reason to believe that similar efforts in these countries may fail in the future.

The nested-game framework also provides one explanation for why it is a mistake to assume that reconstruction efforts are preferable to refraining from intervention. The inability of outsiders to objectively comprehend the payoffs associated with the array of nested games, let alone to find a stable cooperative solution to these various games, provides another reason for erring on the side of humility when considering the possibility of exporting democracy via military occupation.

The general implication for reconstruction efforts is that attempts to export democracy are more likely to be successful when some voluntary solution to the meta-game exists *prior* to occupation. In these cases, nested games are less likely to be an issue. To a large extent, situations of conflict will already be transformed into situations of coordination, and success will be a matter of occupiers solving the coordination problem by coordinating citizens around the "right" conjectures. This was the case in both West Germany and Japan, countries that were held together through widespread voluntary acceptance of political, economic, and social institutions instead of through violence and coercion. The citizens of both countries also shared an underlying national identity that created a relatively strong social cohesion at the meta-level.

In contrast, nested games will be more likely to prevent the transformation of conflict to cooperation, and hence success, in countries where the meta-game has not been voluntarily solved prior to the reconstruction. The cases of Iraq, Afghanistan, and Somalia fall into this latter category. Although the meta-games in Iraq and Afghanistan were solved prior to reconstruction, unification took place through the centralized use of force and coercion. Once the governments in these countries were overthrown, formal institutions quickly unraveled, leaving both countries without many key institutions, including effective police, courts, and utilities. Likewise, these countries lack widespread consensus around a national identity, which increases the costs of coordinating citizens around a shared set of conjectures. In such circumstances, there is no focal change agent at the meta-level to start a countrywide diffusion of good conjectures. To date, conflict has persisted and efforts have failed to transform the reconstruction game into one of coordination and cooperation.

The Problem of Credible Commitment

As noted, the Coase theorem may fail to hold when property rights are ill-defined or unenforceable. Under these conditions, negotiating parties will be unable to reach a mutually beneficial agreement and conflict will persist because there will be no guarantee that agreements will be binding. In the role of mediator, the occupying forces stand ready to enforce the agreements made by the parties involved in the reconstruction process, but typically, this enforcement is only for the duration of the occupation—a successful reconstruction requires the continued enforcement of property rights in the long term, *after* the occupiers exit. In other words, in order to achieve sufficient cooperation to venture forward toward sustainable liberal democratic institutions, indigenous parties must be convinced that agreements reached during the occupation will be binding and enforceable after the occupation ends.

To illuminate the "commitment problem," consider the situation under the Hussein regime in Iraq. Hypothetically, the Shi'a Arabs, who were violently victimized by the Hussein government, could not have offered a one-time payment to Hussein to refrain from violence against them because there could be no credible commitment on the part of Hussein. He could accept payment only to renege and continue to engage in coercion. In the absence of an effective mechanism to enforce the agreement, the hypothetical acceptance by Hussein would not have been credible.

Economists have long recognized the problem of credible commitment within a set of existing formal institutions. For example, Nobel Laureate Milton Friedman, writing in the area of monetary policy, noted not only that policy-makers lack the requisite knowledge to develop and commit to effective discretionary policies but that there is a time lag between the recognition that a policy is needed and the design and ultimate implementation of that policy. The passage of time is itself an issue because a policy that is appropriate in one period may not be appropriate in subsequent periods. Because of these time lags, Friedman's contention was that discretionary public policy will often be destabilizing, and because of this fact, he called for specific rules instead of discretionary public policy.[49]

Along similar lines, Nobel Laureates Finn Kydland and Edward Prescott highlighted the general problem of time inconsistency in public policy.[50] They noted that when governments announce policies, they influence the expectations of individuals in society. For instance, if a government announces a policy

in the absence of credible commitment, individuals will understand the government's incentive to ultimately deviate from the announced policy as time
passes. In other words, policymakers face a commitment problem because the
public will realize that future government policies will not necessarily coincide with policy announced in the current period. To overcome this credibility
constraint, Kydland and Prescott, like Friedman, concluded that committing to
policy rules may be better than allowing discretionary power in public policy.

Peter Boettke has applied similar reasoning to the credibility problem faced
by reformers in the Soviet Union, and concludes that the problem of credible
commitment should be seen as a major factor in failed reform efforts.[51] With
no means of enforcing announced reforms, Soviet policymakers often had an
incentive to either renege or shift their course of action. The result was the
ultimate failure of reform policies leading to increased economic instability.
Boettke's insight can be generalized to apply to all attempts at political, economic, and social reforms.

Similar reasoning applies to credible commitment in the context of reconstruction. Consider, for instance, the first attempt by the United States to
export democracy to the Dominican Republic during the military occupation
of 1916–1924. Horacio Vásquez Lajara was elected president of the Dominican
Republic on the eve of the U.S. exit in 1924. In 1926, a debate began about the
legal length of Vásquez's term. Many possessing positions of political privi-
lege contended that Vásquez and members of Congress had been elected under the constitution of 1908, and therefore, their terms should be extended
two more years, for a total of six. In reality, as the historian Frank Moya Pons
has pointed out, the proposed term extension was not valid because Vásquez
had agreed to, and been elected under, the Evacuation Treaty, which in part
involved his commitment to uphold and respect the new constitution designed under the occupation.[52] The United States, having exited the country
several years earlier, refused to enforce the constitution via a subsequent military intervention.

With no effective mechanism to enforce the terms of the new constitution,
Vásquez and the Congress ignored the constitutionally dictated term limits established under U.S. guidance and chose to remain in office for six rather than
the stipulated four years. This initial disregard for the constitution led to political maneuvering that ultimately resulted in a military-led coup, which in turn
led to the complete unraveling of the reconstructed political institutions and
autocratic rule for the next several decades.

The U.S. occupation and reconstruction effort in the Dominican Republic created some semblance of a cooperative equilibrium, but without mechanisms for ensuring credibility it was not sustainable following the exit of the occupiers. This example illuminates the general insight that parties engaged in long-term negotiations regarding the future of the reconstructed country will require some assurance that any mutually beneficial agreement will be enforced through some combination of rules and checks and balances. In the absence of such assurance, it is less likely that a cooperative agreement will be reached in the first place, and more likely that conflict will persist.

If parties involved in negotiations during the occupation expect others to defect in the future, compromise toward agreement in the present is less likely. As discussed in the previous section, a major issue in the reconstruction of Iraq is the distrust between the various parties—Sunni Kurds, Shi'a Arabs, and Sunni Arabs—involved in the negotiating process. A key fear of these parties is that any agreement reached during the occupation will not be sustainable after the occupiers exit. Each has some concern that the other will renege, which raises the cost of striking a deal in the present period.

Potential Solutions to the Problem of Credible Commitment

Given that the problem of credible commitment is a central issue to the reconstruction negotiating process, is there any way to achieve sustainable cooperation? Social scientists have considered various means of securing commitment between negotiating parties. One of the main conclusions in this area of research is that, under certain conditions, commitment can be secured through the reputation of the players involved.

To understand this premise, let us return to the prisoner's dilemma situation illustrated in Figure 2.1. While defection is the optimal strategy in a "one shot" game, there is the possibility of obtaining a cooperative equilibrium if the prisoner's dilemma game is played repeatedly over many future periods.[53] The logic here is straightforward. In a repeated prisoner's dilemma game, cooperation can be the dominant strategy because players increase the value of their reputation in future periods by cooperating in the current period. As long as the value of one's reputation for cooperating is greater than the value associated with defecting in any one period, a cooperative equilibrium will be obtained.

On the surface, the possibility of reputation serving as a means of achieving the cooperative outcome may be a cause for optimism. However, this is not necessarily the case. Counterintuitively, the desire of negotiating parties to establish a "tough" reputation in the reconstruction bargaining game may actually intensify divisions and contribute to failure to solve the meta-game. The parties involved in the reconstruction game realize that they will be involved in continued interactions with the other parties in future periods. Because of this, they may seek to establish a firm reputation in the hope of gaining an edge in future interactions. In such a case, future interactions and associated gains mean that parties may fail to strike an agreement in the current period.

Such behavior can be observed in many different contexts outside reconstruction efforts, including divorce settlements, child custody cases, and the refusal of governments to negotiate with terrorists and hostage-takers. In all of these cases, the parties to the various "games" attempt to establish a reputation for being a tough bargainer. The key lesson is that, while existing reputation may facilitate cooperation, establishing a reputation may make cooperation more difficult. Within this context, Tyler Cowen notes, "the difficulty arises *precisely because* there will be future transactions, and not because transaction costs are too high."[54] Because the gains from trade in future periods are high, parties may hold out for a greater share of the available surplus, such that an agreement cannot be reached and neither party benefits.

Yet another possibility in repeated games is that players may adopt a "tit-for-tat" strategy.[55] Under a tit-for-tat strategy, players initially cooperate and then respond in kind to the choices made by other players. For instance, cooperation will be met with cooperation, defection will be met with defection, and so forth. If adopted, the existence of a tit-for-tat strategy may effectively substitute for an actual contract. However, in most historical reconstruction cases, it does not appear that parties act in a manner indicative of the tit-for-tat model. In the tit-for-tat model, parties are able to coordinate around cooperative ends and only defect if the other party does so. In many cases of historical reconstruction, we do not observe parties coordinating around a cooperative equilibrium initially only to defect later in response to defection by other parties. For instance, in the cases of Haiti and Somalia, to name but two, indigenous parties were never able to coordinate around cooperative ends in the first place.

In sum, although theoretical solutions to the problem of credible commitment exist, their actual implementation has proven to be a difficult task. Policymakers' knowledge of constitutional craftsmanship is severely deficient, which limits the ability of external actors to overcome the problem of credible commitment. Further, it appears that mechanisms of self-enforcement, such as reputation or retaliation, typically fail to generate the initial coordination necessary for the evolution of sustainable liberal institutions.

Implications for Reconstruction Efforts

The potential problems associated with credible commitment have several important implications for efforts to export liberal democracy. For one, the issue of determining the credibility of commitment calls into question many commonly accepted measures of progress in reconstruction efforts, such as elections and voter turnout, the number of indigenous troops trained, monetary aid, and infrastructure measures. The issues addressed here indicate that such measures may in fact be poor indicators of the long-term sustainability of reconstructed orders. In the absence of binding checks and balances to constrain political actors from defecting once occupation ends, reconstruction efforts will, at a minimum, be dysfunctional, and at the extreme, will unravel. Absent binding constraints on their actions, those in positions of political and military power will have the incentive to engage in discretionary behavior and defect once occupiers exit.

Thus, in attempting to develop workable reconstructed institutions, it is critical to recognize the incentives and informational constraints present. Unfortunately for occupiers, understanding the true credibility of indigenous actors involved in the reconstruction process is a nearly impossible task. Likewise, the knowledge of how to effectively design sustaining liberal constitutions that can provide such checks is severely lacking. In short, the inability to understand which commitments are credible, coupled with the lack of knowledge of a viable solution for how to determine this fact, provides further support for considering alternatives to military occupation and reconstruction as a mechanism of change.

Over-Confidence, Self-Deception, and Expectations Management

A core assumption in economics is that individual actors are "rational," meaning they seek to capture existing gains from exchange. Part of this assumption is that people have a realistic understanding of their abilities, prospects, and limitations. Given an understanding of these constraints, it is assumed that individuals attempt to maximize their position. However, research indicates that in many cases individuals lack a truly realistic understanding of the constraints they face. For instance, many people tend to believe that their values and beliefs—whether political, religious, or moral—are superior to others. Further, individuals typically overestimate their skills and inherent qualities (for example, driving ability, athleticism, and their relative attractiveness and intelligence). This combination is quite problematic when the misinterpretation occurs at the level of the participants in a reconstruction effort, given what is at stake.

The miscalculation regarding an entire nation's true abilities and prospects is perhaps most evident in war. Parties engage in a conflict because each believes it has some chance of winning. Assuming there is an ultimate winner, one side must have erred in its *ex-ante* judgment of its prospects for victory. If parties had a complete and accurate understanding of their abilities and chances, the Coase theorem predicts that they would recognize the difference in power and not engage in conflict in the first place. Instead, they would strike some kind of bargain that reflects their relative power and their prospects in war. Why then do we observe the onset of wars and conflicts?

Overconfidence in Conflict

The political scientist Dominic Johnson has analyzed why we observe overconfidence displayed by the various parties involved in war.[56] According to Johnson, the trait of positive illusions underpins much of that overconfidence. Positive illusions are grounded in human psychology and represent a type of self-serving bias that evolves through self-deception. Typical reasons provided for the evolution of this trait are that it generates persistence, the desire to tackle challenges, and a positive attitude. In other words, positive illusions allow individuals to confidently pursue certain activities that they otherwise would avoid. In situations of conflict positive illusions allow an individual to signal strength and confidence even if the individual is, in reality, weaker than his opponent.

The notion of positive illusions offers one explanation for why we observe war—a preconflict bargain to avoid war can only be reached if both parties agree on their chances of victory if the conflict was to take place. However, the theory of positive illusions indicates that individuals will overestimate their chances of winning, and thus will often choose to fight instead of bargaining to avoid war.

The idea of overconfidence in conflict can be extended beyond physical wars to the post-conflict reconstruction process. In seeking to achieve a mutually beneficial and sustainable reconstructed order around "good conjectures," occupiers attempt to bring relevant parties to the bargaining table. We have discussed the importance of past histories and experiences that manifest themselves in the form of nested games, and the issue of overconfidence introduces yet another potential problem into the negotiation process. In a few words, we should expect parties to be overconfident in their perception of their prospects for success in securing a part of the surplus that is the subject of bargaining.

Let us consider how overconfidence might influence the negotiating process. Each party at the bargaining table will have some view of how the reconstructed country should look. This view is based on an array of factors such as background and upbringing, culture, and historical experiences. Research in the area of self-deception indicates that individuals have a tendency to believe that their worldview aligns with the interests of the world, and consequently, individuals will be overconfident that their vision is the "right" one.[57] Further, social scientists are coming to understand more about how individuals tend to maintain their views and beliefs even in the face of evidence that stands in contrast to that view.[58] Given this tendency, we should assume that individuals will be less likely to compromise regarding their vision of the reconstructed country. As the number of overconfident parties increases, the likelihood of striking a mutually beneficial agreement will tend to decrease.

In short, overconfidence and self-deception can cause the persistence of conflict and can prevent the transformation of situations of conflict into situations of coordination. Parties, each with their own vision of what the ultimate outcome should look like and confident that their view is accurate, will be less than willing to compromise with other participants in the negotiating process—all of whom also hold a vision that they believe to be accurate. In the case of the current reconstruction of Afghanistan and Iraq, the views of the relevant parties on the issues of federalism, Islam, natural resource ownership, language, and the rights of women differ substantially, which would certainly be an obstacle to successful negotiations in the face of these premises regarding overconfidence.

It seems likely that self-deception will be more prevalent in reconstructions motivated by liberation as compared to international wars. In reconstruction efforts following international wars, such as in Japan and West Germany, occupiers tend to impose institutions instead of facilitating bargaining, which minimizes the opportunities for indigenous parties to act in an overconfident manner and engage in self-deception. By contrast, in cases of liberation, bargaining toward self-determination between indigenous parties is a central feature of the process, which makes overconfidence and self-deception far more likely.

Moreover, occupiers can do little to overcome the issue of overconfidence and self-deception on the part of indigenous citizens involved in the negotiating process, which would be tantamount to convincing those involved in negotiations that the world is other than they perceive it to be. Therefore, the main issue for occupiers is accurately gauging when parties are actually engaging in self-deception and overconfidence so as to compensate in some fashion. However, the failures of reconstruction efforts in various locales around the world indicate either that these issues are not under active consideration or that adequate compensation strategies have yet to be discovered.

What Do You Expect?
While occupiers may have little influence over the propensity of individuals to engage in self-deception and overconfidence, they can have some influence over the expectations of the parties involved in the reconstruction process. In fact, expectations of indigenous citizens regarding the reconstruction effort are of central importance for its ultimate success or failure. In general, while the specifics of each reconstruction situation will differ, in each case there is some set of expectations whereby the meta-game is potentially one of coordination rather than conflict. In other words, if the expectations of the citizens of the country being reconstructed are aligned, at least to some degree, with the aims of the reconstruction, there will tend to be a greater degree of coordination and cooperation.

Economics can assist in understanding exactly *how* expectations matter in the larger reconstruction process. Specifically, work in the area of behavioral economics can shed light on the formation of expectations. Behavioral economics attempts to combine insights from psychology with economics to better understand economic behavior. The aim of the behavioral research program is to increase the explanatory power of the economic way of thinking by basing it upon a more realistic psychological foundation.

How can behavioral economics contribute to our understanding of expectations in the reconstruction process? Recent work in behavioral research illustrates that a critical element of expectation management is how outcomes relate to expectations. For instance, psychologist Ed Diener and economist Robert Frank conclude from their work in this regard that individuals value their current state of affairs relative to their expectations.[59]

For example, a millionaire who loses $100,000 in the stock market in a day may, at least for a while, be less happy than a middle-class individual who finds a $100 dollar bill on the street. The central issue is the "frame of reference," the benchmark against which an individual compares his or her current situation, which is a critical determinant of ultimate satisfaction or disappointment. Even though the millionaire is wealthier than the middle-class individual in absolute terms, he is worse off relative to his initial position. His loss, relative to his frame of reference, is greater than the gain realized by the middle-class individual relative to his frame of reference.

Scholars writing in this area conclude that individuals experience improvements by doing well relative to local norms, such as consuming more than in the past or relative to other individuals. This realization can be applied to the situation of reconstruction. A disjuncture between expectations and outcomes can lead to the persistence of conflict. When individuals are forced to participate in an agreement that provides an outcome that is worse than they anticipated, they may very well refuse to act in a cooperative manner. Therefore, understanding the importance of the frame of reference is critical for occupiers in setting expectations.

Setting Expectations

In general, the expectations conducive to a successful reconstruction will vary with the situation. In some cases, it may be better if individuals expect very little. For instance, if expectations in the defeated country are modest, coordination will often be easier to achieve. The Japanese, for instance, expected to be treated very harshly after World War II, and when the Americans treated them relatively well, they reciprocated with cooperation. In other words, the occupying forces treated the Japanese citizens well relative to their frame of reference, which induced further cooperation. If the populace views the occupying forces as firm in their commitment to maintaining social order via force and do not expect quick prosperity, obstacles that arise may be looked upon with less resentment. The signal sent by occupiers regarding the level of force they are willing to use will influence the initial expectations and frame of reference.

If, on the other hand, the defeated citizens expect immediate reconstruction, it may be harder to establish cooperation given the array of constraints that occupiers face in achieving success in reconstruction efforts. If the populace expects the occupying forces to be their immediate benefactor over a wide range of activities, they may very well blame them for each and every mistake made during the reconstruction. Citizens' expectations will be at odds with what is possible. They will feel that they have been cheated relative to their initial expectations, which may elicit non-cooperative behavior in response. Therefore, the occupying forces need to build realistic expectations by clearly signaling their goals and delivering on initial promises.

It might appear that it is always preferable for the populace to have low expectations in order to lessen the potential for a backlash against occupiers.

However, successful reconstruction also requires an investment on the behalf of the citizens of the occupied country in the form of authentic commitment to the process, and insuring this investment requires a certain level of expectations. For instance, in order for impersonal social and economic interaction to take place, individuals must have an expectation that their property rights will be respected. Likewise, in order for citizens to participate in the political process, they must have an expectation that their political and civil rights will be protected. This indicates that a mix of both high and low expectations is needed, depending on the nature of the activity in question.

Overall, low expectations are best when the central question for success is whether the populace will blame the occupying power for every mishap—lack of infrastructure beyond basic necessities, welfare, and other acts of "goodwill" fall into this category. In such instances, there is the real possibility that failure by occupiers will result in resentment and non-cooperation in future periods. In some cases, however, more optimistic expectations will assist the building process. For example, in the case of security and protection from violence, individuals in the war-torn country will expect that the occupying forces provide immediate property rights protection. In the absence of such property rights security, cooperation will be less likely. So the best net recipe includes low expectations concerning "goodwill" but high expectations concerning the provision of basic necessities and property rights. For obvious reasons, this mix can be difficult to achieve.

Another key factor influencing the nature of expectations is the nature of the occupying force's goals. When wars are waged, if the populace perceives that the underlying reason for undertaking the war effort is "liberation," then they will most likely have high (that is, overly optimistic) expectations regarding the speed of the process. Individuals will expect to be made better off then they were under the previous regime relatively quickly. If the reconstruction does not proceed as expected, non-cooperation and continued conflict are real possibilities. If, on the other hand, the reason for the war is retaliation or long-term colonization, expectations will most likely be lower and overly pessimistic.

To illustrate this point, let us consider the case of Iraq. The United States entered the country as liberators of the Iraqi people from the repressive Hussein regime, a role that created a set of expectations on the part of the Iraqis that they would have the opportunity to determine their own future and that their situation would improve relatively quickly. These expectations were evident in the battle over who would draft the interim constitution for the country. Paul

Bremer, representing the United States, chose an appointed twenty-five member Governing Council. However, many Iraqis wanted an election to choose the members of the assembly. The announcement of a council appointed by the United States led to a backlash from many Iraqis. Ayatollah Ali al-Sistani, one of the most respected Shi'a authorities in Iraq, issued a fatwa—a legal pronouncement issued by a religious authority—declaring the appointed council to be unacceptable and calling for general elections. This had the effect of delegitimizing the Coalition Provisional Authority's effort to begin the process of establishing a legitimate government.

Iraqis had the expectation that their participation in the political process would improve quickly, and when it did not, they blamed the occupiers. In contrast, the psychological state of the populace in Japan was one of defeat and despair.[60] The United States made clear that it was occupying the country and that the occupying forces had a monopoly on power and decision making. These factors set a completely different set of expectations compared to those in postwar Iraq.

Again, occupying forces can seek to influence expectations and the frame of reference to some extent, but it must be noted that they cannot completely control the expectations held by the citizens of the occupied country. There is some range over which individuals have preconceived expectations that cannot be significantly influenced. As discussed, individuals may lack a realistic assessment of their prospects in the larger reconstruction game, which may cause expectations to be unrealistically high, and in other cases, historical interactions with other parties involved in the bargain will influence expectations. Even when occupiers attempt to set realistic expectations, the achievement of a long-term, sustainable agreement may be constrained if each side possesses unrealistic and disparate expectations of what they deserve and what they can ultimately achieve. Indeed, the odds of success in such situations are slim at best.

Summation

This chapter has analyzed some of the key indigenous mechanisms that can contribute to the transformation of the reconstruction situation from one of conflict to one of cooperation. Of course, just as these mechanisms can contribute to this transformation, they can also prevent it, resulting in the persistence of conflict. In short, the recipe for successful reconstruction has been shown to be incredibly complex and often unattainable. However, the insights yielded by applying the economic way of thinking to reconstruction can contribute to our understanding of reconstruction on several margins.

One contribution is to the political science literature on this topic. Two of the main models of democratization in the political science literature are "precondition" theories and "bargaining" or "actor-oriented" theories. Precondition theories focus on the prerequisites necessary for democratic consolidation, and studies premised upon these theories typically focus on civil society, economic institutions, the existence of political parties, and a rule of law, among other conditions.[61] In contrast, bargaining theories focus on the role of political and economic actors in shaping the direction of the transition to democracy.[62] Studies based upon these theories typically focus on understanding how the decisions and actions of these actors influence the speed and trajectory of transition.

The economic way of thinking indicates that both preconditions *and* indigenous political and economic actors matter for ultimate success of reconstruction efforts. For instance, the existing art of association is an initial condition that will constrain the ability of occupiers to establish liberal institutions. Likewise, historical experiences will manifest themselves through nested games and expectations. Economic analysis indicates that certain preconditions, such as a certain art of association, solutions to nested games, and experiences that influence expectations in a positive manner, will contribute to a successful reconstruction.

Simultaneously, the actions of political and economic actors influence the outcome of reconstruction efforts. The nature of nested games, and how they relate to the larger meta-game, is influenced by the decisions of actors involved in the reconstruction process. Similarly, issues related to the credibility of reconstructed institutions as well as overconfidence and expectations are directly related to actors' decisions. Finally, occupiers can have some influence over the nature of expectations on the part of citizens in the country being reconstructed. However, as discussed in this chapter, the ability of external actors to influence and guide the reconstruction process is constrained by both preexisting conditions and limitations on their knowledge of how to design the informal and formal institutions necessary for sustaining liberal democracy. Given that, the economic way of thinking indicates that actors are indeed important while concurrently contributing to our understanding of the limitations of their ability to influence ultimate outcomes.

What specific insights can be drawn from this analysis? The mechanisms discussed in this chapter can contribute to our ability to explain why past reconstruction efforts have failed and why future reconstruction efforts may be unlikely to generate the desired effect. Specifically, the analysis is beneficial in providing parameters for what the effective limits are of our knowledge regarding social dynamics. To reiterate one of the main themes of this book, while we have a good understanding of *what* a liberal democratic society looks like, we know much less about *how* to achieve such an outcome where it does not already exist.

This chapter identified some of the major issues for which policymakers suffer from a knowledge problem with no readily apparent solutions. For instance, simply funding the creation of associations does not generate the necessary art of association required to support liberal institutions. Further, policymakers and academics do not know how to overcome the deep cultural and historical constraints that limit the effectiveness of controllable variables such as troop levels, monetary aid, and the timing of elections. The same level of resources employed in different reconstruction efforts will yield very different outcomes due to the varying nature of complementary informal institutions—belief structures, ideas, and values. Unfortunately our understanding of how to create or change the trajectory of these informal complementary institutions where they do not align with formal liberal institutions is nearly nonexistent. What is clear is that the indigenous informal institutions cannot merely be discarded.

Recognizing the limits of our knowledge regarding how to reconstruct countries lacking liberal institutions should not be seen as a negative, however. Instead, acknowledging this limitation is a necessary step in realistically framing both the policy agenda and also the research agenda of those in the academic community. Those in the policy and academic communities need to consider alternative means to military occupation for generating sustainable change toward the desired end of liberal democracy.

4   Exporting Conflict

FOLLOWING THE FORMAL SURRENDER by the Japanese on the
USS Missouri on September 2, 1945, General Douglas MacArthur
officially assumed the position of Supreme Commander for the Allied Powers.
As his title indicated, one of the unique aspects of the occupation and reconstruction of Japan was the near absolute monopoly over decision making that
MacArthur possessed and exercised. Recounting the extent of his position to a
U.S. Senate committee in 1951, MacArthur noted, "I had not only the normal
executive authorities such as our own President has in this country, but I had
legislative authority. I could issue fiat directives."[1]

Indeed, MacArthur had firm control over all aspects of the reconstruction. As the historian John Dower notes, "MacArthur was the indisputable
overlord of occupied Japan, and his underlings functioned as petty viceroys."[2]
MacArthur was also largely insulated from the political process in the United
States, which further allowed him to make decisions quickly. MacArthur and
the occupying forces controlled and filtered information, issued new laws,
and rewrote existing laws covering a wide range of subjects. They also rede-
fined land rights and played a major role in the writing of the country's new
constitution.[3]

The American occupation experience in the post–World War II occupation
of West Germany was different than that in Japan. While the occupying forces
had a relatively free hand compared to more recent reconstruction efforts, they
did face constraints in the form of the Allied forces. Germany was divided into

zones, and each zone was assigned to one of the Allied countries. The United States, the United Kingdom, and France occupied the western zones, while the Soviet Union occupied the eastern zone. One of the notable differences between the reconstruction in Japan and that in Germany was the difference in speed associated with the formulation and implementation of policies. By contrast to MacArthur's near complete control over the occupation of Japan, in Germany, agreement between the various Allied countries was required in order to institute any policy change affecting all zones. Indeed, this need for consensus not only slowed but in some cases prevented policies from being instituted.

The Allied Control Council (ACC), consisting of representatives of the Allied powers, became the main governing body of Germany after the country's official surrender, and there was often disagreement between the members of the ACC regarding policy design and implementation. The range of disagreement included, but was not limited to, central administration and government integration, reparations, monetary aid, and the nature of economic activity. The need for unanimous agreement increased the transaction costs associated with policymaking.

Regarding the resistance from France and the Soviet Union on certain policies, General Lucius Clay, the U.S. military governor in Germany, wrote to Washington D.C., "Unless there is a definite improvement in our ability to obtain results in the next two to three meetings . . . it will be manifest to the press and to the public that the Quadripartite government in Germany has failed."[4] As history tells us, the ACC did ultimately fail: following the merger of the U.S. and U.K. zones into Bizonia in 1947, the Soviets left the council permanently. The less-than-adequate operation and ultimate unraveling of the ACC serves as but one example of the difficulties that can occur between occupying powers in war-torn countries when a multilateral approach is taken.

In addition to the issues with the ACC, another key difference between the reconstructions of Japan and West Germany was the involvement of the U.S. domestic political process, which influenced the reconstruction of West Germany much more than that of Japan. Unlike MacArthur, who was largely insulated from the domestic political process, Clay made frequent trips to Washington, where the War and State Departments, among others, attempted to shape and influence the reconstruction of West Germany. Regarding the United States's reconstruction of West Germany, the historian Edward Peterson notes, "the story of Germany policy formation . . . is an amazing tale of clashing personalities and bureaucratic structures, which together delayed and obscured policy goals to an extraordinary degree."[5] This insight sounds eerily familiar to the pre-war planning and ongoing reconstruction effort in Iraq.

Indeed, there is a growing literature criticizing the current and ongoing efforts of the United States to establish liberal democracy in Iraq. For instance, Larry Diamond, a leading expert on democracy and also a former advisor to U.S. occupation authorities, has criticized the "bungled effort to bring democracy to Iraq."[6] Similarly, David Phillips, a former senior advisor to the U.S. State Department, takes the reader inside what he refers to as the "postwar reconstruction fiasco" in Iraq.[7] Diamond's and Phillips's firsthand accounts of the Iraqi reconstruction paint a picture of poor planning and execution, infighting within the U.S. government, and a lack of appreciation for the nuances of Iraqi culture and history.

As but one example of the unresolved disagreements within the Bush administration, consider the conflicting visions of post-Hussein Iraq that existed prior to the invasion. Vice President Dick Cheney, Secretary of Defense Donald Rumsfeld, and Deputy Secretary of Defense Paul Wolfowitz, as well as other key members of the Bush administration, initially favored the quick transfer of power to Iraqi exile Ahmed Chalabi. In contrast, the CIA voiced their support for Ayad Allawi, a Baath Party defector in the 1970s. Finally, some in the State Department favored Adnan Pachachi, another Iraqi exile, as the next leader of Iraq. The disagreement between these varying visions in the pre-war period contributed to some degree to failure to develop a cohesive postwar plan.[8] The main problem was not the disagreement itself, but instead the failure to find a resolution and coordinate around a unified vision of the new Iraq. Indeed, it is unclear that there was consensus around many if not most key issues prior to undertaking the war and subsequent reconstruction, which has led to subsequent confusion in the postwar period and contributed to the environment of conflict that currently exists in Iraq.

The tension between the various factions of the U.S. government is also evident when one considers the issue of Iraq's possession of weapons of mass destruction. The claim that Saddam Hussein possessed such weapons was the main motivation behind the war, but recent research focusing on the pre-war intelligence indicates that the Bush administration selected the pieces of intelligence that supported its case for war while neglecting those that cut against the case.[9] What have to date turned out to be exaggerated claims of Hussein's possession of such weapons seem, in part, a function of the need to find a focal rallying point for uncoordinated agencies and departments within the U.S.

government. As Paul Wolfowitz noted, "For reasons that have a lot to do with the U.S. government's bureaucracy, we settled on the one reason that everyone could agree on, which was weapons of mass destruction."[10]

These cases highlight the importance of the political decision-making process in reconstruction efforts. The political process in the country sponsoring the reconstruction will have a direct impact on the nature of the effort abroad and will influence overall success or failure. More generally, these examples serve to illuminate the broader fact that reconstruction efforts not only are subject to constraints *within* the country being reconstructed but are also subject to external constraints as well, which, by definition, are those constraints that are peripheral to the country being reconstructed.

As noted earlier, in the case of Japan, domestic politics in the United States had a minimal impact on the day-to-day reconstruction efforts abroad, in stark contrast to Iraq, where domestic U.S. politics continue to have a major influence. Indeed, domestic politics of the occupying country will influence everything from the leadership structure of the occupation to the magnitude and allocation of troops and monetary resources as well as the exit strategy.

Yet another example of an external constraint would be the fact that foreign countries—whether directly involved in the reconstruction or not—can influence the direction and ultimate outcome of reconstruction efforts. For instance, other foreign countries can contribute to the reconstruction by joining a coalition or providing troops and monetary or logistical aid. Likewise, these countries can harm or undermine a reconstruction by criticizing and refusing to support the broader effort. In either case, the influence of these countries serves as a constraint on reconstruction efforts that, while outside the country being reconstructed, will directly affect the ultimate success or failure of the effort.

The motivations of those carrying out the occupation and reconstruction are also of central importance. As noted in the previous chapter, a key aspect of reconstruction is for occupying forces to assume the role of mediator. In this role, the occupiers attempt to bring the relevant parties to the bargaining table to facilitate negotiations toward a mutually beneficial agreement. In doing so, occupiers attempt to reduce the transaction costs associated with bargaining in the hopes of achieving binding rules that will transform situations of conflict into cooperation. However, this assumes that those associated with the reconstruction—political and military leaders, occupying troops, the intelligence community, and so on—will act in a manner to bring this end about.

Ideally, individuals associated with the occupation will undertake activities that minimize transaction costs and provide the greatest possibility for success in transforming the post-conflict situation into sustainable cooperation around good conjectures.

The central question is whether this ideal will be realized. In other words, will those associated with the occupation behave in a manner that maximizes the chances of success? It is unwise to simply assume that they will. Indeed, it is a mistake to assume that those associated with the occupation will serve as neutral mediators, pursuing only those actions that minimize transaction costs while maximizing the overall chances of success. Instead, we need to look at the incentives faced by external actors involved in the reconstruction process to see if they align with the stated ends of the reconstruction effort. A wide variety of external actors are involved in the reconstruction process, including elected political officials, government bureaucrats, military leaders and personnel, voters, and special interests, and these individuals have different interests and face different sets of incentives that may contribute to the persistence of, or increase in, conflict.

For instance, a key characteristic of liberal democracy is self-determination. However, political officials and special interests—both inside and outside the country being reconstructed—often have a vested interest in seeing certain individuals obtain positions of power in the newly reconstructed country. Because of this, they will often have the incentive to influence the political process of the country being reconstructed in order to "pick winners." These interventions, in turn, may reduce the legitimacy of the overall effort and in some cases can generate a backlash against the occupiers. Furthermore, interventions can contribute to conflict by generating negative unintended consequences. In such cases, occupiers may undertake an intervention in the hope of transforming conflict into cooperation, only to further contribute to conflict.

Given this dynamic, a central issue in the reconstruction process is understanding why the political process in the country sponsoring the reconstruction does not necessarily generate benevolent policies that maximize the chances for success in the broader reconstruction effort. The economist Daron Acemoglu has asked, "Why not a political Coase theorem?"[11] Typically, economists consider the Coase theorem in the context of private transactions, and as we saw in Chapter 2, when the assumptions of the Coase theorem hold, we observe the efficient outcome. If the Coase theorem could be extended to the political realm, it would indicate that political policies and institutions were efficient, meaning that the best outcomes were achieved given the needs of society. Indeed, if the theorem did in fact hold in the political realm, this best outcome would exist no matter which political parties or groups were in power. Unfortunately, however, this is not the case. Inefficient and wasteful policies are often generated by the political decision-making process.

Acemoglu concludes that inefficient policies and institutions are chosen because they serve certain political officials and groups whose interests often do not align with the general welfare of other members of society. Similar reasoning applies to reconstruction efforts. The political institutions and political decision-making process in the country sponsoring the reconstruction guide the actions of the array of external actors involved in reconstruction efforts. However, the policies generated will not necessarily be the "best" policies in terms of effectively reconstructing a country along liberal lines, due to the fact that typically a disconnect exists between the interests of the political decision makers in the intervening country and the interests of the citizens both in the sponsoring country and in the country being reconstructed.

This disconnect will manifest itself in inefficient and ineffective policies, which will either slow the reconstruction effort or may, in the extreme, contribute to its failure. One of the aims of this chapter is to explore the causes of this disconnect between the interests and activities of those involved in the political decision-making process of the country sponsoring the reconstruction effort and of those in the country being reconstructed.

As discussed in Chapter 3, those involved in any reconstruction effort face a series of constraints that are indigenous to the country they are occupying and reconstructing. The main point of this chapter is that in addition to these constraints, individuals involved in the reconstruction process simultaneously face external constraints as well. These external constraints often have the counterproductive effect of either contributing to the persistence of conflict or increasing conflict.

In other words, it is possible for foreign countries to export conflict even if the intention of their interventions is to export liberal values and institutions. In the text that follows, I explore the nature of these external constraints and the implications for reconstruction efforts. I seek to understand how those involved in the reconstruction process can export conflict even if that is not their intention. As will become evident, political institutions provide a set of incentives to those acting within those institutions, and often those incentives will not be aligned with the broader aims of the reconstruction effort.

Insights from Public Choice

In the analyses of past and current reconstruction efforts, the motivations of and incentives facing those involved in the occupation and reconstruction (political and military leaders, occupying troops, the intelligence community, government bureaucrats, and so on) are often overlooked. In many cases, it is implicitly assumed that these individuals put aside their own interests and instead act in the "best" interest of both their home country and also the country they are attempting to reconstruct along liberal lines. This line of reasoning assumes that those associated with reconstructions take the most effective steps known to achieve the stated ends of establishing liberal democracy. For instance, this assumption would predict that individuals utilize the best intelligence and information available and follow it in an unbiased manner in initially deciding to reconstruct a country as well as during the subsequent occupation. Further, this line of reasoning assumes that individuals allocate resources such as monetary aid in an effective manner by choosing contractors that can best accomplish the required tasks.

But what if this is not in fact the case? What if the various parties involved in the reconstruction process fail to act in the interest of either those citizens in their home country or those in the country being occupied and reconstructed? The field of economics known as "public choice" can assist us in finding answers to these questions.

Public choice economics developed in the 1950s and evolved from the traditional field of public finance, which focuses on the study of government taxation and expenditure. The central principle of public choice theory is the demand for the symmetry of behavioral assumptions. In other words, public choice theorists apply the same principles that economists use to analyze private actors and extend them to public actors. Economists typically assume that private individuals act in a purposive manner. It is assumed that individuals seek to better their position, given their goals, as best they can within the constraints they face. Public choice requires that we apply this same assumption to actors in the political realm. In other words, we assume that those acting in the public arena, just like those acting in the private markets, pursue their own ends using the best means known to them. This is not to say that public actors never behave in an other-regarding manner, but instead, the postulate is that, like private actors, public actors *tend* to identify with their own wants and concerns rather than those of others.

This has major implications for the study of the public sector. Public choice theory overturns the romantic view, or perhaps the ideal, that individuals in the public sector act in the "public interest." Instead, it introduces skepticism into the study of politics. While public actors may have some concern for others, their dominant motivation is their own well-being and the furthering of their own agenda. The definition of well-being can take on many forms, including monetary or job security, fame, reelection, or promotion within the political system. Only to the extent that their private interests overlap with the broader interests of society will public actors pursue the "public good." Because this field of study focuses on the incentives faced by public actors, public choice theory can contribute to our understanding of the reconstruction process and lend insight into why political constraints may hinder effective reconstruction. Indeed, public choice issues are central to both the initial motivation for engaging in the occupation and the subsequent reconstruction process.

The basic model of politics and democracy developed by public choice theorists is as follows. There are four key groups—private voters, publicly elected officials, bureaucrats, and special interest groups—contending for position as regards policy. Similar to the standard assumptions that underlie economic analysis, it is assumed that individuals have well-defined preferences and pursue their desired ends to the best of their ability given the constraints they face. For example, it is assumed that publicly elected officials seek some mix of maximum votes, fame, power, and income, while individual voters and special interest groups seek to maximize their monetary income. Further, it is assumed that each group wants something that is possessed by one of the other groups, whether it is money, certain policies and regulations, or votes. For instance, individual voters want beneficial policies from elected politicians, who in turn want each voter's support at the ballot box. Likewise, special interests wish to see favorable policies that maximize their income in exchange for votes. Bureaucrats want to maximize their budgets, which typically are controlled by elected officials. Elected officials want bureaucrats to provide their constituents with goods and services in order to gain votes.

How does the basic public choice model manifest itself in the context of reconstruction? Voter behavior and both domestic and international special interest groups will influence the actions and decisions of elected politicians. At the same time, bureaucrats—including those in the military establishment—will also attempt to influence the process by maximizing their budgets and by attempting to create a demand for their services.

The main result of this array of interactions is that those involved in the reconstruction process may fail to take steps to facilitate coordination and cooperation in the country being reconstructed. Instead, the various actors involved
in the political process may actually contribute to the persistence of conflict
as they pursue their own narrow interests at the expense of the larger interests of both their home country and the country being reconstructed. Stated
differently, there is little reason to believe that the most effective and efficient
policies that would maximize the chances of ultimate success will actually be
adopted and implemented. To understand why this is the case, let us consider
the relationships discussed above in more detail.

Voters and Voter Opinion
Consider first how voters and voter opinion influence the behavior of elected
politicians in the context of reconstruction. Social scientists, particularly
those in political science, have developed the "casualty hypothesis" to understand changes in public opinion regarding foreign interventions. In its
simplest form, the casualty hypothesis indicates that the public will not tolerate foreign interventions if they lead to the loss of American lives. In other
words, there is an inverse relationship between the number of casualties and
public support for the intervention.[12] According to this theory, as the number
of American deaths increases, support for the intervention decreases.

The political scientist John Mueller has applied the casualty hypothesis to a
number of U.S. interventions, including the Korean and Vietnam wars, the intervention in Somalia, and the current intervention in Iraq, and it is his contention that the casualty hypothesis does in fact hold.[13] In the case of Iraq, Mueller concludes that American deaths have created an "Iraq syndrome" among
the American public, which may have lasting implications, as the public will
be hesitant to support future foreign interventions. Of course there is some
shelf life for the "anti-intervention" syndrome that follows from the erosion of
public support for foreign interventions. For instance, public opposition during and after the Vietnam War did not seem to have an impact on public support for the second Iraq war in 2003.

To be clear, consensus is far from complete regarding the variables that influence public opinion about foreign interventions. Some researchers emphasize the importance of expectations as they relate to the number of casualties
that will be tolerated by the public. For instance, the political scientists Christopher Gelpi and Peter Feaver contend that Americans will tolerate casualties as
along as they deem them to be necessary to achieve ultimate victory.[14] They also

conclude that the expectations of what are "necessary casualties" have changed over time as technologies have changed. Simply put, technological advances mean that Americans are willing to tolerate fewer casualties because they expect that fewer deaths are necessary to achieve victory.

Although there may not be complete agreement on how public opinion is influenced and shaped, the competing hypotheses discussed above indicate that the opinions of voters are influenced, to some extent, by the choices of political actors and the outcomes of those choices. Likewise, the success of elected officials depends, to some extent, on voter opinions. Given this, elected officials, acting to maximize votes, will consider the impact of their decisions on voter opinion. They will do so both in initially deciding whether to engage in foreign interventions and in deciding on the direction of policies for the subsequent reconstruction effort. Further, one should expect them to respond to voter opinion even if it conflicts with the broader goals of the reconstruction effort. For instance, there may be pressure from voters to reduce troop levels even if success requires maintaining the *status quo* or increasing the number of troops. In short, policies that voters demand from elected officials may cut against efforts to export liberal democracy.

Yet another important insight from public choice theory is the fact that individual voters have the incentive to remain "rationally ignorant," meaning that they are largely uninformed of the specific choices of political actors. The logic here is straightforward. Each individual vote counts very little in the overall scheme of things. For instance, it is unlikely that any one vote will influence the outcome of an election. Further, the more voters that participate in any one election, the smaller the influence of any one vote. Finally, voting is an extremely limited means of expressing one's views and preferences, mainly because one must vote not on specific policy outcomes but upon a bundle of *potential* outcomes.

In addition to the limited influence of any one vote, we must also consider that there are positive costs to obtaining detailed information regarding the candidates and associated issues. It is not that this information is not readily available—much of it is—but rather that there is a cost to actually obtaining and reviewing the relevant information. For instance, one could spend time analyzing the detailed voting record and platform of a candidate, but the individuals incur a cost in that they cannot allocate that time to doing other things. At the same time, the benefit of allocating time to obtaining this detailed knowledge is relatively small because possessing that knowledge will have little bearing on the ultimate outcome given the nonexistent influence of each individual vote. This logic explains why few voters know the detailed voting records of the candidate they support, and instead of seeking out detailed information, individual voters typically rely on focal signals and characteristics—political party affiliation, stance on key issues, and so on—to choose their candidate.

Individual voters have little incentive to become informed regarding issues such as reconstruction efforts. For instance, voters know, in the broadest sense, that an occupation and reconstruction are taking place, but they remain uninformed regarding the particulars such as specific dollar costs, the source of monetary funds, and the allocation of resources. In response to this, politicians have an incentive to engage in showmanship involving activities that are readily visible and easily identifiable to voters. Who doesn't remember President Bush's arrival on the *USS Lincoln* via fighter jet in May 2003? The president, wearing a full flightsuit and standing in front of a banner reading "Mission Accomplished," declared that major military operations in Iraq had ended in success.

This is but one example of the outcomes generated by the rational ignorance of voters. In general, voters will not be fully informed and will demand policies from elected officials regarding reconstruction that will often fail to align with the broader goal of exporting liberal democracy. Stated differently, there is no reason to believe that voters will demand the "best" policies given the goals of reconstruction efforts.

The Logic of Special Interests

Whereas individual voters often lack the incentive to obtain data, organized interests *do* have the incentive to actively seek information. Therefore, public choice theory concludes that special interest groups wield key influence on the decisions of elected politicians. For instance, one could assume that average voters know very little about the steel industry or how their representatives voted on legislation influencing that industry. However, participants in the steel industry most likely do know the details of how representatives have voted in this regard and seek to influence the direction of those votes in their favor.

The logic here is straightforward. The average voter garners little to no benefit from being informed regarding legislation and policy regarding the steel industry. However, members of the steel industry do have a direct interest in such policy and regulation of their industry. They stand to gain a relatively large benefit if policy decisions and legislation are in their favor. Therefore, they have an interest not only in being informed but also in attempting to influence the outcome of the political process so that they realize as much of the potential benefits as possible.

Because of this disconnect between uninformed voters and informed special interests, the latter are often able to manipulate political outcomes to concentrate the benefits of their lobbying efforts on their members while dispersing the costs among the rest of the uninformed taxpaying population. In the preceding example, those in the steel industry stand to gain large benefits from securing political favors while the cost of those benefits are dispersed over a large number of taxpaying voters.

Because the cost incurred by each voter is relatively small, voters have little incentive to seek change. For instance, the average voter has no idea how much of his or her annual tax bill is allocated to steel subsidies, let alone the total amount of subsidies that steel producers receive. The percentage of each individual's total tax bill allocated to steel subsidies is relatively small and so of little interest to most voters, but this small amount aggregated across all taxpayers adds up to a large amount, the benefits of which are concentrated in the hands of said producers.

Because well-informed special interests concentrate benefits on their members while dispersing the costs across a large number of uninformed taxpayers who are not typically aware of what they are paying for, special interests have an incentive to influence and manipulate the political decision-making process in their favor. Stated the other way around, one should not expect the political process to generate policies that benefit the "public interest." Instead, more often than not, policies will be inefficient and a misallocation of resources.

The logic of special interest group politics influences many political decisions, including those associated with many aspects of reconstruction efforts. Indeed, because war and reconstruction are international in nature, special interest politics is not limited to purely domestic actors. Instead, both domestic *and* foreign special interest groups will influence the decisions of political actors as they relate to reconstruction efforts. These interests will seek to secure benefits for their members by lobbying politicians and political officials and by making political contributions to curry favor.

Such influence can range from the initial decision to engage in war to the subsequent occupation and reconstruction efforts. This kind of manipulation will often generate inefficient and ineffective policies that can slow or completely impede the reconstruction process. Moreover, ineffective policies potentially can cause more harm than good by increasing conflict in the country being reconstructed. Considering both domestic and foreign special interests in more detail, along with some specific examples from the current reconstruction efforts in Afghanistan and Iraq, will serve to illuminate this point.

Domestic Special Interests   Domestic special interests are those within a country that have organized for a common purpose and seek to influence domestic political decisions for their direct benefit, even if that benefit conflicts with the broader interests of society. The steel industry is one example of a domestic special interest group in the United States, and another would be domestic defense contractors who seek to influence political decision making regarding military-related appropriations and authorizations. Given that the federal government is the defense industry's main customer, members of this industry gain a direct benefit from any increase in such expenditures and will seek to influence the political process in their favor.

Once started, reconstruction efforts yield many potential benefits that will be sought by special interests. For instance, infrastructure and utilities need to be constructed or repaired. Further, indigenous citizens must be trained to run an array of public services. How are contracts to carry out these activities to be awarded? Ideally, politicians and bureaucrats would choose the contractors who were best able to contribute to the effort to transform situations of conflict to those of sustainable cooperation in the country being reconstructed.

However, public choice theory suggests that this may not be the case and that political connections will play some role in the awarding of contracts. Those contractors that have political ties and who effectively lobby politicians will tend to have the upper hand in securing contracts even if they are not the most effective provider of such goods and services. Those that are able to most effectively curry favor with the appropriate actors in government will tend to be rewarded.

To understand the influence of special interests, let us return to the most recent Iraq war and current reconstruction effort. Specifically, let us consider the six companies that were secretly asked by the United States Agency for International Development (USAID), via the Bush administration, to submit bids on an initial $900 million government contract. This request took place in early March, *prior* to the invasion of Iraq on March 20. The specifics of the contract were to construct and reconstruct infrastructure such as hospitals, roadways, schools, and utilities.

How were these six companies chosen by the Bush administration and USAID? Although some may assume that these contractors were chosen objectively, public choice theory suggests that political connections likely played some role in their selection. Consider Table 4.1.

As Table 4.1 indicates, each of the six companies made campaign contributions over the 1990–2002 period, and five of the six made contributions over $1,000,000. These same five companies hold five of the top six spots in terms of total contract value received for the Iraq reconstruction as of July 1, 2004.

Note that campaign contributions only tell part of the story, however. The strength of political connections is not necessarily captured in contribution figures. In fact, depending on the nature of the relationship, contributions may decrease over time as established relationships replace the need for lobbying via monetary contributions.

To illuminate the importance of political connections and the influence on political decision-making process, consider the case of Halliburton.[16] Much has been made in the popular press about the awarding of major contracts to Halliburton and its construction subsidiary, Kellog, Brown & Root. Indeed, as Table 4.1 indicates, Halliburton has received the largest total contract value to date in the Iraq reconstruction. Halliburton has a long history of close political ties, including the current vice president, Dick Cheney, who was the CEO of the company from 1995 through August 2000.

TABLE 4.1 Campaign contributions and total Iraq contracts: Contractors selected by USAID prior to the Iraqi War[15]

Company	Campaign contributions 1990–2002 ($ millions)	Total contract value, Iraq 2002–July 2004 ($ millions)	Rank, total contract value, Iraq 2002–July 2004
Halliburton Co.	2.4	10,832.0	1
Parsons Corp.	1.4	5,286.1	2
Fluor Corp.	3.6	3,755.0	3
Washington Group International, Inc.	1.2	3,133.1	4
Bechtel Group, Inc.	3.3	2,829.8	6
Louis Berger Group, Inc.	.2	27.7	37
Total	$12.1	$25,863.7	

Cheney had well-established political relationships long before he assumed the chairmanship of Halliburton. He was elected to the U.S. House of Representatives in 1978 and stayed in Congress until 1989, when he was appointed as President George H.W. Bush's secretary of defense. Cheney stayed in that position until 1993, when he assumed control of Halliburton. Government lobbying was a major part of Cheney's efforts as chairman of the company, and indeed, the Center for Public Integrity notes that in the three election cycles prior to Cheney's arrival at Halliburton, the company's PAC and employee political contributions totaled $740,000. Compare this to the $1.6 million that was spent in three election cycles while Cheney controlled the company. During his five years at Halliburton, the company was awarded $2.3 billion in government contracts.[17] This suggests that Halliburton had established political relationships well before the second Iraq war in 2003. Indeed, the fact that Halliburton received significant contracts during the 1990s, when the Clinton administration was in office, further supports the claim regarding existing political relationships.

Since assuming the position of U.S. vice president, Cheney has denied any special relationship or favoritism toward his former company. However, note that since the Bush administration came to power, Halliburton has reduced its lobbying expenses by about a half of its previous levels.[18] Despite this reduction in lobbying expenditure, the company has received more than any other contractor in the reconstruction of Iraq in terms of total dollars. This may suggest that the nature of the relationship between Cheney and his former company is such that the same level of monetary lobbying is not necessary to secure benefits generated by the political decision-making process.

In the present effort in Iraq, the presence of political connections does not stop at Halliburton, however. The Center for Public Integrity has traced the political connections of companies receiving contracts during the reconstruction, and as it turns out, in addition to Halliburton, the other companies that USAID contacted prior to the war in Iraq also have important political connections.[19] Consider the following examples.

James McNulty, the chairman and CEO of Parsons Corporation, which has received over $5 billion worth of contracts in Iraq as of July 2004, served in the U.S. Army for twenty-four years. During his time in the Army, he was the program director for the Star Wars Defense program run by the Pentagon. Philip J. Carroll Jr., the former chairman and CEO of Fluor Corporation, is the main advisor to Thamir Ghadhban, an Iraqi appointed by the United States to head Iraqi's oil ministry. Carroll still has connections to Fluor in the form of retirement benefits that are tied to the performance of the company. Moreover, he owns approximately $34 million worth of Fluor stock. The Bechtel Group, Inc., which has a long history of government connections, hired Marine General Jack Sheehan in 1998 to be the senior vice president in charge of operations in Africa, Europe, Southeast Asia, and the Middle East.[20] In addition to his position at Bechtel, Sheehan sits on the Defense Policy Board. The board, whose members are appointed by the Pentagon, is meant to provide the Secretary of Defense, Deputy Secretary, and Under Secretary for Policy with advice on defense-related issues. As with Halliburton, the political connections of these companies evolved over many years and existed well before the occupation of Iraq in 2003.

Identifying political connections is easier than understanding the magnitude and impact of those connections, however. Because so much of the political decision-making process occurs behind closed doors, it is difficult to pinpoint the exact effect of such relationships. However, economics generally assumes that individuals respond to incentives while public choice theory emphasizes that those incentives are shaped by the nature of the political process. We know that the political process provides incentives for the average voter to remain largely uninformed while special interests not only seek to be informed but also to influence the political outcome in their favor using contributions and personal connections. In the context of reconstruction, these incentives can lead to the failure of reconstruction efforts and the persistence of conflict in the country being reconstructed. Ineffective policies will be instituted, and inefficient or inferior providers of goods and services will often be rewarded at the expense of the overall effort and the interests of citizens of the country being reconstructed.

Foreign Special Interests   Similar to domestic interests, foreign special interests will also seek to influence the political decision-making process of countries either considering an occupation or already engaged in such an effort. Just like domestic interest groups, foreign interests have an incentive to be informed and to actively seek to concentrate benefits and disperse costs across uninformed taxpayers. Indeed, there is evidence that foreign special interests contributed to the decision to go to war in Iraq as well as to postwar planning. Considering the case of one of these foreign interests, the Iraqi National Council (INC), will illuminate how foreign interests can influence reconstruction efforts.

The INC was formed with monetary aid from the United States following the end of the first Gulf War. The aim of the INC was to bring together the various anti-Hussein factions, including members of the Sunni Kurds, Sunni Arabs, and Shi'a Arabs, in order to overthrow the Hussein regime. Ahmed Chalabi, an Iraqi Shi'a Muslim, was elected head of the group in 1992 and was a central figure in the second Iraq war in 2003.

Tensions within the INC in 1994 significantly weakened its effectiveness as a power in opposition to the Hussein regime. Despite this loss of cohesion, Chalabi remained in power and maintained key political ties with the United States, in particular with the Bush administration. In fact, the INC provided information to the Bush administration that directly influenced both the decision to go to war and postwar planning.

For instance, Chalabi's claim that he had a broad network of supporters that would greet American troops as liberators directly influenced postwar troop levels. Further, the claims of the Bush administration regarding ties between the Hussein regime and terrorist organizations were largely based on information provided by Chalabi and sources provided by the INC. In hindsight, it is evident that most of the information provided by Chalabi and his sources regarding these connections, the existence of weapons of mass destruction, and Iraqi support for an American-led war against Hussein was severely misrepresented if not false.

It is important to recognize Chalabi's motivations in this whole process. Although he couched his case in rhetoric regarding the liberation of the Iraqi people, in hindsight, it seems evident that Chalabi was motivated by the desire to see the United States overthrow the Hussein regime so that *he* could control the government of the new Iraq. As David Phillips notes, "After getting the U.S. into Iraq, he [Chalabi] hoped to keep it there to stabilize the country and consolidate his authority as Iraq's new leader."[21] Indeed, for many in the Bush administration prior to the Iraq invasion, Chalabi was the favorite to assume leadership of the new Iraq.

Chalabi was aware of this fact, and it appears that he provided information that supported the case for war, even if that information was inaccurate or fabricated. Despite the Bush administration's trust of the INC, there were critics in the U.S. government who recognized Chalabi's true motivations. The journalist Robert Dreyfuss noted, "At the CIA and State Department, Ahmed Chalabi . . . is viewed as the ineffectual head of a self-inflated and corrupt organization skilled at lobbying and public relations, but not much else."[22]

Chalabi's influence in U.S. political circles is evident when one looks at the amount of monetary aid the U.S. government provided to the INC. Between

1992 and 2004, the U.S. government provided over $100 million to the INC.[23] In 2004, Senators John Kerry and Carl Levin called on the General Accounting Office to investigate the spending of the INC. Specifically, concerns were raised about the use of U.S. government funds to pay the expenses of Iraqi defectors to influence the policies of the United States in directions favorable to members of the INC.

Yet another concern was that the INC violated U.S. lobbying laws as a result of its relationship with the Iraq Liberation Action Committee (ILAC). The ILAC, which Chalabi helped found, was a nonprofit organization that was formed to lobby the U.S. government to take military action to remove the Hussein regime. The accusation was that U.S. taxpayer money that funded the INC was passed through to the ILAC, which in turn used the funds to persuade the U.S. government to take military action against Iraq. Although an earlier audit in 2001 by the State Department's inspector general did not note any violations, the connection between the INC and ILAC is difficult to deny. In addition to playing a key role in the creation of ILAC, Chalabi's nephew, Mahdi al Bassam, was ILAC's chairman and actively lobbied members of the U.S. government.[24]

In May 2004, during the U.S. occupation, the INC headquarters was raided along with Chalabi's villa. The warrants were signed by an Iraqi judge after evidence came to light that officials in the INC were involved in a scheme to obtain state property from the Finance Ministry. A deeper investigation indicated that members of the INC had also been involved in the kidnapping and murder of political opponents.[25] This investigation is still ongoing, and some of the details have yet to come to light. Nonetheless, these charges, along with the misinformation provided by the INC, should add further skepticism to the initial claims made by Chalabi and INC officials that they were aiding the United States in the public interest of Iraq.

Inevitably, more details will come to light regarding the INC's and ILAC's role in the initial invasion of Iraq as well as the reconstruction planning. Both serve as examples of the role of foreign special interests in influencing war and reconstruction efforts. Foreign interests, pursuing their own ends, will seek to manipulate the political process in the country sponsoring the reconstruction in their favor. Such manipulation will not necessarily align with the general interests of those in the country sponsoring the reconstruction or the country being occupied and reconstructed. Further, such manipulation can actually stifle the reconstruction process and contribute to conflict, as the charges of corruption, let alone kidnapping and murder, in this example illustrate.

Bureaucracy

Bureaucrats hold non-elected positions in government. In theory, the general purpose of government agencies is to provide an array of goods and services to the public. A wide variety of government agencies play a central role in the reconstruction process. For instance, the Department of State, Department of Commerce, Department of Defense, Army Corps of Engineers, Central Command, and U.S. Agency for International Development and Federal Business Opportunities, among other U.S. government agencies, are involved in the reconstruction efforts in Iraq and Afghanistan. Because of the key role that bureaucrats play in the political arena in general, public choice theory emphasizes that a complete analysis of the public sector must include an analysis of the incentives that bureaucrats face.[26]

A central insight of public choice theory is that individuals in the private and public sectors are subject to various incentives, but there are key differences between those incentives in each setting. Private actors choose in an environment characterized by private property, prices, and profit and loss, and consequently, those acting in the private sector are subject to market forces. Satisfying consumer wants generates a profit, while the failure to do so results in a loss. In contrast, however, public decision makers utilize the property of others, namely that of taxpayers, and are not subject to profit and loss like private businesses. Absent the profit motive, political criteria and pressures drive the allocation of resources in the public sector.

For instance, agencies receive a budget from elected representatives. Given this fact, we can add bureaucrats to the list of influences on legislators that already includes voters and special interests as discussed previously. In short, legislators respond to the demands of voters and special interests, and the activities demanded by these groups are typically executed by government agencies and bureaus staffed and operated by bureaucrats. Given this, the relationship between legislators and bureaucrats is a key element in political outcomes.

It is important to note that public choice theory does not assume that bureaucrats act with malfeasance. Indeed, many bureaucrats have good intentions and are dedicated to their jobs. Instead, the underlying assertion here is that the symmetry of assumptions that underpins public choice theory implies that bureaucrats respond to incentives just like private actors do. In many cases, the incentive structure in the public sector generates perverse outcomes, even though the intentions of bureaucrats may be completely benevolent.

To understand just a few of the incentives that confront bureaucrats, consider the following. As discussed, elected politicians seek to obtain as many votes as possible. To do so, they need to supply voters—individual voters and special interests—with goods and services. Within the political process, working with bureaucrats is typically the best way to accomplish this.

Within this context, bureaucrats from different agencies compete with one another to secure a part of the limited government budget available at any point in time. Resources are allocated based on relationships with legislators and the stated budgetary needs of the agency. The incentives faced by bureaucrats include signaling to legislators and voters that their services are needed in *greater* amounts than currently exist.

Given these incentives, bureaucrats will tend not only to exhaust their entire appropriated budgets but also to continually seek increases in their budgets in order to increase the size of the agency. Given the absence of the profit-and-loss mechanism, however, agencies are not subject to the need for fiscal discipline as private firms are. Instead, being fiscally prudent is discouraged by the system because it results in budget reductions over time instead of increases.

How do the incentives that bureaucrats face influence the reconstruction process? The nature and extent of bureaucratic influence will vary across efforts, but we can identify some general tendencies. In general, there will often be a conflict between the aims and goals of different agencies and bureaus. Each agency attempts to provide specific goods or services, and these do not always align with those goods and services offered by other agencies. As mentioned, there is continuous competition between agencies as each attempts to maximize and secure its share of the fixed budget, which creates a potentially problematic tension. On the one hand, agencies are supposed to be united in a common goal of reconstructing the country in question, but on the other hand, bureaus are competing with one another and attempting to carve out their niche that differentiates them from other agencies in order to secure a part of the fixed budget. Each will have its own agenda, which may clash with the agenda of other agencies as well as with the overarching goal of achieving a successful reconstruction. These tensions can generate perverse outcomes in the larger reconstruction process and may contribute to the persistence or even exacerbation of conflict.

By way of example, recent analyses of the current reconstructions in Afghanistan and Iraq indicate that competition and tensions between various agencies have had negative consequences on the broader reconstruction efforts. For instance, Michael Scheuer, in his analysis of the current effort in Afghanistan and the larger war on terror, has highlighted the tensions between the missions of the CIA and the FBI.[27] As Scheuer notes, "At the most basic level, the FBI is meant to enforce U.S. law. . . . The CIA, on the other hand, is authorized to break the law to gather information that helps defend the United States."[28] Note that it is the clash between missions that leads to these outcomes and not the malevolence of those within these organizations. Members of each agency pursue their respective missions, which do not mesh with the ends being pursued by the other.

Likewise, the journalist Robert Dreyfuss has documented battles between the Pentagon and the CIA as the United States prepared to go to war with Iraq.[29] The main tension was between those in the Pentagon who supported the war effort in Iraq and those in the intelligence agencies who were largely opposed to the invasion. As Dreyfuss notes, "The war over intelligence is a critical part of a broader offensive by . . . the Bush administration against virtually the entire expert Middle East establishment in the United States—including State Department, Pentagon and CIA area specialists and leading military officers."[30] Along similar lines, Paul Pillar, a former National Intelligence officer, documents how members of the Bush Administration "cherry-picked" intelligence data that supported the case for war with Iraq while neglecting the large amount of intelligence that suggested that refraining from war (and thus subsequent reconstruction) was the prudent course of action.[31] Following the invasion, the reason for the fight over intelligence within the U.S. government became clear, as many of the initial claims regarding weapons of mass destruction and links to terrorist organizations were shown to be overstated or wrong.

David Phillips, who was involved in the early stages of planning for a post-Hussein Iraq, notes that during the postwar reconstruction efforts, "Relations between the Office of the Secretary of Defense (OSD) and the State Department became increasingly acrimonious. U.S. officials vied for control over the Iraq policy."[32] Similarly, Larry Diamond, who was also involved in the reconstruction of Iraq, indicates that "A number of U.S. government agencies had a variety of visions of how political authority would be reestablished in Iraq. . . . In the bitter, relentless infighting among U.S. government agencies in advance of the war, none of these preferences clearly prevailed."[33] Along similar lines, the journalist George Packer has documented the tensions between the Department of Defense and the State Department. Packer notes how members of the Office of Stability and Peace Operations were excluded from meetings at the Pentagon and had their memos ignored as Rumsfeld and Wolfowitz advanced their own agendas.[34]

Again, in theory, reconstruction efforts are meant to transform situations of conflict into situations of coordination and cooperation, as illustrated by the framework developed in Chapter 2. This task becomes extremely difficult when there is conflict within the occupying country that is supposed to facilitate the transformation from conflict to cooperation in the foreign country being reconstructed. Why have the various U.S. agencies failed to coordinate their activities around the overarching goal of establishing liberal democracy in Afghanistan and Iraq? Once more, public choice theory provides important insights into the answer to this question.

Not only does each agency have an agenda that it seeks to pursue, but within each agency there are competing agendas and visions. Bureaucrats seek to maximize their share of the budget not only for a given agency but for a given department within a given agency. Given this fact, it is logical that both representatives of departments within agencies and representatives of the larger agency will attempt to seek positions of influence in major public activities such as occupations and reconstructions. Obviously, each department and agency wants its vision and agenda to be the dominant one in order to secure the maximum amount of resources, which, again, can yield perverse outcomes that run counter to the overarching goal and contribute to the overall failure of the effort. The competition between agencies and the potential outcome of conflict instead of cooperation are not limited to Afghanistan and Iraq and can be generalized to all reconstruction efforts. Considering the broader goals of the reconstruction effort, there is no reason to assume that the most effective policies and strategies will be adopted and implemented by bureaucrats, given the incentives and constraints they face.

Elected Officials and Shortsighted Policies

Yet another central insight generated from public choice analysis is that the decisions of elected politicians tend to be shortsighted in nature. In other words, a temporal disconnect for politicians exists between choices made in the present period and the consequences of those choices in future periods. For those politicians who are constrained by a term of service before the next election cycle, the main focus is on obtaining benefits during their time in office, even if this involves significant costs for the country once they are no longer in office. This disconnect is due to the fact that they do not fully internalize the costs of their actions. Instead, subsequent political actors will incur some of the costs of decisions made by those that preceded them. The shortsighted bias of the political decision-making process indicates that political actors facing a limited time in office will often trade off long-term costs to obtain short-term benefits, even if those costs are substantially greater than the benefits. Policies that are a net cost can have an impact on the long-term interests of both the domestic country carrying out the reconstruction and the country being reconstructed.

In theory, constitutional rules will be effective in overcoming this temporal disconnect. In other words, ideal constitutional rules will create a set of checks and balances that will force political actors to incorporate long-term considerations into decisions made in the present period.[35] However, it is unclear that these rules operate as desired in many instances. For example, public debt is continually used to finance deficits. This debt will need to be retired in future periods, typically once the politician who initially benefited from the deficit has exited office. To pay for this debt, future politicians will need to undertake some policy mix of raising taxes, reducing spending, or issuing further debt.

Other political decisions such as war and reconstruction efforts also have long-term costs that will not be directly incurred by those currently in office, but instead will be incurred by future elected officials. Consider, for instance, the war effort in Iraq. The U.S. Constitution includes a number of checks on the president's ability to utilize the military for war, the major check being that Congress must declare war. The logic behind these checks is straightforward. A war is a major effort that requires the commitment of resources over a potentially long period of time, and further, the consequences of a war effort may potentially last well beyond the term of the president who initially declares war.

In the case of the recent war in Iraq, President Bush evaded this check by utilizing a prior Congressional resolution that allowed the president to engage in military action against Iraq under three scenarios, including the threat of an immediate attack by Iraq against the United States, the passing of weapons of mass destruction from Iraq to al-Qaeda, or if the U.N. Security Council authorized military action against Iraq. It is unclear that any of the scenarios in the resolution existed, but by evading Congress, Bush evaded a key check put in place to ensure the alignment of short- and long-term interests.

The bias toward shortsighted policies that is prevalent in democracies indicates that oftentimes politicians will understate the associated costs of intervention when considering policy alternatives. Emphasis will be placed on current benefits and current costs while neglecting long-term costs associated with the decision. For instance, the original projection by Larry Lindsey, a Bush economic advisor, that the Iraq war could cost in the range of $100–$200 billion was rejected by the administration as an overestimation.[36] It now appears that the costs of the war in Iraq will in fact exceed the upper end of Lindsey's prediction.

There are additional costs, beyond the costs of military operations, that are often excluded from standard calculations of the cost of war, such as health costs and disability for those injured in the war, other veteran costs, the psychological costs of warfare on soldiers, the costs of depreciation and replacing military equipment, and the costs of demobilizing troops and equipment. Estimates that attempt to incorporate these and other costs conclude that the total cost of the war could be in excess of $1–2 trillion.[37] Again, these long-term costs will tend to be excluded from the decision calculus of elected politicians because those "bills" will not come due for many years to come.

This has implications for reconstruction efforts because decisions made with an eye toward the short-term may end up imposing substantial costs over the long-term both in the country carrying out the reconstruction and in the country being reconstructed. These costs will fall on the future leaders of these countries. For instance, it has been argued that the occupation of Iraq has provided a training ground for the next generation of terrorists.[38] If this is indeed true, the costs of dealing with these new terrorists will be felt for years to come by countries around the world.

Granted, any attempt to quantify future costs involves assumptions about the future, and therefore it is difficult to assign a precise cost to the current war and reconstruction efforts. What is important for our analysis, however, is that given the nature of the political decision-making process, political actors will often have a shortsighted bias. Decisions made in the current period will involve costs that will not be fully internalized by the decision maker. Therefore, political actors will have the incentive to consider short-term benefits and short-term costs while excluding, or at least discounting, long-term costs from their decision calculus. This temporal disconnect may result in the adoption of inferior or ineffective policies, the full effects of which will only be realized well into the future.

Implications for Reconstruction Efforts

Obviously, it is a grave error to assume that those involved in the reconstruction process will act in a manner which maximizes the chances of success. Instead a complete understanding of reconstruction requires a consideration of the motivations of actors in the public realm. Public choice theory indicates that those acting in the public realm will often fail to take steps that would facilitate cooperation if those activities fail to align with their private interests. This is not necessarily because the actors are malevolent, but rather, because they respond rationally to the incentives put forth by political institutions and those incentives are often perverse in nature.

Public actors must make choices, in an institutional setting characterized by distorted incentives, on the basis of biased information and a fundamental disconnect between the costs and benefits of political actions. The main takeaway is that, simply put, intentions do not equal results. Even if policymakers are driven by the best of intentions, the political process will distort those intentions, generating perverse outcomes.

So let us review: the political process is one of competition between four key groups—individual voters, special interests, elected officials, and bureaucrats. In this process, voters have an incentive to remain ignorant of many of the facts while special interests attempt to manipulate the political system to concentrate benefits and to simultaneously disperse the costs among the unorganized and uninformed voters. Elected officials have the incentive to cater to special interests and to engage in showmanship to provide signals to a "rationally ignorant" electorate. Finally, bureaucrats have the incentive to exhaust their entire budget, indeed to fail in their mission, in order to secure additional funds, and to overstate the importance of their role in providing goods and services.

This array of insights provided by public choice theory should give further pause to those supporting efforts to export liberal democracy via military occupation. Even if the motivation behind the initial intervention is benevolent, we have little reason to believe that the necessary policies will be implemented and that the desired outcome will be achieved, due to the distortions caused by political institutions. The political decision-making process in the country sponsoring the reconstruction will influence the nature of the reconstruction, and we have good reason to believe that it will distort the situation and may make it worse. The various parties involved in the process trade off the interests of the country being reconstructed, and often the interests of their own country, in the pursuit of their own private interests. The result will often be the persistence of conflict and, at the extreme, the outcomes generated by inferior and ineffective policies can have the counterproductive and harmful effect of increasing the overall level of conflict.

The Dynamics of Intervention and Unintended Consequences

Early in the twentieth century, the economist Ludwig von Mises explored the nature of government intervention in the economic system and developed a theory of the "dynamics of intervention."[39] The main insight was that one intervention creates a new set of incentives for both political and private actors. These new incentives may in turn create a set of circumstances that prevent the achievement of the initial desired goal and require additional interventions on the part of political agents. However, these subsequent interventions again cause the underlying incentive structure to shift. The process then continues in a similar manner in which political actors are forced to choose between revoking the past interventions or implementing additional interventions.

Consider the example of a price ceiling, which is a type of price control that prevents, by law, the price of a good or service from rising above a specific level. Basic economic analysis indicates that the outcome of this intervention will be a shortage. The negative unintended consequences of this intervention will include long lines but also perhaps an increase in black market activity, bribes, and discrimination as producers turn to nonmonetary means of allocating the good or service. In response to these unintended consequences, government actors can either retract the initial intervention or intervene again to attempt to deal with the shortage by some sort of rationing measure. However, subsequent interventions will again create a series of unintended consequences, such as a further increase in black market activity and crime.

The main factor behind the negative unintended consequences associated with interventions is the lack of complete knowledge. Those intervening lack the knowledge of how the intervention will shift incentives, and therefore they cannot accurately predict the full consequences of the intervention, which means that it is possible that interventions will have negative consequences that are both unforeseeable *and* undesirable. In some cases, these unintended consequences may be worse than the initial problem that the intervention targeted for correction. Yet another important insight from the analysis of the dynamics of intervention is that there is typically a time lag between the initial intervention and the manifestation of the unintended consequences resulting from that intervention—it can take years or even decades before the full implications of an intervention become apparent.

Although the theory of the dynamics of intervention has typically been applied to economic systems, the same logic can be applied to foreign policy, and specifically to reconstruction efforts. The political scientist Chalmers Johnson has provided an in-depth analysis of many of the unintended consequences, or "blowback," from America's proactive foreign policy during and after the Cold War.[40] In the context of reconstruction, foreign governments can never have full and complete information regarding the impact of interventions that aim to craft and implement self-sustaining liberal institutions. Policies that appear to generate the desired outcome may in fact have negative undesired consequences in future periods, and these unintended consequences may in turn generate the need for further government interventions that in turn create a new set of unintended consequences, seemingly ad infinitum.

In the context of reconstruction, unintended consequences can manifest themselves in a number of ways. For one, the unintended consequences of past foreign interventions are a contributing factor behind the need for current reconstruction efforts. To illustrate this, consider the case of U.S. intervention in Afghanistan in the 1980s. The aim of the U.S. intervention was to assist the Afghanistan resistance in expelling Soviet Union forces. The intervention took the form of arming and funding Afghani freedom fighters including, among others, Osama Bin Laden, who were fighting against the Soviets. After achieving the desired goal, the United States removed itself from the situation in Afghanistan, with the result that various factions within Afghanistan, many of which the United States had funded and supplied with weaponry, turned against one another. The ensuing civil war created an environment in which the Taliban and al-Qaeda eventually assumed significant positions of control, ultimately resulting in further U.S. interventions in 2001.[41] Yet another unintended consequence of this U.S. intervention in the 1980s is that some of the weapons that the United States had provided to resistance forces to expel the Soviet Union were used against U.S. troops during the more recent war in Afghanistan.

To further support this claim, consider again the work of Michael Scheuer, the former head of CIA's Bin Laden Unit. Scheuer has provided a comprehensive analysis of Osama Bin Laden, al-Qaeda, and the war on terror as presently undertaken by the United States.[42] One of Scheuer's central claims is that al-Qaeda, and other terrorist organizations, are not motivated by a fundamental hatred for the American identity and way of life, but instead by U.S. interventions and policies in the larger Middle East region. It is Scheuer's contention that these interventions are in fact the driving force behind the backlash against the United States.[43] In other words, these interventions in the Middle East have generated negative unintended consequences, such as the 9/11 attacks, that in turn led to further interventions, such as the overall war on terror and the invasion of and subsequent reconstruction efforts in Afghanistan and Iraq.

Current reconstruction efforts will likewise have unintended consequences in future periods, which may contribute to conflict over the long term. Once they manifest themselves, these negative unintended consequences may result in the call for further military interventions. Again, these unintended consequences may take years or even decades to appear.

In general, negative unintended consequences associated with reconstruction efforts can occur along two key margins. The first consists of *internal* negative unintended consequences that cause harm within the country being reconstructed. The second consists of *external* negative unintended consequences that create "neighborhood effects" which cause harm outside the country being reconstructed. I will consider each of these possibilities in turn.

Internal Negative Unintended Consequences

To understand the notion of internal negative unintended consequences, consider the first effort by the United States to establish liberal democracy in the Dominican Republic during the 1916–1924 occupation. A key aspect of the reconstruction was the disarmament of the populace as part of a broader aim to prevent rebellions. However, the disarmament policy had a major unintended consequence that became evident with the rise of General Rafael Leónidas Trujillo to power via a military coup.

Trujillo, who joined the Dominican National Police during the U.S. occupation, rose quickly though the ranks and was eventually named chief of the army. Trujillo would eventually lead the coup to overthrow President Horacio Vásquez, who had been elected during the last days of the U.S. occupation. The coup itself, as well as Trujillo's rule following the coup, made clear a major unintended consequence of the U.S. occupation policy. With the Dominican population disarmed as a result of occupation, there was no military threat to Trujillo. Trujillo had a literal monopoly on force with exclusive control of weapons as well as control over the troops and police that the United States had trained and armed during the occupation. Once in power, Trujillo used this monopoly on force to impose his will on the Dominican populace, using violent force where necessary. This is but one example of how military occupation can generate internal negative unintended consequences.

As another example of an internal negative unintended consequence, consider that reconstruction efforts might unintentionally distort or destroy the evolution of indigenous social structures and governance mechanisms more broadly. To illuminate this, consider the attempted reconstruction of Somalia by the United States from 1993 through 1995, where efforts to establish a central government had the unintended consequence of increasing conflict and preventing the evolution of indigenous governance mechanisms.

As the World Bank economists Tatiana Nenova and Tim Harford have recently discussed, Somalia presents an interesting case study because of the ability of the private sector to operate despite the fact that Somalia is a prototypical failed state.[44] I will discuss the case of Somalia in more detail in Chapter 6, but it is important to note here that, while Somalia lacks a central government, the private sector has developed governance mechanisms to fill the void. These mechanisms have proven to be more effective in generating cooperation and order than previous attempts by foreign governments to impose a central government. Indeed, counter to their intent, attempts by external governments to establish a central government in Somalia have often served to exacerbate conflict instead of generating coordination around cooperative ends.

When occupiers have attempted to construct political institutions, the various clans throughout Somalia reallocated resources from productive activities to secure positions in the new political order and obtain the benefits associated with positions of political power. Many individuals are willing to incur the costs of conflict, oftentimes violent in nature, for the potential benefit associated with political positions. The conflict resulting from attempts to construct a central government erode the private mechanisms that developed prior to the reconstruction effort by shifting the relative payoff to conflict.

External Negative Unintended Consequences

While reconstruction efforts can cause negative unintended consequences within the country being reconstructed, they can also generate unintended consequences that are external to the country being reconstructed. In other words, the actions of occupiers may create neighborhood effects in the form of negative spillovers that cause harm to those outside the occupied country.

One of the most widely accepted wisdoms held by both policymakers and many social scientists is the "democratic peace theory."[45] In its simplest form, this theory holds that democracies do not go to war with other democracies. The idea can be traced back to the eighteenth-century philosopher Immanuel Kant, who noted that a republican constitution was one of several factors necessary for "perpetual peace."[46]

Although academics continue to debate this claim, the democratic peace theory is one of the driving factors behind reconstruction efforts that attempt to establish liberal democracies around the world. In his 1994 State of the Union address, President Clinton noted, "Ultimately, the best strategy to ensure our security and to build a durable peace is to support the advance of democracy elsewhere. Democracies don't attack each other. They make better trading partners and partners in diplomacy."[47] Likewise, regarding Iraq and the larger Middle East, President George W. Bush noted that "the reason why I'm so strong on democracy is democracies don't go to war with each other. . . . I've got great faith in democracies to promote peace. And that's why I'm such a strong believer that the way forward in the Middle East, the broader Middle East, is to promote democracy."[48]

As mentioned earlier, the political scientists Edward Mansfield and Jack Snyder have explored the claim that democracies are less likely to go to war, and their findings have important implications for reconstruction efforts.[49] Mansfield and Snyder do indeed find that democracies are less likely to go to war with one another, but they put forth an important clarification. It is not just democracies in general that are less likely to go to war but specifically mature or consolidated democracies. The authors find that immature democracies making the transition from authoritarian regimes do engage in conflict, and specifically in international wars. Perhaps even more important, immature democracies are in fact *more* likely to engage in international conflict than are authoritarian regimes.

Why do immature democracies tend to engage in conflict while mature democracies do not? In weak democracies the institutions of checks, balances, and accountability have yet to develop completely. In other words, immature democracies are not fully developed liberal democracies, and this means that political institutions are unable to handle the increased demands of widespread political participation.[50] Because of this combination—the demand for political participation and the lack of effective checks on that demand—political actors turn to extreme positions to garner attention and separate themselves from political competitors.

In the absence of institutions that enforce accountability, the relative cost of adopting extreme positions is less as compared to mature democracies, wherein political actors internalize a greater part of the cost of such positions. In immature democracies, these extreme positions often take the form of hardline nationalism. Mansfield and Snyder provide Slobodan Milosevic, who inspired his supporters to rally around the alleged threat of Albanians in Kosovo, as but one example of this type of behavior.

Consider what this means in terms of the potential for negative unintended consequences in the current reconstruction efforts in Afghanistan and Iraq. Let us assume that the United States is able to overcome the array of factors discussed to this point and establish the seeds of democracy in Afghanistan and

Iraq. In other words, let us assume the current reconstruction efforts are able, to some degree, to successfully transform situations of conflict to cooperation. It is safe to assume that even if the groundwork for liberal democracy were established, political institutions would be fragile. One could envision the exact scenario outlined by Mansfield and Snyder as regards a semi-democratized Afghanistan or Iraq. A wide range of political competitors would be looking to secure positions of power without well-developed checks on their behavior. In such instances, the adoption of extreme positions grounded in nationalism against neighboring countries in order to garner political support is also a potential reality.

In the hypothetical scenario just outlined, reconstruction efforts would provide minimal stability and coordination within Afghanistan and Iraq. However, this may also result in an increase in conflict between Afghanistan or Iraq and neighboring countries. Stated differently, the "game" between an immature democratic Afghanistan or Iraq and their neighbors would be characterized by the prisoner's dilemma, discussed in Chapter 2. In such a situation, the United States may achieve the goal of bringing some form of stability and democracy to Afghanistan and Iraq but only by increasing conflict in the wider region.

It is important to note that the two margins discussed here—internal and external negative unintended consequences—are not mutually exclusive either. For instance, one could argue that current efforts in Afghanistan and Iraq will generate "blowback" whereby the attempts to curtail the current insurgent movement will give birth to the future generation of insurgents. In fact, Peter Bergen and Alec Reynolds argue that the war and subsequent reconstruction effort in Iraq will generate a blowback greater than that generated by the Soviet-led war in Afghanistan, which was substantial.[51] The Iraq war not only is a training ground for these future terrorists but also serves as a focal rallying point to bring insurgents together against the United States and other countries involved in the reconstruction effort. It is not difficult to envision these future insurgents seeking targets *both* inside Iraq and in other parts of the world. In this case, the interventions in Iraq would have generated negative unintended consequences along both margins simultaneously.

Unintended Consequences and the Nirvana Fallacy

As noted previously, the economist Harold Demsetz introduced the term *nirvana fallacy* regarding the comparison of real and imperfect markets to ideal and perfect government institutions.[52] This comparison results in the conclusion that, not only is government intervention necessary to correct market imperfections, but the outcome produced by an infallible government is a preferable state of affairs. Demsetz pointed out that such a comparison overlooks the reality that government is imperfect as well and may fail to allocate resources as effectively as even an imperfect market. Indeed, as we saw in previous subsections, political institutions often generate policies that allocate resources in a manner which is grossly inefficient. In short, one cannot compare an imperfect situation to its perfect counterpart and assume that interventions can bring that perfect situation about.

Similar reasoning can be applied to reconstruction efforts. In the context of reconstruction, the nirvana fallacy would take the form of the assumption that, in the face of a weak or failed central government, external occupiers *can* provide a better outcome relative to what exists in the absence of reconstruction efforts. Indeed, policymakers who fail to consider the relevant costs associated with reconstruction efforts, including the potential for negative unintended consequences, fall prey to the nirvana fallacy. The assumption that foreign interventions and reconstruction can generate a preferable state of affairs overlooks several key possibilities, including the possibility that reconstruction efforts may fail and that these efforts can do more harm than good. Another key underlying assumption is that weak and failed states are trapped in a condition of underdevelopment that precludes the possibility of the evolution of endogenous governance mechanisms that are more effective than an alternative government that is fragile and dysfunctional. As the case of Somalia indicates, this may not be the case.[53]

The implication of the nirvana fallacy in the context of reconstruction is as follows. While it may indeed be the case that there is significant institutional failure in countries with weak, failed, or illiberal governments, the failures generated by the interventions of foreign governments may be even greater. Interventions by foreign governments that aim to shift the institutional trajectory of these countries do not necessarily result in a preferable outcome. While liberal democracy, and all the benefits associated with it, may be preferable to the current situation, an effective and strong liberal government may not be feasible given the existing set of constraints.

Implications for Reconstruction Efforts

Negative unintended consequences are a central concern in the attempt to export liberal democracy via military occupation and reconstruction. The theory of the dynamics of intervention does not indicate that negative unintended consequences will always result from interventions, but, to reiterate, it indicates that interventions shift the incentives facing private actors in a manner that cannot be predetermined. Nevertheless, while there may be a benefit to intervention, there are also associated costs that must be considered. The difficulty lies in determining what these costs might be ahead of time. What is clear is that one cannot assume that intervention will be beneficial.

In the context of reconstruction, some of these costs are readily apparent, for instance casualties and some minimal monetary costs that can be predicted in advance. However, the dynamics of intervention indicate that there are also potentially significant costs that cannot be known at the time of the intervention. If the intervention does result in negative unintended consequences along either margin discussed earlier, these costs will not have been sufficiently incorporated into the cost-benefit analysis regarding the initial intervention.

For instance, when the United States funded Afghani freedom fighters in the 1970s and early 1980s, they could not have known the full implications that would manifest themselves many years later. Likewise, while the removal of Saddam Hussein clearly had benefits, we cannot fully comprehend the total costs that will only become evident in the coming years or decades.

The central implication of the nirvana fallacy is that it is not always preferable for foreign governments to intervene in weak or failed states. Indeed, given the insights from the analysis here, one could argue that the preferable policy is to allow these states to completely collapse. As the historical record and constraints discussed to this point indicate, it is more unlikely than not that foreign governments can establish mature liberal democratic institutions via occupation. As a result, to the extent that reconstruction efforts are successful they will typically produce fragile and weak political and economic systems. As discussed, leaders in weak states will tend to exploit the absence of strong political checks and balances to engage in violence against neighboring countries or groups. Given this, it is unclear why attempting to rebuild weak and failed states is the preferable course of action. In some cases, such as Somalia, citizens have been better off since the state completely collapsed.[54]

Given the potential for negative unintended consequences, as well as the real possibility that such interventions can cause more harm than good, refraining from interventions aimed at establishing liberal democratic institutions seems to be the default strategy that should be followed. Of course inaction also has potential costs that must be seriously considered. In some cases, such as the genocide that took place in Rwanda in 1994, there may be substantial humanitarian consequences and costs to refraining from intervention. However, humanitarian motivations for intervention can be distinct from efforts to establish liberal democratic institutions at gunpoint. I will consider humanitarian motivations for foreign interventions in more detail in the concluding chapter.

Credible Commitment, Overconfidence, and Self-Deception

In Chapter 3, I considered how issues associated with the problems of credible commitment, overconfidence, and self-deception serve as indigenous constraints on reconstruction efforts. These constraints raise transaction costs and reduce the likelihood of those engaged in the bargaining process striking a mutually beneficial agreement. The problems associated with credible commitment, overconfidence, and self-deception also serve as external constraints on policymakers and occupiers, albeit with different manifestations. Let us consider this in more detail.

Since the end of the Cold War, U.S.-led reconstruction efforts have been motivated mainly by humanitarian and security concerns. For instance, the reconstruction efforts in Kosovo, Bosnia, Haiti, Somalia, Afghanistan, and Iraq were motivated by some combination of the need for stability; liberation from a brutal regime; and the delivery of aid in the form of financial assistance, food, and health supplies. This humanitarian motivation is drastically different from earlier reconstructions, such as the post–World War II reconstructions of Japan and West Germany, which were motivated by international wars and were longer term in nature. As discussed throughout this book, the motivation and perceived purpose of both the occupation and efforts to reconstruct a country will influence the expectations of citizens of the occupied country and hence the success or failure of the effort.

In addition to influencing expectations, the motivation of occupation and reconstruction efforts is important for yet another reason. Specifically, the stated and perceived motivations of the occupation and reconstruction effort will serve as signals of credibility or lack thereof. Consider for instance the incentives that a reconstruction motivated by liberation produces for citizens of the country being occupied. If citizens expect occupiers to leave after a short period of time, there is little to no incentive for citizens to work with them to bring about stability. In other words, announcing that an occupation is a short-term endeavor motivated by liberation may weaken the credibility of occupiers from the very beginning.

If on the other hand the occupying forces commit to a long-term, dictator-style occupation such as the one that took place in post–World War II Japan, there is a stronger incentive for citizens to work with the occupying forces. In such an instance, occupiers signal that they will attempt to impose the aims of the occupation via force where necessary and are committed to seeing the reconstruction through over the long run. Of course, the stronger incentives created by a long-term occupation are not enough to guarantee success, as occupiers will still face the array of constraints discussed to this point.

Here then is a central dilemma for foreign governments considering undertaking future reconstruction efforts. In the post–Cold War world, the international landscape has changed, and there are few superpowers that pose a realistic military threat. Instead, the main threat is from smaller rogue or disintegrating states or paramilitary groups within those states. It is therefore unlikely that there will be large-scale international wars between superpowers as in World War II. This means that the "international war" motivation used for the post–World War II reconstructions of Japan and West Germany will no longer be viable, severely limiting the possibility for longer-term occupation efforts. At the same time, if foreign governments intervene in these rogue and failing states under the flag of liberation, they will have reduced power and influence in shaping the outcome of the country. In addition to the constraints discussed to this point, occupiers will have minimal credibility and citizens will have little incentive to work with them in bringing about the desired end.

It appears then that the only realistic solution to the problem of credible commitment is for foreign governments to refrain from occupying countries with the aim of establishing liberal institutions. Assuming the absence of an international war, countries most in need of reconstruction along liberal lines will be those where occupiers have the least credibility because the main means of motivating the occupation will be some combination of liberation and humanitarian ends.

In Chapter 3 I also discussed the issues associated with overconfidence and self-deception. To summarize these issues, recall that in order to realize the gains from bargaining, those involved must have realistic expectations regarding their prospects, abilities, and limitations. Further, bargainers must be willing to trade off on the margin in order to reach a compromise. When one of the parties involved in the bargaining process takes an all-or-nothing approach, the likelihood of reaching a mutually beneficial agreement is drastically reduced. In the previous chapter these issues were considered in the context of bargaining between indigenous citizens of the country being reconstructed, but the same logic applies to policymakers and occupiers.

Dominic Johnson has explored how overconfidence and self-deception have had an impact on the most recent war and reconstruction in Iraq. According to Johnson, the United States was not overconfident regarding the initial military operations. Indeed, the United States, with its far superior military strength, easily toppled the Hussein regime. However, the Bush administration *was* overconfident in its assumptions regarding the postwar reconstruction of Iraq. As it pertains to the reconstruction, the United States was overconfident on a wide range of issues including the presence of weapons of mass destruction, the speed and duration of the occupation, and the number of potential allies that would support and contribute to the occupation. As former Secretary of the Army Thomas White indicated, the mind-set of many in the Bush administration regarding Iraq was that "this would be a relatively straightforward, manageable task, because this would be a war of liberation and therefore the reconstruction would be short-lived."[55] In reality, this has failed to be the case.

How did this overconfidence in the ability to reconstruct Iraq along liberal lines come to be? One scapegoat for the failures that have occurred to date has been the intelligence community, which has been chastised for the lack of "good" intelligence. However, closer analysis of the pre-war planning process indicates that there was a large amount of information available that did not support the invasion and occupation of Iraq and that was ignored.[56] It is Johnson's contention that the Bush administration was able to successfully close itself off from debate and avoid many of the checks that are in place to assess the risks of engaging in war and occupation. He notes that the administration's "official line foreclosed debate and preparations that, though they might have made the prospect of war less attractive, might have resulted in a more effective peace."[57] By isolating itself from political and public debate prior to engaging in the war and subsequent reconstruction effort, the Bush administration was able to develop positive illusions about the United States's prospects to transform Iraq into a liberal democracy.

As discussed in the previous chapter, research regarding self-deception has found that individuals tend to believe the universal relevance of their values and worldview and assume that spreading that worldview benefits all. Indeed, this is the underlying assumption of U.S.-led reconstruction efforts—that liberal institutions represent universal values that benefit all and therefore should be spread to all.[58] However, this assumption does not appear to hold true. It is not that others prefer living under brutal dictatorships, but rather that they do not necessarily prefer living under Western-style liberal institutions. Indeed, as mentioned at the outset of this book, there is no reason to assume that democratic elections in the absence of constitutional liberalism will generate liberal outcomes. The recent election dominance of Hamas in Palestine seems to further confirm this contention. In the absence of constitutional liberalism, democratic institutions will fail to produce the desired results.

The United States's steadfast commitment to exporting Western-style democracy causes further problems in the reconstruction process. Although occupiers serve in the role of mediator and oversee the bargaining process, they often play an active role in the bargaining process itself, seeking to influence outcomes and often attempting to pick winners. Further, as noted in last chapter's discussion of nested games, there will potentially be many "mini-games" involving occupiers and indigenous citizens, which implies that, in many cases, occupiers serve in the capacity of mediator over the larger bargaining process while simultaneously participating in parts of that very process. In order for the process to be successful, occupiers, just like other bargaining parties, must be willing to make marginal trade-offs.

To the extent that occupiers are committed to a specific outcome no matter what, it is less likely that parties will reach a mutually beneficial and sustainable agreement. Further, when liberation is the motivation behind reconstruction efforts, a firm commitment to the construction, or reconstruction, of specific institutions with certain characteristics is problematic. Given that self-determination is a key aspect of liberation, foreign governments must be willing to allow indigenous citizens to determine their future. However, if policymakers and occupying forces are unwilling to make marginal trade-offs, self-determination is only possible over a certain limited range of outcomes.

If the outcome of self-determination cuts across the broader aims of the reconstruction, policymakers and occupiers will be forced to choose between either accepting or rejecting the outcome. Accepting the outcome may very well produce illiberal results, but rejecting the outcome raises the risk of creating a backlash and a loss of credibility. This poses yet another constraint on undertaking foreign interventions under the banner of humanitarian liberation and yet another reason to give policymakers in a would-be occupying nation pause.

Implications for Reconstruction Efforts

The problem of credible commitment will continue to hamper the ability of foreign governments to successfully export liberal democracy via military occupation. Reconstructions motivated by humanitarian liberation create a set of incentives whereby policymaker and occupier influence are severely reduced. At the same time, it is unlikely that there is international and domestic support for long-term colonization that relies on brute force to impose liberal institutions. Even if there was such support for long-term occupation, it is unclear that policymakers and occupiers can overcome the multitude of constraints discussed to this point.

Likewise, one should expect that the issues associated with overconfidence and self-deception on the part of the occupiers will continue to hinder current and future reconstruction efforts. Perhaps the best solution to overcoming these problems is to ensure the presence and enforcement of checks and balances that prevent any one branch of government from isolating itself from critical review and discourse so that key actors are less prone to fall prey to positive illusions. However, as evidenced by the case of Iraq, existing checks and balances may not be enough to prevent overconfidence from influencing policy decisions that generate perverse outcomes.

As further evidenced by Iraq, even if the initial intervention is based on realistic expectations, the subsequent reconstruction effort can suffer from the problems that are generated by overconfidence. In fact, given this dynamic, there does not seem to be a clear solution to overcoming the problems caused by overconfidence and self-deception, and in the absence of a clear and effective solution, these issues should further contribute to skepticism regarding the potential of military occupation and reconstruction as the midwife of liberal democracy.

Summation

These past two chapters have focused on understanding the mechanisms that can either contribute to or prevent the transformation of situations of conflict to those of coordination and cooperation. While Chapter 3 focused on indigenous mechanisms operative within the country being occupied and reconstructed, this chapter focused on exogenous mechanisms that are external to the country being reconstructed. Together, these mechanisms indicate two broad barriers to successfully exporting liberal democracy via military occupation.

The first major hurdle is the knowledge problem. In short, policymakers and academics lack the knowledge of *how* to construct liberal democratic institutions where they do not already exist. The second hurdle is the political decision-making process. Policymakers must act within a set of political institutions that will tend to distort the policies driving the reconstruction process. It is critical to realize the implications of this second impediment to successful reconstruction. Even if policymakers possessed the necessary know-how regarding the construction of liberal institutions, we have good reason to believe that the political process would distort the actual implementation of the policies and directives based on that knowledge and information. In addition, those involved in the political decision-making process will suffer from problems of unintended consequences, credible commitment, and overconfidence as discussed earlier.

When we realize that in reality policymakers face incomplete knowledge, imperfect information, and a non-neutral political system, we have a very strong argument for refraining from foreign interventions aimed at exporting liberal democracy. Policymakers lack the knowledge of how to construct liberal democracy and also will have their policies distorted by the political process. When we understand the magnitude and extent of these two hurdles, it becomes evident why a majority of U.S.-led reconstruction efforts have failed. In fact, given these hurdles, we should wonder why one would expect reconstruction efforts to succeed in their stated end. This discussion also provides good reason why the policy and academic communities need to explore alternative means of spreading liberal democracy abroad. Considering such alternatives will be the focus of the concluding chapter.

In the next three chapters, I will discuss the mechanisms developed in the past two chapters relative to past and current reconstruction efforts. Specifically, I will seek to understand how these mechanisms can illuminate past cases of success and failure. The cases considered cover a wide range of reconstruction efforts: the post–World War II reconstructions of Japan and West Germany, the humanitarian motivated reconstructions of Somalia and Haiti in the 1990s, and the current reconstructions of Afghanistan and Iraq. Although I recognize the intricate nuances of each specific situation, the following case studies focus specifically on illustrating how the previously discussed mechanisms contribute to either the successful transformation of situations of conflict into cooperation or the persistence of conflict.

5   The Pinnacle of U.S. Imperialism: Japan and West Germany

THE POST–WORLD WAR II, U.S.-led reconstructions of Japan and West Germany serve as the benchmarks against which all subsequent reconstructions are compared. In both cases, foreign military occupiers were successfully able to bring liberal democratic institutions to these respective countries, and thus these Allied postwar efforts are typically cited as evidence that foreign occupiers can indeed achieve the objectives of reconstruction. Given the success of these efforts and their subsequent importance in the argument to justify current reconstruction efforts in other countries, it makes sense to look at each case in the context of the framework and mechanisms developed in previous chapters.

Japan

Overview

Following the use of nuclear bombs by the United States in Hiroshima and Nagasaki, the Japanese government announced its surrender to the Allied forces on August 14, 1945, signing the official surrender document aboard the *USS Missouri* in Tokyo Bay on September 2, 1945. This document specified the terms of the surrender that the Allies had agreed upon and offered to the Japanese in the Potsdam Declaration in late July. General Douglas MacArthur, the Supreme Commander for the Allied Powers, was the key representative of the United States but also of the Allied Forces in general. The surrender

called for an Allied occupation, and the occupiers were charged with democratization and demilitarization. More specifically, the terms of the surrender included the purging of leadership and trials for war criminals, military
disarmament, and the creation of liberal democratic institutions that would
protect freedom of speech and religion, among other individual rights.

The magnitude of the devastation resulting from the war was significant.
Estimates place the total number of deaths—civilians and service personnel—
in the range of 2 to 2.7 million. Japanese industry was also affected by the extensive bombing campaign, and it has been estimated that the war destroyed a
quarter of Japan's wealth. The major Japanese cities were heavily damaged due
to the bombings, and approximately 9 million Japanese citizens were homeless
at the conclusion of the war.[1] It is within this context—complete and unconditional surrender coupled with significant physical and psychological devastation—that the Allied Forces, led by MacArthur, carried out the successful reconstruction of Japan.

The Art of Association and Nested Games

Perhaps the most striking characteristic of pre-war Japan was its relatively
high level of economic, political, and social development.[2] For instance, Japan
had a highly industrialized economy with the requisite knowledge of the relevant production, organizational, and management techniques. The shift
from a largely agricultural economy to a modern industrial society took place
following the Meiji Restoration of 1868, well before the U.S. occupation in the
mid-1940s.[3] This evolution of the Japanese economy included large-scale investment in infrastructure, including ports, harbors, lighthouses, a system
of telegraph lines, and a postal system. Further, although private investment
played a major role in the development of a rail system, the government had
spearheaded the building of that system and had been proactive on a number
of other infrastructure fronts.[4]

Although the war caused significant physical devastation, the fundamental
endowment of knowledge, skills, and customs, which had evolved well before
the war and occupation, remained in the postwar period. Indeed, one of the
central occupation policies was aimed at dissolving the existing *zaibatsu*, the
large financial and industrial conglomerates that had emerged in the nineteenth century. Although the occupiers did take steps to break up the *zaibatsu*,
including seizing assets and holdings that were sold to the public, they never
completely succeeded in dissolving them. The important point for this analysis
is that the prerequisites for an industrialized economy and society were in place

prior to World War II and the subsequent occupation, and this endowment of existing know-how served as the foundation for many of the economic and social institutions reconstructed by occupiers.

Another important characteristic of Japanese society was the existence of a shared national identity. This shared identity was reflected in well-developed political institutions that had evolved, like the country's economic and social institutions, prior to the war. Many of these same institutions continued to exist in the postwar period and played a major role in the success of the effort. In terms of the mechanisms discussed in Chapter 3, Japan was characterized by an art of association that allowed for weak ties and a general cooperative solution to the Japanese meta-game. Therefore, although nested games existed, they did not serve as a barrier to coordination at the national level, and the reconstruction of Japan was largely a matter of occupiers solving the "coordination problem."

One example of the art of association that characterized Japan is the previously mentioned *zaibatsu* structure. The conglomerates, which initially emerged from close-knit family ties, evolved to rely on external professional managers to run many of their operations.[5] Francis Fukuyama has argued that firm scale and the employment of professional managers is one indication of a society's trust because it requires the shift from reliance on close-knit family members to reliance on strangers.[6] In other words, firm owners must trust those outside their familial network to increase the scale of their business in an effective manner. Employing laborers and managers outside one's consanguineal network requires trust because the performance of the company is directly tied to the performance of strangers. As one indication of the long history of Japan's art of association, Fukuyama traces the employment of professional managers in Japan over several centuries. Given that a cooperative equilibrium was already in place at the meta-level, the preexisting art of association lowered the transaction costs associated with the reconstruction and was a central factor in the overall success of the effort.

MacArthur was well aware of the existing political and social institutions and their importance for the sustainability of a cooperative solution to the larger meta-game in the postwar period. This is evident when one considers how MacArthur and the occupying forces carried out the implementation of their orders and directives. Instead of utilizing a military government to implement policies and directives, as was the case in West Germany, the reconstruction of Japan was carried out through the use of existing government institutions and relied, to a large extent, on indigenous actors.[7] These individuals had local knowledge of the language, culture, and history of the country. Given this, they were able to implement changes in a manner that was considered legitimate by most Japanese citizens.

One important illustration of the occupiers' awareness of the importance of existing institutions is represented by the role that Emperor Hirohito played in the reconstruction of the country. A poll conducted several weeks after the end of the war showed that 70 percent of Americans supported either harsh punishment or death for the emperor. Further, prior to the U.S. occupation, there was still debate among policymakers regarding what should be done with the emperor. In a series of reports from MacArthur to policymakers in the United States, the general noted the importance of the institution of the emperor for the maintenance of social order and cohesion. Despite the popular support for removing and punishing the emperor in the United States, MacArthur ultimately decided to incorporate the emperor into the reconstruction process.[8]

Although the emperor lost his power under the new constitution, he remained in a position of symbolic power in the new Japan. A key part of this role was serving as the mouthpiece for communicating the directives and orders of the occupying forces to the Japanese populace. Given his historical position and his consequent credibility in Japanese society, the emperor was effectively able to convince many Japanese citizens, who may have otherwise been reluctant, to adopt the reconstructed order desired by the occupiers.[9] In other words, the emperor was able to reduce the transaction costs associated with solving the coordination problem of shifting from the pre-war order to the new postwar order.

The incorporation of indigenous actors into the reconstruction process was not limited to the emperor. For instance, Japanese diplomat and prime minister Yoshida Shigeru, politician and journalist Ishibashi Tanzan, and politician Ashida Hitoshi were three other leading indigenous figures who played central roles in the broader reconstruction of Japan.[10] The historian John Dower has noted how many of the preexisting Japanese political, economic, and social institutions "passed through" from the pre-war to postwar period.[11] Although the reconstruction influenced these institutions, their core compositions, both formal and informal, remained intact.

In sum, to a large extent, the ultimate success of the reconstruction of Japan can be traced to the existing endowment of know-how and skills related to social relations, organizational forms, and production techniques that survived the war and carried through to the postwar period. This existing endowment served to complement those institutions established by the occupiers. The stability created by preexisting formal and informal institutions carried over to the occupation and postwar period. This is not to suggest that the occupying forces did not shift the institutional trajectory of Japan. They clearly had an impact on many fronts, including the new constitution, the court system, education, the structure of business and land ownership, and the purging of some members of the previous regime.[12] However, occupiers were able to work within a preexisting institutional framework that generated a sustainable solution to the larger Japanese meta-game. This existing cooperative solution allowed occupiers to focus on coordinating the Japanese populace around a specific set of institutions instead of having to focus their efforts on transforming situations of conflict into a situation of cooperation.

Expectations

The expectations of the Japanese populace, which played a central role in the ultimate outcome of the reconstruction effort, were influenced by two key factors. The first major influence was the fact that the occupation was the result of an unconditional surrender on the part of the Japanese government. The terms of surrender were explicit: the Allied Forces would occupy Japan with the aim of democratizing and demilitarizing the country. MacArthur carried out the reconstruction in a dictatorial manner, engaging in reforms that included the drafting of a constitution in a relatively short period of time, the redefinition of property rights, and the extensive censorship of information, among other activities.[13] The expectations of the Japanese populace were shaped by the full awareness of the surrender of the emperor to the Allied Forces as well as the emperor's continued involvement throughout the reconstruction, as discussed above.

The second major influence on the expectations of the Japanese populace was the impact of the war itself. As mentioned at the outset of this chapter, the physical devastation to the country due to the war was significant. Related to this fact, and perhaps of equal if not greater importance, was the psychological damage caused by the war.[14] Starting in 1931, with the conquest of Manchuria, Japan had been at war for fifteen years. Many Japanese citizens had lost family or friends during this period, and exhaustion from the extended war effort had had a devastating effect on many citizens.[15] Moreover, the absolute devastation of the nuclear weapons dropped on two of their cities must certainly have had a damaging psychological effect. In addition to the lives lost and homes destroyed, the decade and a half of war destroyed or perversely affected many of the country's distribution channels, and as a result, malnutrition, starvation, and disease were very real concerns for many Japanese citizens.[16] The occupiers had their own difficulties distributing food rations, and black markets developed for a wide array of goods and services. The overall effect on the population was both weariness and uncertainty in regard to the future.

Despite the devastation, the prolonged war effort and unconditional surrender had at least one positive effect from the occupiers' standpoint: a willingness on the part of the populace to consider personal and social change and a break from the past. John Dower notes of the Japanese in the postwar period, "People behaved differently, thought differently, encountered circumstances that differed from what they had previously experienced. . . . People were acutely aware of the need to reinvent their own lives."[17] At a minimum, this awareness contributed to the willingness of Japanese citizens to embrace the changes introduced by the occupiers, especially because they were grounded in existing institutions that were considered legitimate.

To be clear, the Japanese populace did have some minimal expectations of the occupying forces. Public protests were held over certain issues, such as food rationing and delivery. For instance, in May 1946, a series of "Food May Day" demonstrations were held throughout the country. The number of participants in these protests has been estimated to be in the range of 1.25 to 2.5 million.[18] There also were demonstrations by members of labor unions and the Communist Party in Japan. Overall, however, the protests remained peaceful, and for the most part the Japanese populace acquiesced to the directives of the occupying forces. Again, this can be connected to the fact that institutions existed prior to the occupation that had facilitated the transformation from conflict to coordination. The main issue for occupiers therefore was working within existing institutions to shift the equilibrium of the broader coordination game.

Credible Commitment

The issue of credible commitment is a central problem in any reconstruction. The fundamental dilemma is that occupiers must create political, economic, and social institutions that citizens view as credible and constrained in what actions they can take. If citizens do not view constructed, or reconstructed, institutions as being credible, they will fail to make the investment necessary to make such institutions self-enforcing over time.

Credible commitment was not a significant barrier to achieving sustainable cooperation around reconstructed institutions as regards the occupation and reconstruction of Japan, primarily due to the fact that many involved in the reconstruction had established reputations of credibility in the pre-war period. In other words, occupiers largely relied on existing mechanisms to signal the credibility of reforms to the Japanese public.

Perhaps the best example of the use of existing mechanisms of credibility is the first meeting between General MacArthur and Emperor Hirohito on September 27, 1945, at the U.S. Embassy in Tokyo. Although the meeting itself was important, it was the picture of MacArthur and the emperor that had a substantial and lasting impact on the populace. The picture, considered by many to be the most famous picture of the postwar occupation period, shows MacArthur standing next to the emperor in MacArthur's quarters. The picture, published in all of the major newspapers, established MacArthur's authority and signaled to the Japanese populace that the occupiers would work with, and through, the emperor to achieve their goals.[19] In other words, this single photograph legitimized MacArthur and the larger occupation in the eyes of the Japanese populace.

The use of existing credibility went beyond the initial meeting between Mac-Arthur and the emperor, however. The occupiers utilized the Diet, the Japanese Parliament, to pass laws as well as to ratify the new Japanese constitution. Again, utilizing an existing legislative body allowed the occupiers to take advantage of the existing credibility linked to that institution from the pre-war period. Indeed, the members of the Allied Forces respected the Diet as an established institution of great importance, and they allowed for debate regarding the specifics of the new constitution prior to its adoption. It is estimated that 80 to 90 percent of the changes suggested by members of the Diet were accepted and incorporated by MacArthur, whose approval was required.[20] The Allied Forces also organized a widespread public relations campaign, including tours by the emperor throughout the country to meet with citizens. These tours further served to legitimize the larger reconstruction effort by again employing the existing credibility of the emperor.

Note also that the occupiers themselves did not suffer from an issue of credible commitment in carrying out the reconstruction. As stated in the terms of surrender, the Allied Forces were occupiers who would stay the course until success was achieved. Interestingly, MacArthur's dictatorial management style served to reinforce the Japanese public's perception of the commitment of occupiers. This commitment, signaled through the surrender document and Mac-Arthur's actions, coupled with the motivation for the occupation, increased the incentive for the Japanese populace to cooperate with the occupiers.

Public Choice Issues

I have already made reference to MacArthur's dictatorial leadership of the reconstruction of Japan. As the Supreme Commander for the Allied Forces, MacArthur oversaw the entire reconstruction process. However, it must be noted that while MacArthur had much leeway regarding how the occupation would be implemented and its day-to-day operation, the overarching policies and reforms of the effort had been debated and agreed upon by U.S. policymakers *prior* to the end of the war and had been approved by President Truman.[21] MacArthur also kept in constant contact with Washington, D.C., through the issuance of reports regarding the status of the reconstruction effort.

Nevertheless, the freedom that MacArthur had to implement directives as he saw fit should not be downplayed. As mentioned in Chapter 4, MacArthur recounted to the U.S. Senate in 1951 his ability to issue fiat directives. Along similar lines, an advisor to MacArthur noted, "Never before in the history of the United States has such enormous and absolute power been placed in the hands of a single individual."[22] The power MacArthur possessed, as well as his flexibility in implementing the general aims of the reconstruction effort, allowed the occupation to overcome many of the public choice issues discussed in Chapter 4. Further, it is important to keep in mind that the broader context of Japan—the existing art of association, solution to the meta-game, and political institutions—reduced the scope of the activities required by MacArthur and the occupiers for ultimate success.

Although he was largely insulated from the public choice issues associated with the political decision-making process back home in the United States, there were some pockets of disagreement and tension between policymakers and occupying forces. One area where this was evident was in MacArthur's attempt to dissolve the *zaibatsu* network. As previously discussed, the *zaibatsu* were business conglomerates that had existed long before the war and occupation. The dissolution of the *zaibatsu* network, which was viewed as monopolistic and supportive of the centralized and militaristic pre-war order, was one of MacArthur's main objectives during the reconstruction.

Resistance to MacArthur's anti-*zaibatsu* program came from two sources. The first was from within the U.S. policymaking bureaucracy. MacArthur had initially enacted an aggressive program to break up and decentralize the existing *zaibatsu* network, but not all U.S. policymakers agreed with the program. For instance, William Draper, who was the Under-Secretary of the Army and also a Wall Street banker, advised MacArthur to cease the program because of the implications for Japan's economic recovery.[23] In 1947, George Kennan, a State Department official, traveled to Japan to "impress upon MacArthur the reorientation of Washington's thinking" regarding the anti-monopoly measures.[24]

The second source of resistance came from both Japanese and U.S. special interests. On the one hand, many Japanese business and political interests argued that the program would lead to economic instability and would make the Japanese economy dependent on external aid from the United States.[25] On the other hand, U.S. business interests sought to restore trading relationships with the *zaibatsu* and argued that the program to dissolve the conglomerates was stunting the economic recovery of the country.

The influence of bureaucrats and special interests, coupled with the threat of communism, led to the ultimate abandonment of the anti-*zaibatsu* program prior to its full implementation. This case serves to illustrate that even in instances in which the power to direct a reconstruction is centralized, the overall process will still be influenced to some degree by the public choice issues discussed in Chapter 4. Despite the existence of such cases, however, public choice issues did not heavily influence the reconstruction of Japan and were not a significant barrier to ultimate success.

West Germany

Overview

On May 7, 1945, Germany surrendered unconditionally to the Allied Forces, which consisted of the United States, the Soviet Union, and the United Kingdom. The terms of the surrender and occupation had been developed and agreed upon prior to the surrender in a series of meetings between the Allies at Casablanca in January 1943, at Yalta in February 1945, and at Potsdam in August 1945. The specifics included unconditional surrender, democratization and denazification, the purging and trial of war criminals, the reconstruction of liberal economic institutions, reparations, and disarmament. It was also agreed that Germany would be divided into zones that would each be occupied by a separate Allied country. Specifically, it was determined that the United States, United Kingdom, and France, which was absent from the initial series of meetings between the Allies, would occupy the zones in western Germany while the Soviet Union would occupy the eastern zone of the country.

Similar to the case in postwar Japan, Germany was physically devastated. It is estimated that the "war destroyed one-third of German wealth, nearly one-fifth of all productive buildings and machines, two-fifths of the transportation facilities, and over one-seventh of all houses."[26] Given the widespread damage, much of the emphasis of the reconstruction effort was on rebuilding physical infrastructure. Despite these constraints, the reconstruction of West Germany had the same outcome as that in Japan—liberal democratic institutions were successfully reconstructed.

One of the most common explanations for the ultimate success of the reconstruction of West Germany is the monetary aid provided through the Marshall Plan. There is ongoing debate regarding the magnitude of the effect of the Marshall Plan on the recovery of the country and of Europe in general.[27] My goal here is not to resolve this debate but rather to highlight that the economics of reconstruction developed in earlier chapters can contribute to our understanding of the ultimate success of the reconstruction of West Germany. Further, the economics of reconstruction indicate that, to whatever extent that aid is deemed to have been effective, preexisting complementary institutions were in place that allowed for that success.

The Art of Association and Nested Games

Germany was an industrialized country with well-developed economic, social, and political institutions that had evolved prior to both World War II and the Allied occupation of the country. In other words, the German meta-game was solved prior to the reconstruction effort. Similar to the circumstances in Japan, in spite of the fact that the war had caused physical destruction to much of the infrastructure of the country, the existing endowment of skills, knowledge, and the art of association was conducive to the establishment of liberal democratic institutions in the postwar period.

The industrialization of Germany can be traced back to the early nineteenth century, when members of the German Confederation began to liberalize their economies. The result of these reforms, which began with Prussia in 1818, was the creation of the German Customs Union (the *Zollverein*) in 1834. The Union created an open economic space between members of the German Confederation who agreed to join.[28] The openness between Union members significantly reduced barriers to trade and lowered the transaction costs associated with developing and maintaining economic ties, which in turn fostered further industrialization and the further development of an art of association.

Germany's industrialization was evident in the development of the country's infrastructure, but perhaps more telling was the development of firms of significant size. These firms moved beyond the family ownership structure and relied on professional managers outside a close-knit circle of trust.[29] As Francis Fukuyama notes, "the Germans were very quick to move from family businesses to professional management, building rationally organized administrative hierarchies that turned into durable institutions."[30] Similar to the case of Japan, the beginning of the move toward weak bonds of trust with strangers outside family circles can be observed over a century prior to the post–World War II occupation and reconstruction.

Further support for the claim that the art of association present in Germany solved the larger meta-game prior to occupation and reconstruction can be found in the country's established political institutions. Although the Nazi regime was ruthless, it is important to keep in mind that it assumed its position of power through existing political institutions. Further, once in power, the regime did not engage in a widespread dismantling of state institutions and bureaucracies, but instead utilized them to carry out its rule.[31] These institutions had a long history of legitimacy among the German populace and served as the foundation for reconstructed institutions at the meta-level.

Evidence also indicates that there was a strong existing commitment to democracy and self-governance at the local level.[32] For instance, a 1944 *U.S. Civil Affairs Guide* indicated that governments at the local level had a strong tradition of self-governance when it stated that local politics were to be the springboard for political reform throughout Germany.[33] Along similar lines, writing on British plans to democratize Germany, the political scientist Barbara Marshall notes, "It was recognized, however, that beneath the nationalist and aggressive policies perpetuated by German central governments, there had existed a healthy democratic tradition at the local level. . . ."[34]

Allied advisors, many of whom were experts in German history, recommended retaining particular indigenous traditions. The reconstruction process, for instance, included many native Germans. The military governments in the U.S. Zone appointed Germans in villages, towns, and cities to assist in the implementation of the Allied policies. In choosing natives for these positions, emphasis was placed on past administrative experience and the perceived ability to cooperate.[35]

It should be noted, however, that it would be a mistake to believe that the social, political, and economic institutions that evolved in Germany prior to the war and occupation mirrored those of the West; but the more fundamental point is that an art of association that allowed for a cooperative solution to the

German meta-game had evolved and was solidified in durable institutions prior to World War II and the subsequent reconstruction efforts. This meant that Germany was characterized by an existing endowment of the requisite knowledge, skills, and organizational forms to serve as a foundation for liberal reconstructed orders. In other words, mechanisms of self-governance along liberal lines already existed prior to the arrival of the occupiers. It is true that the Nazi regime stifled many of these mechanisms, but once that regime was removed, these mechanisms were once again allowed to operate. As the historian Edward Peterson notes, "The [U.S] occupation worked when and where it allowed Germans to govern themselves."[36] In sum, while the war effort and occupation clearly served as an exogenous shock to Germany, the foundation for sustaining liberal institutions was already in place. The preexisting solution to the meta-game greatly eased the task of U.S. occupiers, whose main concern was working within existing institutions to overcome the coordination problem.

Expectations and Credible Commitment

The issues of citizen expectations and credible commitment do not appear to have been barriers to the successful reconstruction of West Germany either. Similar to the case of Japan, the physical and psychological damage caused by the war effort had a devastating effect on many members of the populace. In addition to the physical damage outlined earlier, it was estimated that there were twenty-one million displaced individuals throughout Europe.[37] Furthermore, food production and delivery systems were severely damaged, which led to shortages and the threat of starvation.[38]

Julian Bach, a news correspondent who wrote a firsthand account of the occupation, noted that "apathy is widespread," and recorded how the Allies from all four zones were "struck by the 'docility' of the population. . . ."[39] Another account described German citizens as "dazed or sullen or spiritless" and noted, "The devastating bombardments . . . the years of tension, had left them drained of energy and emotions."[40] In addition to the physical exhaustion and devastation of the German citizens, it was evident that the Allied forces were occupiers and not liberators.[41] Because of this fact, German citizens expected change and were willing to accept forced demilitarization and denazification in exchange. As the historian Edward Peterson notes, "Unlike most Military Government measures, these [demilitarization and denazification] prohibitions were successful, but they were because the Germans were ready to accept them."[42] In other words, to the extent that the occupiers' actions aligned with the expectations of citizens, they were successful.

To the extent that it issued policies and directives, the U.S. Military Government utilized many existing political and social institutions. For instance, the Bonn Constitution (in other words, the basic law), which was written and adopted during the occupation, drew heavily on the existing Weimar Constitution, a well-established document grounded in indigenous norms and laws.[43] Although a military government was established, occupiers largely relied on indigenous citizens and grassroots support for democracy and self-government. By utilizing existing institutions, occupiers were able to overcome the problems associated with achieving credibility. As will be discussed, while part of this reliance on indigenous institutions was by design, it was also due to internal conflicts and tensions that developed both between the Allies in general and between policymakers in Washington and occupiers in the U.S. Zone. However, the point remains that there were institutions in place that allowed for the implementation of effective reforms by the occupiers.

Public Choice Issues

Although few would disagree that the post–World War II reconstruction of West Germany was ultimately a success, a closer look at the U.S. occupation indicates that the reconstruction process was far from smooth. There is evidence that ultimate success was achieved not because of the occupation but despite it.

Public choice issues plagued the reconstruction on two fronts. On the one hand, there was confusion among and division between U.S. policymakers in Washington, D.C., and the occupiers. On the other hand, difficulties arose due to coordination problems between the Allied Forces. Consequently, conflicting ends and correlative goals, both between those within the U.S. domestic political decision-making process and among the Allied occupiers, influenced the reconstruction.

As noted earlier, the historian Edward Peterson has advanced a thesis that the U.S. occupation worked best when occupiers and policymakers did least and allowed German citizens to engage in self-government.[44] Peterson notes that confusion and conflict occurred at all levels of U.S. domestic policymaking, which slowed the reconstruction and had the unintended benefit of allowing German citizens to self-govern. It appears that one obstacle was the fact that many of those in the United States who achieved positions that either influenced or determined policy were awarded those positions because of personal ties or because they could be easily manipulated by those in power, and not because they were the best candidates to establish policies that would bring liberal democracy to West Germany.[45]

Further, policymakers largely ignored experts in the State Department who were in the best position to develop a cogent German policy, which was part of a greater problem of general confusion between agencies within the U.S. government.[46] As John Hilldring, the Civil Affairs Division commander at the time, noted, "There wasn't even a clear and lasting decision as to what civilian departments and agencies of the government should participate in the making of policy. . . . This very bitter and troublesome controversy was never resolved."[47] This confusion at home greatly slowed the speed of the reconstruction efforts abroad.

General Lucius D. Clay was the central administrator of American policy during the U.S. occupation. As Clay spent time in West Germany, he became increasingly informed regarding the needs of German citizens and the nuances of the German way of life. This knowledge influenced both the manner in which he implemented policy and the specifics of those policies. Oftentimes, this knowledge of the cultural facts and economic and political necessities on the ground put him at odds with both policymakers in Washington, D.C., and the other Allied Forces.[48] Moreover, the policies of the occupiers were only effectively implemented to the extent that they aligned with the desires and wants of the German citizens. As Peterson notes, "Without the assistance of his [Clay's] alien subjects, assistance which was given if his policy accorded with their felt needs, little would have been accomplished."[49]

Although the reconstruction of West Germany is often viewed as a successful exercise in the central planning of economic, political, and social institutions, this is far from the case. In reality, occupiers were largely unable to effectively govern the German population during the occupation let alone centrally design and implement sustainable liberal institutions. Indeed, the German reconstruction should be seen less as an exercise in imposing liberal institutions and more as an exercise in overseeing emergent indigenous institutions of self-government.

Peterson notes that "OMGUS [Office of Military Government, United States] was never able to govern. At best it could only supervise aspects of German self-government. Clay's top level staff had a variety of skills, but sufficient skill to govern foreigners was rare."[50] He goes on to argue that only after the occupiers retreated from programs of forced denazification and economic planning was West Germany actually able to rebuild sustaining institutions.

Even the retreat from economic controls was unintended and not the result of the actions of occupiers. In the immediate postwar period, occupiers maintained many of the price and economic controls that had been implemented during Hitler's regime. This was part of the larger goal of planning the West German economy. However, these controls were eventually removed, not because occupiers realized that they were stifling economic recovery but because Ludwig Erhard went behind the backs of occupiers to abolish the controls. Erhard, who was appointed Bavarian Minister of Finance in 1945 and then elected Director of Economics of the bizonal Office of Economic Opportunity in 1948, orchestrated sweeping economic reforms that included currency reform, the removal of price controls and other regulations, and tax reforms.

Occupiers did not even have knowledge of many of these reforms in advance. For instance, Erhard announced the end of price controls during a radio address without having informed the occupiers. When he was called on the carpet for overstepping his bounds—Erhard did not have the power to change the military government's regulations—he responded that he had not changed any regulations, but rather, had abolished them and therefore violated no rules.[51] When Clay asked Erhard why he hadn't gone through the proper channels, Erhard responded, "[I]f I had told your officials, they would have stopped me."[52] One should not underestimate the impact of Erhard's reforms on the reconstruction and recovery of West Germany, which also serves as a shining example of how the reconstruction and recovery of West Germany took place not necessarily because of the military occupation by the Allied Forces but despite it.[53]

In addition to conflict and confusion internal to the U.S. occupation of West Germany, there was also tension between Allied forces that slowed the speed and effectiveness of the occupation.[54] In contrast to the case of Japan, where MacArthur had unilateral control of the occupation, agreement between the various Allied countries was required for designing and implementing broad and general policies that affected all zones in Germany.

Following Germany's surrender, the Allied Control Council (ACC), which consisted of representatives of the Allied powers, was the main medium for coordinating a reconstruction policy. There was disagreement between the members of the ACC on a number of issues, including economic reform, reparations, aid, and the design and administration of reconstructed political institutions. The need for consent between ACC members increased the transaction costs associated with coordinating on a policy, which in turn slowed both policy design and implementation. The result of these high transaction costs was that "Official U.S. German policy was stalemated until early 1947, with . . . economic integration stalled by Russian and French reluctance to move."[55] In fact, the transaction costs associated with coordinating around unified policies were ultimately stifling. Indeed, with the merger of the U.S. and U.K. zones into Bizonia in 1947, the Soviets left the council permanently.

Clay retired from his post in May 1949 with the major policies of the reconstruction implemented. Describing Clay's time in charge of the U.S. Military Government, Edward Peterson notes that "Clay became less and less a 'master' of Germans for Washington and more and more a 'first servant of the state' for Germans against Washington and the Allies. With the organization available to him he had no chance of being a master of even his own zone."[56]

As indicated, Clay spent much of his time maneuvering between competing interests and agendas both within the United States and between the Allies. The end result was Clay's limited ability to exert the powerful influence over social, political, and economic institutions that is normally assumed. Again, perhaps the most interesting aspect of the reconstruction of West Germany is the fact that success was ultimately achieved *despite* the fact that the dynamics of the occupation often contributed to preventing the desired end.

Summation

The post–World War II reconstructions of Japan and West Germany are the standard bearers for all subsequent U.S.-led reconstruction efforts. However, it is important to recognize that a very specific set of circumstances characterized both of these countries. In both cases, an art of association existed that provided a solution to the overarching meta-game well before the war and subsequent occupation. Therefore, occupiers did not need to allocate resources to transforming situations of conflict to situations of cooperation, but instead could make marginal changes to existing institutions. In other words, the transformation from conflict to cooperation had taken place prior to occupation, and reconstruction efforts were largely an exercise in shifting the equilibrium in the coordination game.

The economist Luigi Zingales has likened the situations in post–World War II Japan and West Germany to a firm whose plant had been destroyed by fire.[57] This is a sound analogy. The fundamental skills, knowledge, and organizational forms of the firm's employees that had evolved prior to the fire will carry over to the reconstructed plant, allowing the firm to eventually achieve its prior level of productivity. Although the resources to invest in rebuilding the plant are indeed important to achieving success, it is the underlying endowment of skills and knowledge that allow the firm to be productive in the first place. Without these complementary institutions (that is, the skills and knowledge of how to organize production activities), the plant would be nothing but an underutilized or empty building. In the context of reconstruction, countries lacking complementary institutions to serve as a foundation for formally reconstructed institutions will fail to be sustainable liberal democracies.

As mentioned, there is ongoing debate regarding the role of aid associated with the Marshall Plan in the ultimate success of the reconstruction of West Germany. While this debate is beyond the scope of this book, the present chapter indicates that, to the extent aid did have a positive effect, the complementary institutions were already in place so that that aid could be used effectively. To return to Zingales's analogy, to the extent that the Marshall Plan did contribute to the success of West Germany, it did so because it allowed the West German "plant" to be rebuilt.

However, it was the preexisting complementary institutions that allowed the rebuilt plant to be used effectively. In short, even if aid was indeed a major factor in the successful reconstruction of West Germany, that success does not imply that injecting aid into weak, failed, and war-torn states will generate a similar outcome, because the existing endowment of skills, culture, and know-how will vary across cases. Where the necessary endowment is lacking, a plant can be built using monetary aid, but few will know how to utilize this infrastructure.

As the case of West Germany indicates, even where the requisite complementary institutions exist, occupiers still suffer from the most basic knowledge problem: how to construct liberal institutions. Further, the reconstruction effort is still subject to the potentially negative effects generated by the domestic and international political decision-making process. As discussed, many aspects of the West German occupation had the effect of slowing the speed of the overall reconstruction process, and this in a country with an effective basis for liberal institutions in place; further, the successes of reconstruction were often achieved despite the actions of occupiers, not because of those actions. One can envision how these same problems in a country lacking the complementary institutions that existed in West Germany can generate perverse outcomes of an even greater magnitude.

One implication is the need to reconsider how the reconstructions of Japan and West Germany are viewed relative to more recent efforts to export liberal democracy via occupation. Along these lines, the political scientist Eva Bellin argues that the reconstructions of Japan and West Germany are in fact not suitable benchmarks against which to compare more recent U.S. reconstruction efforts due to the fact that the countries where these most recent efforts have taken place possess very different endowments of skills and knowledge as compared to the post–World War II reconstructions.[58] To reiterate a central theme of this book, simply looking at the level of controllable variables in past reconstruction efforts tells us very little about the potential for success in current or future efforts because of the large variance in the endowment of complementary institutions, the absence of which constrains the effectiveness of technical resources such as troops, aid, and the reconstruction of physical infrastructure.

Recognizing and understanding the unique characteristics of Japan and West Germany will continue to be of utmost importance in the consideration of future reconstruction efforts. It is unlikely, at least in the near future, that there will be significant threats from countries that have reached relatively high levels of development. Instead, at least in the near term, the main threat appears to be from weak, failed, and conflict-torn states or rogue groups within those states. Post–World War II Japan and West Germany are extremely poor points of comparison for these modern threats, and employing them as a baseline will generate faulty and inaccurate analyses of the potential for success in future reconstruction efforts.

6   Fool's Errands: Somalia and Haiti

U NDENIABLY, the problems generated by weak and failed states are among the most relevant issues in the world today. The potential chaos that these states can produce poses a threat to global political and economic security and stability. In addition to these issues, however, humanitarian concerns within weak and failed states are also a central concern of the international community. Weak and failed states typically are characterized by a lack of government-provided security, the absence of basic services and infrastructure, and the weak or nonexistent protection of civil freedoms.[1]

Given the potential difficulties caused by these states, understanding what can be done to remedy the situation in these countries is a central policy issue facing the international community. These concerns, for example, were the motivation for such programs as the World Bank's Low Income Countries Under Stress (LICUS) initiative, which focuses on countries that fail to provide even the most basic services to their citizens.

As illustrated by the cases of Afghanistan, Bosnia, Cambodia, Haiti, Kosovo, and Somalia, U.S. and international policymakers have often sought to address the concerns generated by weak and failed states by engaging in reconstruction efforts. Indeed, in the post–Cold War period, a large majority of U.S.-led reconstruction efforts have been motivated by either humanitarian or security concerns related to such states. Although the United States is still involved in several of these efforts (for example, in Afghanistan, Bosnia, Iraq, and Kosovo), many of the cases in which U.S. occupiers have permanently exited, such as

Cambodia, Haiti, and Somalia, must be considered failures. Given that, it makes sense to consider reconstruction efforts in weak and failed states in the context of the economics of reconstruction developed in earlier chapters.

Specifically, this chapter focuses on the recent reconstruction efforts in Somalia (1993–1995) and Haiti (1994–1996). Both countries are part of the previously mentioned World Bank LICUS initiative, and as such, represent many of the general characteristics of weak and failed states. In addition to illuminating the specific mechanisms that influenced the outcomes in Somalia and Haiti, however, this chapter will also shed light on some of the central issues facing the policy community in dealing with other states in this category.

Somalia

Overview

Following the overthrow of Major General Muhammad Siad Barre's regime in 1991, Somalia fell into a state of civil war as various dissident groups turned on one another. The combination of civil war and a widespread drought and famine led to United Nations (UN) intervention in April of 1992.[2] The UN Operation in Somalia (UNOSOM I) was created to oversee the cease-fire in the capital city of Mogadishu, to provide security for UN personnel, and to deliver humanitarian assistance. In August 1992, the mandate originally granted to UNOSOM I was expanded to include not just the capital city but also the distribution centers throughout Somalia. However, it quickly became evident that UNOSOM I could not provide the required security and protection for the delivery of humanitarian assistance. The original UN-mediated cease-fire failed, as both sides refused to compromise in regard to positions of political authority. Moreover, each side engaged in looting and interference in the delivery of humanitarian supplies and services, claiming that the humanitarian activities would assist the enemy.

Responding to these difficulties, the UN Security Council authorized a U.S.-led Unified Task Force (UNITAF) for deployment in December of 1992. The initial U.S. involvement was limited and aimed at providing security along the lines of UNOSOM I. Eventually, in May 1993, the mandate granted to UNITAF expanded under UNOSOM II to include reconstruction and democratization efforts.[3] Specifically, the expanded mandate under UNOSOM II, which lasted until May 1995, gave UNITAF personnel the authority to seize weapons and to rehabilitate and construct political and economic institutions along Western

lines. The mandate also included directives to attempt to foster national reconciliation and stability.[4] UNITAF was successful in delivering some humanitarian assistance to Somalis, but ultimately, UNITAF was not able to effectively
end conflict and generate sustaining political, social, and economic change.[5]

The Art of Association and Nested Games

The existing art of association and resulting nested games that characterized
Somalia constituted the main constraint on attempts by external occupiers to
successfully create national liberal democratic institutions. Indeed, Somalia's
art of association constrained the formation of national political institutions
from the country's inception. Under the direction of the United Nations, the
Republic of Somalia was formed in 1960 by the joining of former colonies of
British and Italian Somalia. The Republic was initially modeled after Western
democracies, with a prime minister, a National Assembly, and an elite bureaucracy. However, political institutions failed to operate in the manner desired
by their designers. To understand why, consider in more detail the network of
indigenous institutions that existed prior to the creation of the Republic.

The physical landscape of Somalia was a major influence on the development of indigenous institutions. The land is characterized largely by desert with
an arid climate, brush vegetation, and little rainfall. The main economic activities include farming and pastoralism. The viability of farming is largely constrained by the amount of rainfall, while the available brush supports grazing
livestock. Due to the difficulties posed by the physical environment, Somalia's
pastoralists were divided into clans as an evolutionary response to their environment, enabling collective support and the enforcement of property rights.
Clans and the subgroups within clans continue to be fundamental aspects of
life in Somalia and, as such, are critical to understanding the evolution of the
social, economic, and political landscape.[6]

Clan membership is determined by patrilineal descent, and clan membership can be as large as several hundred thousand members. Within the
larger clan structure, smaller groups, known as *diya*-paying groups, also exist.
Ranging in size from several hundred to several thousand members, the *diya*-
paying group is an alliance of related lineages formed via contract. The contract
states that members of the alliance should pay and receive blood compensation
(*diya*[7]) as a group. That is, any injury suffered by or caused by any member of
the alliance implicates all members of the contract. For instance, if a member
of Group A kills or injures a member of Group B, Group B will collectively
claim compensation from Group A. When injuries occur and compensation is

due, the contract states who is to accept what portion of the burden and thus who is to pay what portion of the compensation.

Of all the relationships an individual Somali might have, membership in and loyalty to a *diya*-paying group is the most binding and thus the most frequently invoked. In fact, the *diya*-paying group is the basic political and judicial unit. The individual members of a *diya* group provide support for other members through collective political and judicial means, and they also provide a form of social insurance whereby members present goods and services to other members who are negatively affected by personal crisis, drought, or harvest failure. The *diya*-paying groups also serve to protect members' property from other clans through the threat of retaliation from the entire group. Elders make key decisions and act as leaders in political matters.

While the *diya*-paying group provides the means of governance within clans and also the threat of collective action against other clans, *heer* provides a means of contracting between clans. *Heer* refers to agreements between clans and can be viewed as an unwritten but binding contract that states the responsibilities of each group and the penalties for failing to act in the stated manner. *Heer* serves to govern the interaction between clans regarding such issues as the common pool of resources. The interclan council of lineage leaders, the *Guurti*, enforces sanctions against violators of the *heer*. Although governance institutions that are internal to clans (that is, *diya*-paying groups) operate relatively effectively, interclan mechanisms do not always operate as smoothly. Many disputes are resolved, but minor infractions have occasionally escalated into full-fledged conflict between clans.[8]

Given that individual identity and the daily operation of society are derived from clans and the subgroups within clans, Somalis have no experience with a centralized liberal democratic form of government. Stated differently, no meta-game around a central Somali state has ever evolved endogenously. Instead, numerous smaller games that involve a wide array of actors have evolved and developed over time. The actors include the clans themselves (as in the relationships within and between clans), warlords, Muslim clergy, and NGOs, among others.

The dynamics of these mini-games serve as a major constraint on any attempts to settle the meta-game and establish central political institutions. As the political scientist Kenneth Menkhaus notes, "a broad section of Somali society possess veto power over state-building, peace-keeping and law enforcement. This makes negotiating towards those objectives all the more difficult. . . ."[9] Understanding the prevalence of these nested games, and the associated transaction costs for solving the larger meta-game, provides key insights into why the centralized political institutions created in 1960, and attempts to create similar institutions in the 1990s, failed to operate as desired.

With the creation of the Republic of Somalia in 1960, political affiliations quickly developed along clan-based lines. Prior to independence, two parliaments existed—one in the North and one in the South. A unitary parliamentary republic governed the independent Republic. The majoritarian parliament created a set of incentives that led to constant struggles wherein clans would attempt to form coalitions and then create disputes among other clans in order to establish a majority. Regional differences between northern and southern clans also constrained the extent of cooperation. As Maria Brons notes, "Parliamentarians perceived the central state framework as a source of opportunities and enrichment. . . . The political system . . . became another layer in the personalized and/or clan-oriented arrangements. . . ."[10] In short, the establishment of a central government of the Republic of Somalia did not yield benefits to members of Somali society at large. Instead, the central government was seen as a tool to be used by a few to expropriate from the many. As such, the political system was characterized by constant fragility and eventually resulted in a military coup in 1969.

Following the assassination of President Abdirashid Ali Shermarke in October of 1969, Major General Muhammad Siad Barre seized power via a bloodless coup. The result was a centralized state developed along totalitarian lines. Barre ruled over the revolutionary council composed of his family's clans. The council banned certain clan activities and exploited the weakness of interclan norms to divide any potential threats to his power. In some cases, the government provided arms to feuding clans. In short, the activities of Barre's regime significantly damaged the strong norms of governance within clans while also eroding governance mechanisms and prior agreements that had existed between clans. Despite the repressive measures, the informal economy still functioned throughout Somalia, serving as the central means of survival for most Somalis.[11] The Barre regime was able to settle Somalia's meta-game for two decades by relying on continual force, coercion, and repression. Parties did not voluntarily coordinate around the central political institutions, but rather, were forced to do so.

The Barre regime was relatively stable until the late 1980s. The regime's policies had resulted in repression and inequities throughout the country, and over time, dissident groups in various parts of the country gained sufficient size and strength to wrest control of certain areas from the regime. These groups included the Somali National Movement (SNM) in the northwest, the Somali Salvation Democratic Front (SSDF) in the northeast, the United Somali Congress (USC) in central Somalia, and the Somali Patriotic Movement (SPM) in the south. The civil unrest caused by these dissident factions eventually spread to the capital of Mogadishu and resulted in the collapse of the Barre regime in 1991.

The collapse of the regime resulted in a power struggle among competing clans for control of the central government. Although the various dissident groups had agreed to act as a united front in their fight against the Barre regime, cooperation did not continue in the wake of its collapse. One faction of the USC formed an interim government in Mogadishu without consulting the other faction of the USC or the other dissident groups. In response to the interim government, the SPM and the SSDF formed a loose alliance to contest the USC, which led to violent conflict both between factions of the USC and also between the governing USC faction and the SPM-SSDF alliance. In April of 1991, the USC and the SPM-SSDF alliance agreed to a cease-fire, but the agreement was fragile and eventually broke down.

In the northern region, the SNM refused to recognize the USC interim government as legitimate or to participate in USC-led unification talks. The SNM consolidated its position and assumed all local administration in the northern region, but governance did not go smoothly even in this SNM-controlled enclave, primarily because of tension between clans located in the region. The SNM consisted mainly of members of the Isaaq clans, and members of other clans in the northern region, specifically the Gadabursi and Iise clans, resisted the authority of the SNM over their territory. Following some violent conflict between these groups, the leaders of the SNM convinced the leaders from all of the major northern clans to attend a conference in Burao in April of 1991. At the Burao conference, several resolutions pertaining to the future of the northern region were debated and passed. The key outcome of the conference was the creation of the independent Republic of Somaliland in the northern part of Somalia in May of 1991.[12]

Continued violent conflict in the southern part of Somalia led to divided control of the capital city of Mogadishu itself. As mentioned above, the resulting civil war, as well as humanitarian concerns, resulted in foreign intervention by the United Nations, which was followed by occupation by the United States, an occupation that ultimately failed. With the exit of foreign occupiers in 1995, many expected Somalia to collapse into a violent state of chaos. In fact, the opposite occurred. Although one could argue that the lack of a central government has contributed to some problems, it is not "inherently linked to other crises in Somalia such as criminality and armed conflict."[13] Indeed, a closer look illustrates that many individuals can enjoy an environment of peace, lawfulness, and security in the absence of a central government.[14]

With the exit of occupiers, several autonomous states within the larger Republic of Somalia have emerged. As discussed above, the independent state of Somaliland had formed prior to the UN occupation. While not recognized by any foreign government as a legitimate state, Somaliland has remained stable and has instituted a constitution.[15] The autonomous region of Puntland, which has been self-governing since 1998, consists of the regions of Bari, Nugaal, and northern Mudug. Finally, Southwestern Somalia, a self-proclaimed state as of 2002, consists of the Bakool, Bay, Gedo, Jubbada Dhexe, Jubbada Hoose, and Shabeellaha Hoose regions.

Upon close inspection, one observes widespread order with pockets of conflict in these regions. In other words, the Somalis themselves have found endogenous solutions to many of the nested games, which allows for some semblance of order, although the resultant institutions have taken a very different form from those found in Western countries. The extent of order is even more evident when compared to those that existed under the Barre regime and foreign occupation, which are the relevant points of comparison.[16] In fact, one can make a strong argument that attempts by foreign governments since 1991 to revitalize a central Somali state have only served to increase the level of armed conflict. As Kenneth Menkhaus indicates, it is "the process of state-building which appears consistently to exacerbate instability and armed conflict."[17]

As already noted, the UN-facilitated peace agreement of 1991 was short-lived, eventually unraveling into violent conflict. Further attempts by foreign policymakers to generate central institutions have had a similar result. Consider, for instance, the Kenya-mediated peace process sponsored by the Intergovernmental Authority on Development (IGAD) in 2002. Attempts to gain positions of political power prior to the IGAD talks were at least partially responsible for the violent conflict that took place in previously peaceful regions of the country. Indeed, the selection of indigenous individuals to participate in talks regarding the future of the country is a contentious issue. Indigenous actors view participating in peace talks as a key ingredient in securing a favorable position in any future government that may evolve from the talks, and with positions of political power and the associated benefits up for grabs, individuals are willing to engage in high-cost activities, including violence.[18]

In sum, the art of association that characterizes Somalia is such that it precludes the achievement of a feasible solution by foreign occupiers to the larger Somali meta-game. Somalis tend to identify with their clan affiliation instead of with a national identity or national institutions. The associated transaction costs preclude occupiers from generating sustainable cooperation at the national level. Given that, efforts by external occupiers to impose national institutions have met with failure. Somalia is an ideal illustration of the previously discussed nirvana fallacy, which occurs when policymakers assume that reconstruction efforts can generate a preferable state of affairs. In reality, reconstruction efforts in Somalia have had the perverse effect of increasing the level of conflict in addition to generating other negative unintended consequences discussed in the next section.

Expectations, Credible Commitment, and Unintended Consequences

Yet another constraint on the efforts of foreign policymakers and occupiers to establish central liberal democratic institutions is the expectations of the Somali populace. There were seventeen foreign-led efforts (not all by the United States or UN) to achieve national reconciliation in Somalia between the collapse of the Barre regime in 1991 and 1995.[19] Given the historical experiences with clan-based loyalties, past exploitative regimes, and conflict resulting from past efforts at constructing a central government, most Somalis view national politics as a zero-sum situation.

Rather than providing mutually advantageous benefits to society at large, many Somalis expect any central political structure to create clear winners and losers. Given this, any effort to generate a central government leads to conflict as individuals and clans attempt to become the political winners. Because of the expectation that reconstructed institutions will be zero-sum, most are unwilling to make the necessary investment to establish sustainable positive-sum institutions. In general, when the situation is such that the indigenous populace is unwilling to make the necessary investment in the reconstruction process, the transaction costs of striking a sustainable solution to the meta-game are prohibitive.

The problem of credible commitment faced by occupiers is yet another reason that reconstruction efforts in Somalia have failed repeatedly. Given that there are no legitimate national institutions in place, there are no existing mechanisms for occupiers to utilize to shift the existing equilibrium to something considered credible. Recall that existing meta-institutions in both Japan and West Germany lowered the costs associated with social change. In both cases, occupiers were able to rely on preexisting meta-institutions and legitimate leaders to overcome the problem of credible commitment. Somalia's meta-game was solved under the Barre regime, but only through the use of coercion and force.

However, when the coercive regime collapsed, the meta-solution was unsustainable. The combination of a lack of preexisting legitimate meta-institutions and the expectation that constructed central political institutions will be zero-sum in nature has drastically increased transaction costs to a point at which success in reconstruction efforts has not been possible. Because policymakers lack an effective solution to this fundamental problem, future efforts can be expected to have the same outcome as those in the past.

In addition to issues related to expectations and credible commitment, the U.S.-led reconstruction effort in Somalia also suffered from problems related to negative unintended consequences. For instance, reports indicated that sanitary conditions near refugee camps established by occupiers were so bad that the mortality rate actually increased in those areas.[20] Likewise, the larger program of disarmament took weapons from those who were hired by humanitarian agencies to serve as guards, which increased the vulnerability of these agencies to attacks from warlords.[21] As mentioned, the presence of occupiers shifted the incentives facing the indigenous populace and generated the unintended consequence of fostering increased conflict. This outcome is due to the fact that the payoff to engaging in conflict actually increased with the presence of occupiers because each party wanted to secure a position of power to maximize their spoils from the reconstruction effort.

The motivation behind the desire of many Somalis to secure as much as possible as quickly as possible from reconstruction efforts can be traced back, at least in part, to the negative unintended consequences created by historical foreign aid. Prior to the collapse of the Barre regime, foreign aid accounted for 70 percent of Somalia's budget.[22] In addition to propping up a brutal regime, the aid created what James Buchanan, a Nobel Laureate economist, called the "Samaritan's Dilemma."[23] In providing assistance, the "Samaritan" provider of aid shifts the incentives facing those receiving aid, and in doing so, provides a disincentive to save and invest while providing a positive incentive to become dependent on aid. In the case of Somalia, while the intention of those providing aid may have been to better the lot of Somali citizens, the aid had the negative unintended consequence of creating a dependency that actually made the shift toward self-sustaining liberal institutions that much more difficult in later years.

For instance, the expectation of aid is at least partially responsible for the conflict that has occurred in the capital city of Mogadishu. As the political scientist Karin von Hippel notes, "Many Somalis erroneously believe that a restored central government, based in Mogadishu, will once again cause the foreign aid floodgates to open at similar levels to those prior to state collapse. Mogadishu therefore remains the most hotly contested piece of real estate in the country. . . ."[24] As the example of foreign aid indicates, the best of intentions can generate perverse results that ultimately cause more harm than good, in the present but also well into the future.[25]

Public Choice Issues

In addition to the internal constraints discussed previously, the U.S.-led reconstruction effort in Somalia also suffered from public choice issues on a number of fronts. There were tensions regarding Somalia within the United Nations even before the United States became involved. Once the United States did become involved, there were further tensions between the UN and the United States, which stifled the reconstruction effort. Although Somalia's indigenous constraints, including the absence of the complementary institutions necessary for sustainable liberal democratic institutions, were the main cause of the failure of reconstruction efforts, the associated public choice issues contributed to the magnitude of that failure.

The initial intervention in Somalia was a UN-led humanitarian effort in 1992. Only later, when that initial effort was deemed inadequate to meet the specified goals, did the United States become involved. This increased intervention added additional layers of bureaucracy to the reconstruction effort. Prior to U.S. involvement, issues within the UN already existed that carried over to the subsequent joint effort, including infighting and turf wars between the UN staffs in New York and Mogadishu. Many senior UN staffers would take orders only from the UN headquarters located in New York, not from field directors.[26]

Further, there was squabbling over the allocation of monetary and personnel resources. Ultimately, the UN allocated many resources to the capital city of Mogadishu while neglecting other key areas of the country. Other problems associated with the continuity of management across the two UN operations— UNOSOM I and UNOSOM II—further contributed to difficulties with the broader effort in Somalia.[27]

When the United States joined the effort in 1992, the increased complexity of including another participant further exacerbated many of the same issues that had plagued the previous UN effort. For instance, not only did the pre-existing tensions between staff members of the UN continue, it was unclear to many UN forces if they were taking orders from the UN or from the Pentagon. Moreover, U.S. forces would often undertake missions without informing the UN, which led to further discord and confusion.[28] In addition, there was constant conflict between the UN and the United States as to who was responsible for the actual reconstruction of the country, which led not only to a lack of coordination in the efforts of the troops on the ground but also to much energy being expended by politicians and policymakers to place blame instead of focusing on the actual reconstruction effort.

After committing troops, Presidents Bush and Clinton repeatedly stated that the United States did not support the reconstruction aspect of the mission and therefore was not responsible for establishing political institutions.[29] However, a closer look at the related government documents, many U.S. authored, indicates that U.S. government officials had indeed approved the reconstruction aspect of the effort from the start. As Walter Clarke and Jeffrey Herbst indicate, "The allegation that the United Nations greatly broadened the mission that the United States had outlined is simply not true. In fact, all the major Security Council resolutions on Somalia, including the "nation-building" resolution, were written by U.S. officials, mainly in the Pentagon, and handed to the United Nations as *faits accomplis*."[30] The overall effect was that instead of coordinating efforts to reduce fighting in Somalia, policymakers in the United States and the UN allocated much of their effort to infighting and protecting themselves in the event of failure. This detracted from the overall coordination of the effort and served to exacerbate the difficulties posed by indigenous constraints.

Haiti

Overview

The United States has a long history of intervening in Haiti. In 1915, President Woodrow Wilson authorized the use of military troops for means of occupation. Those troops would remain in Haiti until 1934. In 1961, President John Kennedy introduced the Alliance for Progress program, which provided aid to Latin America to foster democracy in the region. The program provided aid for Haiti to construct and update infrastructure as well as to modernize its army to protect it against Cuba, among other threats. Both efforts failed in their overarching goal of generating sustainable liberal democratic institutions in Haiti.[31]

The most recent U.S.-led effort to bring liberal democracy to Haiti took place under the direction of the Clinton administration in 1994, which followed a military coup in 1991 that forced President Jean-Bertrand Aristide from his position of leadership. The United States, along with the broader international community, refused to acknowledge the leader of the coup, General Raul Cedras, as the legitimate president of the country. Following political and economic pressures, coupled with an imminent U.S.-led invasion, Cedras agreed to allow U.S. troops, in conjunction with UN involvement, to enter Haiti to restore Aristide to power.

The overarching goal of the U.S. occupation, known as *Operation Uphold Democracy*, was to restore democracy to Haiti, but while the restoration of President Aristide was one important aspect of this mission, ultimate success would require much more.[32] Many aspects of what Westerners would consider the building blocks of liberal democratic institutions—the rule of law, stable and uncorrupt judiciary and bureaucracy, and a well-functioning police force—were either dysfunctional or altogether absent. In addition to facilitating the safe return of Aristide to his position of leadership, occupiers had to engage in the construction of a wide range of institutions required for a sustainable liberal democracy. Although the effort, which lasted until 1996, was ultimately successful in restoring President Aristide, little else was accomplished in terms of planting the seeds of sustainable liberal political, economic, or social institutions.

The failure of this effort is even more evident when one considers that Aristide resigned and was forced into exile in February of 2004. After failing to broker a political compromise between Aristide and opposition groups, the United States and several other countries refused to defend him from these groups, forcing him to resign. Following his resignation, the United States and the UN Security Council again sent peacekeeping troops to Haiti to oversee the transfer of power. To this day, Haiti remains in a state of disarray. It is the poorest country in the Western hemisphere and relies on peacekeepers for much of its security. Further, political elections continue to be marred by accusations of corruption and fraud.

The Art of Association and Nested Games
Haiti does not suffer from ethnic and religious cleavages that characterize many other weak and failed states.[33] The population is largely homogenous—95 percent of the populace are descendents of African slaves.[34] Instead, the

main divisions within Haitian society are between two distinct classes, the political elite, which make up a small minority of Haitians, and the peasants, which make up a majority of the populace. To understand this division, one must consider the history of the country from its origins.

Haiti became independent in 1804 following a slave revolt, which began in 1791. The revolt was successful, and national institutions evolved out of the military apparatus that carried out the rebellion. Following the revolution, the mulattos assumed the oligarchy previously held by the white slave owners, while the hatred of repression by the black majority shifted from the white elite to the mulatto elite.[35] This tension between the elite minority and peasant majority, which is at the foundation of much of the historical conflict in the country, continues to this day.

Of course, the evolution of statehood through the use of military force and a resulting military apparatus is a common historical occurrence, as evidenced by the examples of Britain, Spain, and Portugal, as well as much of Africa and the Middle East.[36] The key issue, at least in the context of the goals of U.S. foreign policy toward weak and failed states, is whether the institutions that evolve from the initial military state apparatus do so in a manner that produces legitimate liberal institutions and outcomes. In the language used throughout this book, the question is whether institutions evolve that solve the larger meta-game through voluntary coordination around liberal ends instead of an illiberal solution achieved through continual coercive military force. In Haiti's case, institutions have evolved along the lines of the latter. As proof of this assertion, one need only consider the fact that since its independence in 1804, Haiti has had twenty-one constitutions and forty-one state leaders. Further, of those forty-one leaders, twenty-nine have been either overthrown or assassinated.[37]

The widespread use of military force to maintain Haiti's institutional stability continues to this very day. The end result is that the political, social, and economic institutions that have evolved are not positive-sum for Haitian society at large. Instead, they benefit a small segment of the Haitian population—the elite—at the expense of the larger Haitian population. The use of the national Haitian institutional apparatus as a tool of predation by and for the elite has created what the political scientists Brian Weinstein and Aaron Segal call "the two worlds" of Haiti.[38] The first world consists of the previously mentioned minority elite who control the national institutions of the country. According to Weinstein and Segal, "The first world is exploitive and paranoiac, seeing politics and economics a zero-sum game. . . . This world . . . relies on patronage and coercion for control, disdains and despises democratic values, and is manipulative and hierarchical."[39]

Although a very small portion, approximately 5 percent, of Haitians occupy this first world, their actions set the rules of the game for what Weinstein and Segal call the "second world," which consists of the rest of Haitian citizens.[40] In short, the second world of Haiti consists of peasants who are excluded from participating in the first world but who are subject to its rules and control. In contrast to those who inhabit the first world, those in the second world are traditionally illiterate and poorly educated, speak Creole, and practice voodoo.

Those in positions of power in the first world of Haiti historically have wielded repressive force to maintain their positions of power over those in the second world while simultaneously attempting to keep potential opponents from the first world in check. Thus, nested games exist at multiple levels. These games are oftentimes characterized by conflict, as individuals currently in power seek to maintain their established positions and challengers frequently attempt to overthrow those in power, both factions typically employing violent means.

At the same time, nested games exist that include actors in the first and second world that are often solved through violence and repression. Finally, nested games exist between those in the second world who must determine some means of surviving under the repressive policies of the first world. This array of nested games and the resulting art of association are not conducive to central liberal democratic institutions and constrain reconstruction efforts along these lines.

This basic segmentation between the political elite in the first world and the poor peasants in the second world underpins the basis of Haitian political, economic, and social relations. Given the widespread predation by those in the first world, coupled with a lack of investment and production of infrastructure as well as effective police and courts, those in the second world invest a relatively large amount of their resources in avoiding the state apparatus. For instance, the corruption and predation that characterize the national apparatus provide incentive for many in the second world to live a subsistence lifestyle to avoid the predation of profits and wealth by the state. Further, in the absence of state-provided law, an underground customary law has developed that regulates daily activities between peasants and communities.[41]

Those in the second world of Haiti have developed an art of association that allows for some semblance of cooperation. In other words, the nested games involving players in the second world appear to have a cooperative solution. However, the evolution of that art of association is constrained beyond some certain point of development by the rules and incentives created by those acting in the first world.

Although a small minority of the total population, the actors in the first world have used violent coercion to solve Haiti's meta-game. Summarizing the first hundred years of the country's history, Weinstein and Segal put it as follows: "In the first 111 years between independence and occupation [in 1915] the first world ruled the second the way pirates control a captured ship."[42] It appears that this would also be an adequate description for the decades following U.S. occupation. Indeed, the period between the exit of U.S. occupiers in 1934 and the next occupation in 1994 was characterized by the brutal regimes of François "Papa Doc" Duvalier (1957–1971) and his son, Jean-Claude "Baby Doc" Duvalier (1971–1986), which were followed by a series of unstable regimes overthrown by military juntas.[43]

In sum, an art of association conducive to liberal democratic institutions has failed to develop in Haiti because of predatory institutions that have existed since the country's independence. The predatory state apparatus constrains the ability of those in Haiti's second world to make the necessary investment in the movement toward durable liberal institutions. As discussed, those acting in Haiti's first world have created a set of incentives that produce a higher payoff for those in the second world to pursue a subsistence living and to invest resources to evade predation instead of in productive activities that produce real increases in living standards and support liberal political and social institutions.

Attempting to correct this ongoing conflict between Haiti's two worlds has been one of the main motivations behind U.S. interventions in the country. Unfortunately, such efforts have been abject failures, if the benchmark of success is the establishment of liberal democratic institutions. The array of nested games results in transaction costs that prohibit a sustainable shift in the institutional trajectory toward the desired ends. In addition, given the knowledge problem faced by foreign occupiers and policymakers of exactly how to construct liberal institutions where they do not already exist, reconstruction efforts have been unable to provide a cooperative solution to the conflict between Haiti's two worlds.

Expectations, Credible Commitment, and Unintended Consequences

The repressive history of national institutions summarized in the previous section has shaped the expectations of the majority of citizens in Haiti's "second world" as they relate to efforts to reconstruct liberal democratic institutions. Given the long history of repression, the expectations of Haitian citizens regarding reconstructed institutions are not those of Western-style liberal democratic institutions, which the country has never experienced. Instead, Haitians have come to expect institutions characterized by further coercion and predation. The historical experience with predation by the central state contributes to the lack of credibility and legitimacy associated with attempts to construct liberal democratic institutions. As the anthropologist Michel-Rolph Trouillot notes, "Because of the lack of legitimacy of the Haitian state, every single political leader, from the president to a minor legislator, always has to renegotiate [a social contract] from scratch [to establish] his or her right to govern."[44]

The problem that occupiers face, and which they have been unable to overcome, is that those in the second world have absolutely no reason to believe that reconstructed institutions will be credible. In other words, even if it is announced that reconstructed institutions will provide basic services and protect rights, citizens expect, with historical experience as a reference point, defection on the part of those in the political elite once occupiers exit. Trouillot contends that efforts to establish sustainable democratic institutions will continue to be met with failure until the elite class recognizes the need for an enduring social contract that establishes a "national sameness" with the rural peasants.[45]

However, as discussed in Chapters 3 and 4, policymakers lack the knowledge of how to establish credibility and legitimacy where it does not exist. Two examples of the knowledge problem, specific to Haiti, are the attempts by the United States to train an effective police force and judiciary. In fact, attempts to reconstruct both the security sector and justice system have failed miserably despite large investments of monetary support.[46] When one considers the difficulty of attempting to design even more complex institutions, in many cases from scratch, the magnitude of the task at hand becomes clear.

Similar to Somalia, the case of Haiti also serves to illuminate the unintended consequences of providing monetary aid to weak and failing states. This aid is typically proffered with the best of intentions, to provide humanitarian and development assistance to those countries most in need. Unfortunately, such aid often causes additional unintended problems. I have already discussed the issue of the Samaritan's Dilemma, whereby the recipient of aid becomes dependent on that aid, reducing the likelihood of the establishment of the requisite self-sustaining institutions. Yet another effect is that aid often ends up in the hands of corrupt regimes that funnel the aid from the intended recipients to line their own pockets. This is indeed the case in Haiti.

Consider for instance that Haiti received the most standby loans—a loan conditional on the government revising its finances so that it can repay the loan—from the International Monetary Fund (IMF) over the past half-century. But more important for our purpose, twenty of the twenty-two standbys were awarded during the 1957 to 1986 period, when the Duvalier family was in power.[47] This credit from the IMF further allowed the Duvalier regimes to engage in brutal activities while having no recognizable impact on Haiti's development.

One may wonder why the IMF funded the Duvalier regimes, given their brutal nature. The answer lies in the IMF's charter, which prevents the consideration of domestic politics in making funding decisions.[48] This illustrates a more general problem. In an effort to preserve neutrality by ignoring domestic political conditions, the IMF and the broader international aid community often generate perverse effects by extending the scope and strength of illiberal regimes.

However, the corruption that characterized Haiti's political institutions did not end with the Duvalier rule. Indeed, under Aristide, on whose behalf the United States carried out the mid-1990s occupation, Haiti was one of the most corrupt countries in the world.[49] Similar to previous regimes, Aristide diverted foreign aid into personal holdings as well as lined the pockets of allies. And similar to the previous regimes in Haiti, Aristide's was unsustainable, as he was forced from office in 2004. Even the single success of the U.S. reconstruction effort in Haiti in the mid-1990s—the restoration of Aristide to office—ultimately proved a failure.

Summation

The cases of Somalia and Haiti serve to illustrate that attempts by foreign occupiers to export liberal democracy may do more than fail. Indeed, these attempts often have the perverse outcome of inducing greater conflict and instability. There are several general themes applicable to weak and failed states that can be drawn from these cases.

For one, these cases serve to highlight the dual barriers of the knowledge problem: how to construct liberal institutions and the political decision-making processes that influence actual policies. In both Somalia and Haiti, occupiers were unable to design the complementary and formal institutions necessary for sustainable liberal democracy. Further, the effort in Somalia was plagued by infighting and discord both within and between the United States and the UN. Even in the case of Haiti, where it has been argued that coordination between the United States and the UN was better as compared to what took place in Somalia, the end result was the same, failure.[50] This further highlights that even when the problems associated with the political decision-making process are not the binding constraint, the lack of knowledge of how to construct liberal institutions severely hampers the ability of occupiers to achieve any semblance of success.

Another important theme evident in these two cases is the need for occupiers to focus on alternative forms of governance and order, which is especially important given the potential that foreign intervention can create more harm than good. Given the inability of foreign governments to exogenously construct effective institutions, focus must shift to the evolution of endogenous mechanisms for governance. Such endogenous institutions can provide a cooperative solution to nested games and serve as a foundation for the evolution of sustainable formal institutions. The generic one-size-fits-all template utilized in past reconstruction efforts not only neglects these indigenous forms of governance but may stifle their evolution, resulting in less cooperation than there was before the intervention.

Along these lines, much can be learned from exploring the private means of governance that have emerged in Somalia. These indigenous institutions have proven to be relatively successful when compared to attempts at centralized government, and scholars have begun to pay attention to the fact that Somalia is doing better than expected following the collapse of the Barre regime.[51]

For instance, in the absence of an effective state, which typically provides trust-enhancing institutions such as a court system, Somali citizens have turned to the use of clans and local networks of trust coupled with the simplification of transactions to get things done. Further, a system of brokers has emerged that facilitates trade in the cross-border cattle market. Brokers (called *dilaal*) reduce transaction costs by matching buyers and sellers for a fee.[52] Entrepreneurs operating in a range of services simplify transactions in order to make them manageable. For instance, in the absence of large-scale utilities, entrepreneurs provide electricity via generator to smaller sets of clients, which allows them to build a relationship with their clients and also to monitor usage. Existing social networks are also used to provide social insurance to members of the group.

In addition to relying on existing networks of trust, Somalis have overcome the problem of an absent state by importing governance from abroad. Perhaps the best example of this is the telecommunications industry. Initially, the indigenous telecommunications companies used the preexisting infrastructure, much of which had been damaged or destroyed during the civil war. Over time, however, the local companies partnered with established companies such as Sprint, ITT, and Telenor, and in doing so, they were able to offer Global Systems for Mobile Communications, a leading digital cellular system, and build new landlines. In addition to traditional phone services, these companies also offer fax and Internet services. Competition in the telecommunications industry has driven prices down in Somalia to a level that is lower than in most African countries. For instance, international calls have fallen from $5 to $7 per minute in the 1990s to $0.50 per minute in the larger cities and $1.50 per minute in small cities. To punish nonpayers, telecommunications providers have agreed to share a list of defaulters, which is certainly an instance of cooperation.[53]

Similar techniques of importing governance from abroad have been used in the airport sector, where carriers lease well-respected brands such as Boeing and import flight crews from Eastern Europe to signal credibility and safety. By importing the standards developed by these international companies, indigenous entrepreneurs have effectively circumvented the need for standards and regulations that are usually set by a central government.

World Bank economists Tatiana Nenova and Tim Harford conclude that "Somalia's private sector experience suggests that it may be easier than is commonly thought for basic systems of finance and some infrastructure services to function where government is extremely weak or absent."[54] Given the widespread failure of reconstruction efforts to establish basic infrastructure and governance mechanisms, the viability of such endogenous alternatives must be considered. Indeed, given the very real possibility that reconstruction efforts may either fail or cause more harm than good, such alternatives must be considered as potentially superior to the outcomes generated by reconstruction efforts. Although well-functioning liberal democratic institutions would produce superior outcomes compared to the existing situation in Somalia, this option is not feasible in the short run for the reasons considered in previous sections.

As discussed, the standard response to weak and failed states has been some mix of foreign intervention and occupation as well as monetary aid aimed at solving humanitarian and development issues. Whereas the analysis of this book has focused on the ineffectiveness of occupation and reconstruction efforts, the evidence seems to indicate that monetary aid is also largely ineffective in overcoming the problems posed by weak and failed states. As discussed in the cases of both Somalia and Haiti, monetary aid can generate perverse incentives and outcomes that can foster the sustainability of illiberal institutions without any related economic development.

The economist William Easterly has provided a detailed analysis of the many problems with foreign aid, emphasizing the dual issues of incentives and delivery mechanisms. First, statesmen and policymakers in the country receiving aid must have the incentive to utilize the aid in an effective manner.[55] Easterly demonstrates that oftentimes the incentive structure created by the provision of foreign aid directs officials and policymakers toward unproductive activities that generate perverse outcomes and cause more harm than good.

Even if the correct incentives are in place, many underdeveloped, weak, and failed states lack the delivery mechanisms to allocate aid effectively.[56] For instance, feedback loops that provide information as to accountability and effective allocation of resources are typically absent or lacking in scope. As such, even if the right incentives are in place, getting the aid to those who need it most presents an additional problem.

A brief review of the performance of aid to those countries that experienced complete state failure seems to support the claim regarding the ineffectiveness of aid. As Table 6.1 illustrates, engaging in IMF programs for an extended period of time correlates with a greater risk of complete state collapse.[57]

Of course, the countries listed were dysfunctional even before receiving IMF loans and may very well have collapsed absent these loans. The data indicate nothing about causation, and the magnitude of the effect of IMF programs relative to state collapse is unclear. Nonetheless, as the data suggest, there is no reason to believe that monetary aid is a suitable mechanism for generating widespread sustainable change toward liberal democratic institutions.

Despite the failures of past attempts to remedy the problems associated with weak and failed states through aid, it does not appear that the international community will cease utilizing this policy tool any time soon. In March 2004, after Aristide left power, the World Bank held a donor meeting in Washington, D.C., that generated a joint government/multidonor Interim Cooperation

TABLE 6.1 All eight cases of state failure worldwide
as of 1990s and prior IMF programs

Country	Approximate year of onset of state failure	Time under IMF programs in preceding ten years (%)
Afghanistan	1977	46
Angola	1981	0
Burundi	1995	62
Liberia	1986	70
Sierra Leone	1990	59
Somalia	1991	74
Sudan	1986	58
Zaire	1991	73
Average		55
Average for developing countries 1970–90		20

Framework *(Cadre de Coopération Intérimaire, CCI).* The aim of the CCI is to coordinate a "national reconstruction plan covering both short- and medium-term priorities" for Haiti.

This leads to the final theme that emerges from the analysis of Somalia and Haiti. It typically is assumed that the international community should work to strengthen weak and failed states through some mix of monetary support and/or interventions and occupation. But it is far from clear why this is the case, for the regimes and institutions in these countries are often dysfunctional beyond repair. As the cases of Somalia and Haiti illustrate, such regimes are typically characterized by predation and the inability to carry out basic services such as providing infrastructure, security, and justice. Citizens living in these countries incur the full cost of a dysfunctional state, which stifles or prevents productive activities and provides little or no benefit. It is unclear why efforts should be undertaken to prop up or strengthen these states. One alternative that at least must be considered is the possibility of letting weak and failed states collapse altogether.

There is a school of thought in political science that echoes this realization and contends that state failure is due to erroneous sovereignty.[58] In other words, state collapse is due to the imposition of centralized formal institutions on an indigenous foundation that was not adequate to support those formal institutions. The analysis put forth in this book supports this line of thought. The main implication is that the focus of any subsequent reconstruction effort must shift from exogenously imposing formal institutions to recognizing the indigenous emergence of mechanisms of governance. As will be discussed in the final chapter, this does not mean that there is no role for the United States. It does however mean that the United States's role would be severely constrained.

7 Post-9/11 Imperialism: Afghanistan and Iraq

FOLLOWING THE ATTACKS on the World Trade Center and the Pentagon on September 11, 2001, the United States began military operations that were followed by reconstruction efforts in Afghanistan and Iraq. In contrast to the humanitarian motivation behind the occupations in the 1990s—Somalia, Haiti, Kosovo, and Bosnia—the post-9/11 occupations were motivated by security concerns posed by the governments of Afghanistan and Iraq and rogue groups residing within their borders. Ostensibly, these ongoing efforts to export liberal democracy to Afghanistan and Iraq are part of the larger "war on terror." More specifically, Western officials and policymakers believe that directing such efforts to spread liberal democracy will contribute to the ultimate eradication of the terrorist threat.

While it is too early to conclusively declare these efforts decisive successes or failures, some general trends can be observed. For example, in each case, the initial military operations were extremely successful, as the superior U.S. military easily toppled the respective government regimes. However, the subsequent reconstruction efforts have been met with great resistance due to insurgency groups, problems with resource allocation, and a lack of coordination between coalition members and agencies within the U.S. government. Along these lines, *The Iraq Study Group Report*, produced by a bipartisan panel in late 2006, notes that "The situation in Baghdad and several provinces is dire. . . . [T]he [Iraqi] government is not adequately advancing national reconciliation, providing basic security, or delivering essential services. The level of violence is high and growing. There is great suffering, and the daily lives of many Iraqis show little or no improvement. Pessimism is perverse."[1]

The goal of this chapter is not to predict the ultimate outcome of the reconstruction efforts in Afghanistan and Iraq. Instead, the goal is to utilize the mechanisms developed in previous chapters to highlight some of the major barriers that occupiers and policymakers will continue to face, both now and in the future, in attempting to export liberal democracy to these countries. Given that these reconstruction efforts currently overlap, I will consider both cases simultaneously within the discussion of each general category.

Afghanistan and Iraq

Overview

Military operations in Afghanistan, which were a direct response to the 9/11 attacks in the United States, began on October 7, 2001. The initial operation designed to eliminate the Taliban government and the al-Qaeda organization was indeed effective in ousting the central government, although the effect on al-Qaeda's ability to carry out operations remains open to discussion (which will be apparent in the discussion of Iraq). In fact, by mid-November, the United States had taken control of the capital city of Kabul. At a meeting held in Bonn, Germany, in December 2001, representatives from the United States and Afghanistan produced the Bonn Agreement, which provided a roadmap for the future of the country. On May 1, 2001, U.S. officials declared the end of major military operations and announced that subsequent efforts would focus on stabilization and reconstruction.

Since that declaration, key successes include the drafting of a new constitution, which was approved in January 2004, and presidential elections, which were held in October 2004. The result of those elections was that interim president Hamid Karzai was officially elected by Afghani citizens to lead the reconstructed country. Slightly less than a year later, in September 2005, parliamentary elections were held.

Despite these achievements, however, serious problems still plague the country and the larger reconstruction effort.[2] For instance, the completion of infrastructure projects has been slower than originally planned, partially due to poor planning and execution and in part to insurgency and terrorism. Acts of insurgency threaten not only damage to physical infrastructure but also injury to the contractors and engineers who carry out those projects.[3]

There continues to be a strong insurgency in the southern part of the country, where terrorist acts are common. In addition, much of the insurgency is not based in Afghanistan but in neighboring Pakistan.[4] The fact that insurgents are dispersed across borders makes efforts to battle and eradicate the threat that much more difficult.

To understand the continued threat posed by the insurgency, consider that more U.S. troops were killed in Afghanistan in 2005 than in each of the previous three years.[5] However, the insurgent violence is not merely ideological in origin, for related to the prevalence of violence is the continued production of opium, which is a profitable business for many Afghani citizens.[6]

Much of the continuing violence is most certainly politically motivated, however. For example, there were nineteen separate attacks at polling stations during the recent parliamentary elections.[7] A correlative problem that contributes to this violence, whether ideologically or economically motivated, is that indigenous security and justice institutions, including the police and court systems, are largely corrupt and ineffective.[8] It is within this context that the U.S. troops, who make up the majority of the occupying force, which includes a smaller number of NATO peacekeeping forces, and U.S. military leaders, who direct the overall reconstruction, continue the effort to make over Afghanistan along liberal democratic lines.

In March 2003, while the effort in Afghanistan was already under way, the United States began a military operation in Iraq. Similar to the initial operation in Afghanistan, the initial Iraqi operation went smoothly and met little resistance from a comparatively ill-equipped Iraqi army. The Hussein regime quickly collapsed, and President Bush publicly declared that Iraq had been "liberated" in April 2003. Similar to the situation in Afghanistan, occupiers in Iraq have achieved several key successes, but also as in Afghanistan, these successes have been counterbalanced by several obstacles that must be overcome if success is to be achieved.

First, let us consider the successes. After several extensions during the drafting process, a constitution was put forth by the transitional government and officially approved in October 2005. General elections were held in December 2005, and six months after the elections a national-unity government was announced, under the leadership of Prime Minister Nouri al-Maliki, the third prime minister of Iraq since sovereignty. Although al-Maliki has attempted to draw from across ethnic and religious groups to fill the top leadership positions in his government, the new government is, as expected based on demographics, dominated by the Shi'a.[9] Only time will tell whether the new government has the legitimacy and strength to convince the Sunni minority and insurgents that it is in their long-term interest to participate in the new Iraq. Other notable successes include the capture, trial, and execution of Saddam Hussein and the killing of Abu Musab al-Zarqawi, an al-Qaeda leader in Iraq.

Despite these successes, however, there are major ongoing concerns. For example, as emphasized in *The Iraq Study Group Report*, the insurgency remains strong throughout Iraq.[10] The failure to effectively curtail violence is due, to a large extent, to multiple and overlapping sources of conflict. These include the battle for political power that stems from sectarian and tribal differences, dissatisfied Sunnis who are unhappy with their loss of power, concerned Kurds who fear the loss of their independence, and jihadists who seek to disrupt the reconstruction with the aim of establishing an Islamist state.[11]

Efforts to train self-sufficient Iraqi police and military forces to deal with the continued violence have yielded mixed results. Estimates place trained soldiers in the 140,000–200,000 range, but in practice, the quality of training and ability of these forces varies greatly, with many lacking the necessary skills to be effective. Further, many police forces have been infiltrated by insurgents, further adding to concerns regarding the ability of the police to contribute to the sustainability of the new Iraq.[12] Finally, the issues of federalism, the rights of women, the role of Islam in politics, and especially the distribution of oil ownership rights remain unresolved issues that could be a source of contention both within Iraq and between that country's new government and the West, which has a distinct vision of how the reconstructed country should look.

The Art of Association and Nested Games

Throughout its history, Afghanistan has been at the center of conflict. As the political scientist Barnett Rubin notes, "Today's state of Afghanistan developed as a buffer state between competing empires (Russian and British) and then competing alliance systems (Soviet and American)."[13] In the nineteenth century, Afghanistan became involved in the efforts of the Russian and British empires to expand through India and Central Asia. Following three Anglo-Afghan wars (1838–1842, 1843–1880, 1919), Afghanistan officially gained complete independence from Britain in 1919. To understand the current plight of the country, it is important to recognize the magnitude of conflict that historically has plagued Afghanistan. Summing up the nineteenth-century history of the country, the Middle East scholar Larry Goodson notes that "the entire century in Afghanistan was a mosaic of warfare, with different conflicts so overlapping that it is almost impossible to tell where one began or ended."[14]

Conflict did not come to an end with independence. Tribal revolts in 1929 overthrew King Amanullah Khan, who had led his country to independence. According to Rubin, the subsequent rulers "encapsulated rather than confronted social resistance, imposing an external administration laid over existing society."[15] These subsequent rulers, all of whom received significant economic and military aid from the Soviet Union from 1955 through 1978, did not build national institutions that represented the citizens of the broader Afghan society.

Instead, political institutions were constructed to protect the central regime from the tribal forces that had caused instability for governments in the past. Although this process of insulation was successful, it had the negative consequence of segmenting the country. Rubin contends that "rather than incorporating the various sectors of the population into a common national political system, the political elite acted as an ethnically stratified hierarchy of intermediaries between the foreign powers providing the resources and the groups receiving the largess of patronage."[16] This outcome contributed to the disconnect between state and society that exists in Afghanistan to this very day.

To better understand the art of association and the evolution of nested games in Afghanistan, it is important to understand the importance of kinship ties for most Afghan citizens. These ties have served to fill the void left by a central government that historically was ineffective in representing the larger population. Afghanistan is a patrilineal society, and relationships within the extended family dictate property rights and inheritance, among other things. It is important to note that the patrilineal family does not stand in isolation, however. Instead, the family blends with other units of identity, including ethnic and village and communal groups. Together, these units form what is known as a *qawm*, which is central to Afghanistan's social system.[17]

The *qawm*, which is often translated as "tribe," is the core mechanism through which Afghan citizens carry out their social relations and activities. The loyalty of individuals is to the *qawm* to which they belong instead of the Afghan "nation" per se. The *qawm* is governed through the *shura*, a council consisting of the elders of the *qawm*. The members of the *shura* develop laws that apply to the *qawm* and settle disputes. The elders also select representatives to act as intermediaries between the state and the *qawm*.

Attempts by the central government to impose laws that are in opposition to the social code and existing precedent within the *qawm* historically have been met with resistance, which in some cases has turned violent.[18] The result is a clear separation between the state and the wider socioeconomic sphere, which consists of the *qawms* and has existed in this fashion since independence in 1919. The difficulty that this disconnect between the state and socioeconomic space poses for anyone trying to find a sustainable solution to the larger Afghan meta-game through the creation of sustainable national institutions should be evident.

The Soviet invasion in 1979 and the resulting war, which lasted until 1989, had a devastating impact on the political, social, and economic operations of the country. Following a military coup by the Marxist People's Democratic Party of Afghanistan (PDPA), a civil war broke out in the county as rebel guerrillas attacked the PDPA. In turn, the PDPA turned to the Soviet Union, which had supported the initial military coup, for further financial and military support. In addition to providing aid and military equipment, the Soviet military entered the country but was unable to gain control outside the capital city of Kabul.

The impact on Afghani society of the Soviet war is of central importance to any understanding of present-day Afghanistan. This negative impact occurred along several fronts. Perhaps first and foremost, the devastation of the traditional economy contributed to the development of the opium-driven economy that emerged to take its place. As mentioned earlier, the production of opium—Afghanistan is the world's largest opium producer—and the resulting problems associated with drug lords and the drug trade remain a major issue for current occupiers.[19]

The physical destruction included the death of an estimated 1 million to 1.7 million citizens and the displacement of millions more.[20] Cities, schools, mosques, and other physical infrastructure were destroyed, resulting in an extraordinary fact: "at least half of Afghanistan's twenty-four thousand pre-war villages were destroyed and turned into ghost towns. . . ."[21] This destruction contributed to the erosion of existing social and economic relationships, as described earlier, which had evolved prior to the Soviet invasion and which were the main source of social order and cohesion.

The erosion and destruction of social ties contributed to an overall increase in violence throughout the country. The erosion and collapse of social institutions, which previously had served as key mechanisms for the peaceful adjudication of disputes, led to a greater frequency of the use of violence for dispute settlement. In addition to the erosion of social institutions, violence intensified due to the injection of modern weaponry throughout the country. It is estimated that the Soviets provided between $36 and $48 billion in military equipment to the communist regime between 1978 and the 1990s. The United States and its allies provided between $6 and $12 billion in military equipment to the mujahideen to combat the communists.[22] The presence of these modern weapons throughout the country lowered the cost of engaging in conflict to resolve disputes.

The war also had an impact on the political institutions that had existed prior to the invasion. The war displaced the pre-invasion political elites, thereby creating an environment ripe for new political elites—the mujahideen (the Taliban are one of the mujahideen groups)—to rise to power. The devastating impact that these new elites had in terms of human rights violations, conflict, and a lack of investment in infrastructure and education is well documented. Of course, these new elites also created an environment wherein al-Qaeda could develop as an organization, which was the primary reason for the initial U.S. invasion in 2001.

Yet another outcome of the Soviet war was that group affiliations became increasingly grounded in ethnic, linguistic, and sectarian differences, divisions that exist to this day.[23] To understand the ethnic composition that characterizes present-day Afghanistan, consider that the Pashtuns currently constitute an estimated 42 percent of the population, Tajiks constitute about 27 percent, and Uzbeks and Hazaras each constitute 9 percent of the total population, while smaller ethnic groups make up the final 13 percent. Further, estimates indicate that 99 percent of Afghanis are Muslims, with about 80 percent being Sunni and the rest Shi'a.[24] Ethnic, linguistic, and sectarian differences have created an array of nested games in Afghanistan that must be solved before any meaningful solution to the larger meta-game can be achieved. These meta-institutions will need to be constructed from scratch given that they are not already present, as was the case in the post–World War II reconstructions of Japan and West Germany.

In addition to finding a solution to Afghanistan's meta-game, occupiers must also deal with the geography of the country. Afghanistan's terrain is rugged and includes mountains, plateaus, and hidden valleys that limit mobility and the construction of infrastructure. This further increases the difficulty of a new national government broadcasting its power over the entire country in an effective manner. For instance, the physical terrain will raise the cost of resource mobilization associated with even the most basic tasks, including administration, law enforcement, and building infrastructure.

In Chapter 3, I explored the array of relations in Iraq to illustrate the importance of the art of association and the resulting nested games as a central issue in any reconstruction. To briefly reiterate what was discussed earlier, Iraq suffers from divisions along ethnic and religious lines. It is not these differences by themselves that pose a continued problem, however. Instead, tensions and conflict are a result of the fact that these different ethnic and religious groups have been forced to live under a national government that has, from its beginning, repressed the majority for the benefit of the minority. Further, from the inception of the country, the minority has had a vested interest in strengthening the *status quo* to maintain their position of power, which has further contributed to the intensification of divisions.

Following World War I, The League of Nations granted the area that is present-day Iraq—composed of the former Ottoman regions of Basra, Baghdad, and Mosul—to Britain. In 1921, the British installed the Hashemite Amir Faisal as the king to rule over their new acquisition. One of the key problems in this arrangement, evident from the start, was ethnic division. Whereas the majority of the population of the Basra and Baghdad regions were ethnic Arabs and divided along Sunni and Shi'a religious lines, the Mosul region consisted mainly of ethnic Kurds. Due mainly to these divisions, early efforts by the British to create a unified state, efforts which were implemented through Faisal, failed. As Liam Anderson and Gareth Stansfield note, "Crafting a coherent national identity from a deeply divided and factious society proved beyond the politically experienced and . . . very able Faisal."[25] These fundamental divisions, which have existed from the country's birth and have only strengthened over time, are at the core of much of the conflict in present-day Iraq.[26]

As discussed in Chapter 3, the array of nested games—the Kurds with the Shi'a, the Kurds with the Sunnis, and the Shi'a with the Sunnis—makes finding a solution to the larger Iraqi meta-game that much more difficult. Magnifying the issue are both the intragroup nested games that exist as individuals seek positions of power and the presence of occupiers, which creates yet another set of nested games. Finding solutions to these nested games is of primary importance if one hopes to find a sustainable solution to the broader Iraqi meta-game. Given the array and dynamics of these nested games, however, this is at best a daunting task but one that will need to be resolved if a successful outcome is to be achieved.

Expectations and Credible Commitment
To be ultimately successful, the reconstructions of Afghanistan and Iraq must also overcome problems associated with expectations and credible commitment on several fronts. Consider first the situation in Afghanistan, and specifically

a 2005 ABC News Poll, the first national poll in that country sponsored by a news organization. The poll found mixed results regarding the views and expectations of Afghani citizens.

On the positive side, 77 percent of respondents indicated that they felt the country was on the right track, and 87 percent felt that the removal of the Taliban was a good thing. However, although 83 percent of respondents had a favorable view of the United States, 30 percent felt that attacks against the U.S. occupiers could be justified. Of import, 25 percent responded that, given the circumstances, poppy production was acceptable. Further, 46 percent said that cheating, corruption, and intimidation characterized the recent parliamentary elections. The poll also raised concerns about other things such as security, infrastructure, and clean drinking water.[27] Overall, the findings of this poll seem to indicate cautious optimism on the part of respondents. That is, the removal of the Taliban was viewed as positive, but respondents obviously believe that serious concerns still exist.

As discussed in earlier chapters, institutions must ultimately be designed that are viewed as credible and legitimate by a wide array of groups and actors in Afghani society. One promising occurrence toward this end is the national election of President Hamid Karzai, who had formerly been the interim president of the country. His election by indigenous citizens provides some sense of credibility and legitimacy to the new political institutions being constructed.

However, the election of Karzai (and more recently, a parliament) does not mean that a credible equilibrium has been obtained. Western leaders have expressed concern that warlords and drug lords are among those elected to parliament, which suggests that the goals the new parliament will pursue may be suspect at best from the perspective of the United States. Further, it remains to be seen how members of the parliament will work with Karzai. In previous chapters I discussed the many difficulties with designing credible institutions from scratch. These problems cover a wide range in terms of their nature and magnitude, but they must be overcome if a succesful outcome in Afghanistan is to be achieved.

To provide one example of these problems, let us consider the previously mentioned parliamentary elections, and more specifically, the design of the parliament. As one would expect, Afghanistan's executive branch, headed by Karzai, is relatively weak given that it is still in its infancy. However, as a strategy to combat this weakness, Karzai was successful in banning political parties from the 2005 parliamentary elections, and candidates were required to run as independents. From Karzai's viewpoint, the logic behind this move was straightforward—to prevent the rise of a dominant party that could potentially present strong opposition to the executive branch.

Karzai's move can be seen as positive in that it insulates the currently weak executive branch, allowing for it to sustain itself and evolve. However, outlawing parties also had negative consequences. As discussed in Chapter 4, the average voter utilizes political parties to reduce the information costs associated with understanding a candidate's positions and views. With all candidates required to run as independents, the information costs facing voters regarding candidates' positions were far greater and led to reports of confusion among some voters.

Yet another negative consequence was that, by weakening the parliamentary opposition, Karzai also weakened a key check on the executive branch. A central characteristic of a liberal democratic system is the presence of effective checks and balances that, in theory, prevent one branch from obtaining too much power. By weakening potential opposition by the parliament, Karzai has given disproportionate strength to the executive branch, which makes the country reliant on a small number of "good" leaders. Given the constant threat of violence and assassination that exists in the country or the possibility of a future leader who is not committed to liberal values gaining executive powers, this could be problematic over time.[28]

A final concern is the ultimate credibility and legitimacy of the parliament and broader political institutions. If warlords and other leaders in Afghanistan do not feel that they can engage in legitimate and peaceful opposition to the executive branch because the parliament is disproportionately weak, the benefit to participating in the new Afghanistan will decrease. Therefore, the possibility exists that efforts to create a sustainable executive branch in the current period may result in the ineffectiveness of other branches of newly constructed political institutions in future periods.

The specific issues discussed above serve to highlight the difficulties associated with constructing sustainable liberal institutions. Specifically, there is a continual trade-off between creating an environment wherein newly constructed, and therefore fragile, institutions can develop and credibly constraining those institutions so that they do not ultimately become illiberal.

Expectations and credibility also pose a significant barrier in the reconstruction of Iraq. As discussed, historical relations between the various groups within the country raise the cost of bargaining toward a mutually beneficial end. Each group is skeptical of the others, in many cases with good reason, as well as of the possibility that reconstructed institutions will be a positive-sum for Iraqi society in general. Along these lines, given the historical context, many Iraqis view majority rule as a formula for gaining positions of power over other groups in the country. Others fear that majority rule will result in forfeiting the privileged positions that they held prior to the war and reconstruction.

In addition to creating credible institutions within Iraq, the United States also faces issues of credibility in the broader Middle East. As the Middle East scholar Shibley Telhami notes, "The U.S. has a legacy of decades that is based in part on our policy and in part on impression; it is not going to be able to change the paradigm overnight simply by a charm campaign. . . . People are not going to trust the message if they don't trust the messenger."[29] Along similar lines, Michael Scheuer indicates that the lack of U.S. credibility in the Middle East "encapsulates the consequences of a half-century of U.S. Middle Eastern policy that moved America from being the much-admired champion of liberty and self-government to the hated and feared advocate of a new imperial order. . . ."[30] Overcoming preexisting stereotypes of U.S. policy, whether they are accurate or not, will pose an additional challenge to the ongoing reconstruction efforts, both in Iraq and in the broader Middle East region.

Public Choice Issues

In Chapter 4, I focused on the array of public choice issues that have influenced the reconstruction effort in Iraq. As discussed previously, we observe numerous examples in Iraq of corruption, faulty assumptions, overconfidence, and the awarding of contracts to providers with political connections, all of which have contributed to the current problems. It seems unnecessary to review those here in detail, but it is important to note that these issues will continue to pose a problem for occupiers and will be a major barrier to the ultimate success of the reconstruction effort. In particular, success will require some means of surmounting the problems created by the political decision-making process within the United States.

Similar issues have, to date, had a negative impact on the reconstruction of Afghanistan as well. The waste related to the misallocation of resources associated with constructing physical infrastructure is but one straightforward example. In a 2005 *Washington Post* article, journalists Joe Stephens and David Ottaway documented the progress of a $73 million program to construct Afghani schools and clinics.[31] They reported that the program suffered from a lack of coordination and poor planning due in part to the desire to have something done before the 2004 Afghan presidential elections. In short, those running the program traded off coordination and, ultimately, quality for quick completion in order to signal progress. Afghanistan's physical environment presented further difficulties, as U.S. roof designs used by contractors were not sufficient in strength to support snowfall during the winter season.

Stephens and Ottaway further report that the United States Agency for International Development (USAID), which headed the project, was unable to identify the actual location of many of its projects within the broader program. Further confusion stemmed from the lack of coordination between USAID and U.S. officials outside that organization. Initially, the aim of the reconstruction program was to construct or refurbish 420 schools and clinics by the end of 2004, but this number was eventually increased to 1,000 by officials outside USAID who were motivated by the perceived need to show progress in the reconstruction effort at home.

Along similar lines, a 2005 U.S. General Accounting Office report that analyzed the broader reconstruction effort in Afghanistan noted that "despite partial improvements to U.S. tracking of financial data after the publication of our 2004 report, complete and accurate information was still not readily available; consequently, U.S. efforts to plan, assess progress, and make informed resource allocations were impaired."[32] The report went on to note, "As in fiscal years 2002–2003, USAID lacked a comprehensive operational strategy to direct its efforts in Afghanistan in fiscal year 2004. . . ."[33]

Of course, the waste and lack of coordination associated with the initiative discussed above will not, in itself, make or break the broader reconstruction in Afghanistan, and the $73 million allocated to this project is a minor part of the overall reconstruction budget. However, this basic example does provide important insights that can be generalized. Specifically, this example serves to illuminate the difficulties faced by occupiers, not just in constructing physical infrastructure but also in the broader reconstruction effort. The difficulties associated with reconstructing basic physical infrastructure, such as clinics and schools, would seem to indicate that the barriers to constructing vastly more complex institutions—political, judicial, and economic—would be concomitantly greater, and failure would be even more likely.

In short, if the design and building of effective schools and clinics poses problems, why should one expect that constructing an extended sustainable liberal democratic order will be any easier? Indeed, the problems that plague the construction of basic physical infrastructure are but a small subset of the more complex issues facing the broader reconstruction effort. Success will require some means of reducing the costs associated with bureaucracy and the perverse incentives and knowledge problems that come with it. As discussed throughout this book, policymakers and academics lack effective solutions to these problems.

A final issue that will influence the reconstruction efforts in both Afghanistan and Iraq will be the U.S. election cycle. Determining an exit strategy for U.S. occupiers has become a key political topic, as indicated by the congressional mid-term elections in November 2006. The outcome of these elections, as well as the presidential elections in 2008, will affect the length and magnitude of U.S. involvement in the reconstruction of both countries, and therefore will influence the ultimate outcome in both cases.

Unintended Consequences

Negative unintended consequences associated with the reconstruction efforts in both Afghanistan and Iraq are another issue of importance. Given that many of these unintended consequences will not become evident for years, and perhaps even for decades, one should expect this to remain an issue over the long run. Recall from the several examples of the dynamics of intervention considered in Chapter 4 that negative unintended consequences can both be internal to the country being reconstructed and also create "neighborhood effects." That is, the occupier's actions can create negative spillover effects in the broader region or even beyond. To reiterate the importance of considering negative unintended consequences as well as highlight the issue that occupiers in Afghanistan and Iraq currently face, I will briefly focus on two specific examples.

First, and perhaps most important, a central negative unintended consequence of the occupation of Afghanistan and Iraq is that these actions may actually contribute to creating the next generation of terrorists. This claim will seem counterintuitive to most given that one of the primary reasons the United States is involved in these efforts is to reduce the terrorist threat. However, it appears that U.S. government officials are aware of this very real possibility. For instance, in a January 2005 report, *Mapping the Global Future*, the National Intelligence Council, the CIA director's think tank, noted that Iraq had become the new training ground (Afghanistan was the previous training ground) for future terrorists.

Specifically, the report indicated that those currently engaged in the Iraq insurgency could eventually go home and take their training from the battlefields with them, resulting in an increase in conflict in other regions. In oral comments during a briefing associated with the release of the report, David B. Low, the National Intelligence Officer for Transnational Threats, noted that "there is even, under the best scenario, over time, the likelihood that some of the jihadists who are not killed there [in Iraq] will, in a sense, go home, wherever home is, and will therefore disperse to various other countries."[34] Along similar lines, in a hearing in front of the Senate Intelligence Committee on February 16, 2005, then CIA Director Porter Goss noted that Iraq was being used to recruit "new anti-U.S. jihadists," and he went on to say that those "who survive will leave Iraq experienced and focused on acts of urban terrorism. They represent a potential pool of contacts to build transnational terrorist cells, groups, and networks."[35] Finally, Peter Bergen and Alec Reynolds warn that "the current war in Iraq will generate a ferocious blowback. . . . Foreign volunteers fighting U.S. troops in Iraq today will find new targets around the world after the war ends."[36]

The potential blowback of a new generation of terrorists is but one example of the negative external effects associated with the occupation of Iraq. To the extent that those currently engaged in the Iraq conflict take their training home, the war could have the unintended consequence of increasing conflict in other regions, both within and beyond the Middle East. If this is indeed the case the current effort in Iraq would have the counterproductive effect of increasing the terrorist threat in new regions instead of achieving the desired goal of eradicating terrorism.

Another poignant example of the unintended consequences of the occupation of Iraq is the broader effect on the balance of power in the Middle East of the toppling of the Hussein regime. In removing Hussein from power, the United States hoped to free oppressed Shi'as and create an environment conducive to the formation of a liberal democracy. However, one unintended implication has been a backlash against the Shi'a in the broader Middle East region.

The Middle East scholar Vali Nasr has pointed out that the toppling of the Hussein regime has brought hope to Shi'as for increased freedoms not just in Iraq but also in the broader Middle East region, where they comprise a significant part of the population.[37] For instance, Shi'as constitute about 90 percent of the Iranian population, 70 percent of the population residing in the Persian Gulf, 45 percent of the population of Lebanon, and 75 percent of the populations of Azerbaijan and Bahrain.[38] However, while the fall of Hussein is cause for optimism among Shi'as, it has caused a backlash among Sunnis, who feel threatened by the potential for Shi'a dominance through democratic majority rule. Along these lines, Nasr notes, "The Sunni backlash has begun to spread far beyond Iraq's borders, from Syria to Pakistan, raising the specter of a broader struggle for power between the two groups that could threaten stability in the region."[39]

However, Nasr is careful to point out that the growing backlash does not necessarily have to result in instability in the Middle East. Instead, he notes that "[the Shi'a revival] presents Washington with new opportunities to pursue its interests in the region."[40] This, however, will require a complex balancing act on the part of the United States, involving cooperation and diplomacy with Iran, among others. Given the existing tensions between the United States and Iran in relation to the latter's nuclear program, among other issues, entering into a cooperative partnership in the near term may be problematic.

The specific dynamics of these and other unintended consequences will become clearer over the coming years. However, the potential for unanticipated negative outcomes presents yet another barrier to ultimate success in the reconstruction of Afghanistan and Iraq. Even if current efforts establish some semblance of liberal democracy in these countries, negative unintended consequences that emerge in the future may be potentially destabilizing both within these countries and in the surrounding regions. In other words, current efforts may reduce conflict on some margins while simultaneously increasing conflict on others. The magnitude of each of these two effects will not become evident until the future.

8 Liberal Means to Liberal Ends

T HE MAIN ARGUMENT of this book is that policymakers and occupiers face an array of constraints, both internal and external to the country being reconstructed, that make reconstruction efforts more likely to fail than to succeed. Further, the extent of these constraints is typically greatest in those countries that are most in need of the political, economic, and social change that reconstruction efforts attempt to engender. The irony for policymakers is that reconstruction efforts are least likely to work precisely where they are needed most.

As mentioned previously, the main threat to Western nations, at least in the foreseeable future, will not come from a national superpower but rather from weak, failed, and conflict-torn states and rogue groups within those states. Obviously, the threats posed by these states are potentially formidable and cannot be ignored. However, given the fact that reconstruction efforts are more likely to fail than to generate sustainable change toward liberal democracy, alternative mechanisms for fostering social change in such weak, failed, and conflict-torn states must be considered; this chapter will offer a discussion of competing alternatives to the current approach to reconstruction.

Brute Force

One alternative is for the United States to embrace the role of empire, including the use of its overwhelming military and economic power to spread peace (another irony, of course) and liberal democracy throughout the world, by brute force where necessary. Those who support this position argue that it is not only in the interest of the United States but also its duty as an empire to bring stability to the world. Niall Ferguson, perhaps the most recognizable advocate of this position, argues that the United States should not just occupy countries but set up long-term colonial administrations to oversee and run weak, failed, and conflict-torn states. Along these lines, Ferguson notes, "A country like—to take just one example—Liberia would benefit immeasurably from something like an American colonial administration."[1]

The logic behind this call for colonization is straightforward. Typically, weak, failed, and conflict-torn states lack the basic foundations required for liberal democratic institutions. Therefore, a short-term military occupation that attempts either to quickly establish such institutions or to work within existing institutions, which are by definition fragile or dysfunctional, will not accomplish the desired task of creating sustainable change. Instead of abandoning what Ferguson calls "the liberal imperial project," he contends that *greater* levels of effort and of force relative to what has been utilized in recent efforts must be employed for the project to succeed.

In fact, in contrast to the current "light-footprint approach," which is based on minimal direct intervention and self-determination by indigenous citizens, colonization would *rely* on brute force to impose liberal institutions in weak, failed, and conflict-torn states. Emphasis would not be on the present standard benchmarks, such as the timing of elections and the specifics of an exit strategy, but rather, on establishing order within the context of a military administration no matter what the necessary time frame. Although Ferguson recognizes that not all cases of colonial administration will be successful, he argues that, in many cases, a liberal empire, wherein the countries in question would be managed colonial-style, can achieve better results than attempts at establishing a nation-state in the short-run.[2]

On the face of it, the brute force alternative does indeed appear to have some benefits. For instance, one potential benefit of this approach is that it will overcome the issue of credible commitment discussed in earlier chapters. By committing to a long-term colonial administration, occupiers would signal to citizens that they intend to remain in control of the country's operations until the desired goal is achieved, which may provide some incentive for citizens to work with the occupiers, given their extended presence. Further, by establishing a long-term colonial administration, occupiers do not have to worry about establishing infrastructure or holding elections in the short-term to signal progress. Given the longer time frame of the endeavor, and combined with the clear motivation of colonization, occupiers would not feel pressure to signal progress and quickly make the transition to indigenous actors. While offering these potential benefits, however, the brute force approach also suffers from several major problems.

To begin to understand these issues, let us consider historical colonization efforts. Compared to more recent reconstruction efforts, historical colonial efforts had drastically different motivations. For instance, the goal of many such efforts was to secure resources for the benefit of the empire instead of planting the seeds of self-sustaining liberal democracy, which is the ostensible motivation of more recent reconstruction missions. Therefore, there was less emphasis on human rights and practically no emphasis on the part of colonizers on self-determination.

Although recent support for a return to empire calls for the imposition of liberal institutions, which protect human and civil rights as well as private property, much can be learned from the methods that were required to maintain control over the occupied populace in historical colonization efforts. For instance, in reviewing the U.S. colonial project in the Philippines from 1898 to 1946, the political scientist Kimberly Zisk Marten notes, "Despite instructions from home to use minimal force and to respect the local population, the 'men on the spot' in colonial operations could violate human rights arbitrarily with a great deal of impunity."[3] In fact, they needed to employ such force to overcome resistance to establish and maintain order.

This highlights a more general point: colonization efforts require a complete commitment to the use of brute force to impose order and to establish the desired institutions. This use of force runs the risk of producing a backlash not only in the country being reconstructed but also from the international community. For instance, one would expect the existing international dissent toward the current U.S. reconstruction effort in Iraq to be even greater if the means being employed included the use of unchecked brute force that was perceived as consistently violating human rights. Unfortunately, the use of such force is likely to be necessary to implement even fundamental order in countries such as Iraq, which is characterized by widespread conflict. One could envision the need for force being greater in other weak, failed, and war-torn states where a central government, a police force, and a military force are either severely dysfunctional or completely lacking.

Here, then, is one central dilemma of a return to colonialism. Although there may be some incentive to cooperate with occupiers because they announce they will remain in the country in question for a prolonged period, one should also expect foreign governments that choose this strategy to be met with a backlash. Ferguson recognizes this when he notes that the imperial era did not always go peacefully, as illustrated, perhaps not all that coincidentally, by the British post–World War I invasion of Iraq. That invasion was met by resistance similar to that characterizing the current U.S.-led effort.[4] Such a backlash may extend beyond the country being occupied to the international community and the populace of the empire carrying out the colonization effort.

In attempting to establish their credibility, which is to say their willingness to use brutality, colonial administrators will need to send a strong signal that defection in the form of disobedience, insurgency, or terrorism will be met with force. That is, to be truly credible, such a signal would need to involve the use of force equivalent to, if not greater than, the initial defection. It is clear how such a situation could quickly unravel into circumstances similar to those that characterized the past U.S. effort in the Philippines, where troops often employed brute force with impunity.

As mentioned, a key difference between historical colonization and more recent reconstruction efforts is the emphasis on human rights. Current efforts take place in the context of universal international law, and while human rights violations have occurred in these efforts, there are typically legal mechanisms to deal with such violations, such as courts-martial, that are in place in the country executing the occupation. To be effective, colonial administrators would need to find some balance between the need to employ brute force to impose and maintain order and simultaneously balancing the existing legal structures and expectations of the citizens of the country being occupied, the citizens of the empire, *and* also the international community. Given the various dynamics at work, this is a daunting problem, the solution for which is unclear and perhaps even unobtainable.

Even if one puts aside the issues raised above, colonization efforts would still suffer from the array of issues discussed in previous chapters. For instance, colonial administrators would still suffer from the most daunting of knowledge problems—how to construct liberal democratic institutions from scratch. Further, controllable variables—troops, aid, timing of elections, and so on— would still be constrained in their effectiveness by uncontrollable variables such as the existing art of association, nested games, and expectations. Colonial administrators, just like occupiers utilizing the more recent light-footprint approach, would fail to possess adequate solutions to these problems, which may require them to further rely on the use of brute force to achieve some semblance of stability.

Moreover, colonial efforts, also just like recent light-footprint efforts, will suffer from public choice issues as well. Colonization efforts will be intertwined with the political decision-making process in the empire executing the administration of the colonial effort. The array of various actors discussed in Chapter 4—voters; special-interests; elected officials; and bureaucrats, including those staffing the colonial administration—will influence the direction and outcome of the overall effort. As discussed previously, the incentives created by the political decision-making process will often generate perverse policies that fail to align with the broader goals of the effort. The existence of perverse incentives poses a problem no matter what the specific nature of the military occupation.

In his call for the United States to accept its role as an empire, Niall Ferguson has noted America's "attention deficit disorder" toward foreign military interventions, which "seems to be inherent in the American political system. . . ."[5] This disorder manifests itself in the form of short-term military occupations that typically end prematurely, in relation to their desired goal. Indeed, Ferguson recognizes this lack of sustained attention as a key factor preventing the kind of ongoing military interventions in the form of colonial administrations that he advocates. Public choice theory sheds light on exactly how the dynamics of this "attention deficit disorder" operate.

To the extent that the opinions of voters and special-interests influence the behavior of elected officials and bureaucrats, changes in opinion will also change related behaviors and polices. As discussed earlier, this creates a bias in the American political decision-making process toward short-sighted "solutions," in as much as elected officials are more concerned with the short-term rather than the long-term effects of their actions. The result is that policies will often fail to align with the longer-term goals of reconstruction efforts, no matter what approach to reconstruction is taken. Effective long-term colonization would require a significant commitment that is not likely given the U.S. political system, in which elected officials must either run for reelection or leave office at the conclusion of their term. This reality constrains the possibility of a consistent and stable colonization policy, which would be required for a successful long-term occupation.

There are further issues with the brute force strategy, however. It is unclear how such long-term efforts would avoid creating the "Samaritan's Dilemma," mentioned in Chapter 6. One could envision colonial efforts creating some fragile institutions that were continually dependent on U.S. monetary and military support over the long run if they were to survive at all. In such a situation, it is unclear how the transition to self-sustaining institutions would ever take place.

In sum, the main issue with the notion of a U.S. liberal empire is that such a strategy ultimately requires a strong commitment to the use of brute force to both establish order and impose liberal institutions. This necessary use of force runs the risk of creating a backlash on several fronts. Further, for reasons discussed throughout this book, attempting to impose liberal democratic institutions where the necessary foundations (art of association, solution to nested games and the resulting meta-games, credible rules, and so on) are not already in place will generate a constant struggle. Where voluntary cooperation is absent, the continued use of brute force will be required. The costs of maintaining and enforcing order will be relatively high while the probability of success, measured by the emergence of self-sustaining liberal institutions, will be relatively low.

Moreover, even if the colonial administrators can overcome this problem, the overall reconstruction effort will still need to deal successfully with other constraints discussed throughout this book in order to achieve the stated goals. Given this array of issues associated with the use of illiberal means to achieve liberal ends, it is far from clear that the brute force alternative is superior to the means that have been employed to date to export liberal democracy.

Peacekeeping

Peacekeeping is another alternative means for exporting liberal democracy to weak, failed, and conflict-torn states. In its most basic form, peacekeeping involves foreign intervention but limits the use of military force to maintaining peace and stability. In other words, peacekeeping interventions are more passive than colonization, and they are also more passive than recent reconstruction efforts relying on the light-footprint approach. Peacekeepers attempt to remain neutral while serving the main purpose of providing humanitarian aid and a stable environment.

The political scientist Kimberly Zisk Marten is a key advocate of the peacekeeping position, and she has put forth a strategy she calls "security-keeping."[6] In theory, security-keeping would not utilize military occupiers to forcefully impose liberalization and democratization upon weak, failed, and conflict-torn societies. Instead, the one and only purpose of military forces would be to serve as peacekeepers who provide general security until indigenous institutions evolve sufficiently to assume the provision of security and other basic functions. In short, the objective of security-keeping is to provide an environment wherein indigenous institutions can emerge without military forces actively imposing them.[7]

Peacekeeping as a strategy for the eventual establishment of liberal democracies is premised upon the realization that sustainable Western-style liberal democratic institutions cannot be imposed by outsiders at the point of a gun. Although peacekeeping strategies attempt to provide a more realistic approach by recognizing the limitations of external occupiers to impose liberal democratic institutions, such strategies are ultimately unsatisfactory as effective means for generating sustainable change. In fact, the peacekeeping alternative to exporting liberal democracy suffers from several important problems.

For example, effective peacekeeping requires military forces to remain neutral while simultaneously maintaining some semblance of order. However, even if military forces have announced that they intend to stay neutral, indigenous actors or groups may not view them in that same manner. Recall that the initial intervention in Somalia in the early 1990s was motivated by purely humanitarian concerns. Military forces initially entered the country because of widespread famine, which was due mainly to civil war, and not the desire to construct liberal democratic institutions. However, warring factions within Somalia did not view military forces as humanitarian. Instead, they viewed the delivery of humanitarian aid as assistance to enemy groups and responded violently toward peacekeepers.

When humanitarian supplies were stolen by members of the warring factions in Somalia, the United States decided to respond with force and a program of disarmament. However, this response by the U.S. military required military leaders to pick target groups to attack and disarm, which cut against the initial goal of remaining neutral. In addition to the backlash experienced from these groups, the collateral damage to innocent civilians caused a shift in the support of the Somali populace away from peacekeepers and their mission.[8] As discussed in earlier chapters, the indigenous backlash against the Somali peacekeeping mission ultimately resulted in the deaths of U.S. servicemen and the withdrawal of U.S. forces well before the initial, let alone subsequent, missions were achieved.

In general, when peacekeepers are threatened or attacked, they must decide whether to respond in kind with violence or exit the country. Obviously, exiting will result in the ultimate failure of the peacekeeping mission. However, maintaining peace will require responding with force, which in turn means that occupiers must ultimately choose a side and discard their neutrality. In such an instance, indigenous citizens and groups will come to view peacekeepers as being "for" or "against" their cause. Historically, warring factions have attempted to draw "neutral" peacekeepers into combat by giving the appearance that other factions are a threat or by blaming peacekeepers for the deaths of civilians, thereby turning the populace against both the peacekeepers and the broader peacekeeping effort.[9]

A related result is the onset of "mission creep," which occurs when the specifics of activities associated with a military intervention expand in nature and magnitude. As the discussion in this book of the dynamics of intervention (see Chapter 4) indicates, even the initial intervention shifts the incentives that the actors involved face. These new incentives can often create a new set of problems that require further military intervention. In other words, these new problems will require military forces to change the nature of their mission, and in many cases, the focus will shift away from the narrow task of peacekeeping.

To the extent that the mission of intervening forces does suffer from mission creep and moves beyond the initial aim of peacekeeping and toward more traditional reconstruction, the various mechanisms discussed in previous chapters come into play. As but one example of this point, let us return again to the aforementioned intervention in Somalia. As discussed in Chapter 6, when it became clear that the initial peacekeeping mission was not able to provide the necessary security, the mission was expanded to include disarmament and the establishment of liberal democratic institutions in addition to peacekeeping. The various constraints on reconstruction efforts then became a major issue. The inability of occupiers to find an adequate solution to these constraints contributed to the ultimate failure of the effort.

Even if peacekeepers are not drawn into combat and are able to effectively maintain peace, other issues may arise as indigenous institutions emerge. For instance, what are peacekeepers to do if the indigenous institutions that evolve are illiberal in nature? If the mandate of neutrality is to be maintained, there is little that military forces can do in response to such institutions. In reality, maintaining neutrality in the face of the emergence of illiberal outcomes is unlikely to happen.

Even if the stated motivation is neutrality, peacekeeping missions are influenced not just by humanitarian concerns but also by the political decision-making process in the country carrying out the mission. The various groups that participate in the political process will have their own agendas and motivations, and consequently, peacekeepers may be forced to intervene to shape the direction of the country and "pick winners." Again, this move comes at the expense of maintaining neutrality and can be a result of, and further contribute to, the problem of mission creep.

A final problem facing peacekeeping missions is the same "attention deficit disorder" discussed when considering the use of brute force. Even if we assume that peacekeepers are able to provide some form of stability, it is unclear that liberal institutions will emerge at all, let alone that they will emerge within some realistic time frame. Again, given the nature of the U.S. political process, a long-term peacekeeping mission is unlikely. This realization, coupled with the very real possibility of peacekeeping forces being drawn into the conflict, reduces the likelihood of the peacekeeping alternative to be effective in achieving its proposed ends.

Non-Intervention and Free Trade

Non-intervention combined with a commitment to free trade is yet another alternative approach to dealing with weak, failed, and conflict-torn states. I contend that this approach will be the most effective in spreading liberal democracy around the world. In an ideal scenario, this strategy involves refraining from the use of military forces to occupy and reconstruct weak and failed states while simultaneously removing *all* barriers to trade with as many countries as possible.

While reconstruction via military occupation is one form of exogenous shock aimed at altering the course of a nation, the proposed strategy offers an alternative mechanism for shifting the trajectory of these countries, one that does not entail brute force and that avoids many of the pitfalls to which the other strategies for liberal democratic nation building are prone.[10] Within the framework put forth in Chapter 2, free trade is a means through which mechanisms can develop to transform situations of conflict into situations of cooperation. The dual result of the proposed strategy will be the creation of material wealth in relatively poor countries while also exposing others to Western institutions, ideas, and values without "force feeding" them these ideals at gunpoint.

Economic Benefits of Free Trade

Economists have long recognized the benefits that arise from free trade, and in fact, the intellectual discussion surrounding these benefits can be traced back over two centuries.[11] Today there is widespread agreement among economists that free trade produces a net economic benefit. As the economists David Dollar and Aart Kraay write, "Openness to international trade accelerates development: this is one of the most widely held beliefs in the economics profession, one of the few things on which Nobel prize winners on both the left and the right agree."[12] Free trade allows parties to specialize in those areas where they have a relative advantage and to exchange with others who have a relative advantage in producing different goods and services. The end result is that more total goods are produced and exchanged as compared to a situation wherein each party is self-sufficient. The parties engaging in free trade are made better off in terms of material wealth than in the absence of those trade opportunities.[13]

Indeed, the economic impact of free trade on wealth is significant. William Cline, an economist, estimates that worldwide free trade could help five hundred million people escape poverty while simultaneously injecting $200 billion annually into developing nations.[14] Typically, through no coincidence, weak and failed states are also the poorest countries in the world. In contrast to the evidence that indicates that monetary aid is not an effective cure for the major ills that assail these states (as discussed in Chapter 6), removing barriers to trade *does* appear to be an effective means for bettering the situation in these countries. Given the clear economic benefits of free trade, the question then becomes what specific policy should be followed in order to move toward this ideal end.

When considering barriers to trade, a common, yet incorrect, assumption is that only bilateral free trade (a situation wherein both countries simultaneously remove barriers to exchange) is beneficial. In other words, it is assumed that free trade is an all-or-nothing proposition—either all parties agree to reduce barriers or none should. However, while a bilateral reduction in barriers to trade is indeed a preferable state of affairs, unilateral reductions also produce substantial benefits and are preferable to maintaining bilateral trade barriers.[15]

For instance, consider the fact that, if the United States unilaterally reduced its trade barriers, it would reduce the cost of foreign goods entering the country. This in turn would reduce the costs for U.S. producers that use foreign goods as inputs in their final products, as well as the cost of final foreign goods sold directly to U.S. consumers. A subsidiary effect of lowering the cost of foreign-produced goods is that this would tend to increase the incomes of foreign producers as U.S. consumers purchased their goods, which would not only contribute to economic development abroad but also provide these foreign producers with additional means to purchase U.S. goods and services. In short, even if the United States's trading partners maintained barriers to their markets, unilateral reductions in U.S. trade barriers would be beneficial to many individuals both in the United States and abroad.

What this single broad example highlights is that there are very good reasons for the United States to take steps to remove barriers to trade with foreign countries—both developed and undeveloped—on purely economic grounds. Because of the economic benefits associated with free trade, opening U.S. markets to people around the globe is more likely to have a greater impact on growth and development in other countries than efforts to export liberal institutions, and the benefits associated with those institutions, via gunpoint. As I will discuss shortly, although there is much room to do more, the United States has already taken steps along these lines through the commitment to negotiating and implementing free trade agreements.

Cultural Benefits of Free Trade

When analyzing free trade, the significant benefits beyond the economic gains discussed above are often overlooked. The economist Tyler Cowen has analyzed the impact of globalization on culture, and he concludes that free trade makes societies better off not only in terms of increases in wealth but also in terms of the array of cultural products available.[16] Cowen's core argument is that cross-cultural trade has the dual effect of allowing cultures to simultaneously maintain and develop certain aspects of their unique identities while partially merging with other cultures and becoming similar in other aspects. In other words, the impact of globalization on culture is not an all-or-nothing proposition whereby a culture must either remain isolated or be destroyed. Instead, although globalization admittedly destroys certain aspects of culture, it simultaneously allows other aspects of culture to grow and flourish.

To illuminate this point, Cowen cites the restaurant market. On the one hand, chain restaurants continue to increase their overall market share in the global marketplace, which tends to make cultures more homogenous. On the other hand, the overall increase in dining has also increased the number of ethnic and niche restaurants that are able to remain profitable in the broader restaurant market, which has made the options available in the overall restaurant market more diverse and heterogeneous.[17] Although one can find a McDonald's restaurant in many places around the world, many ethnic and niche restaurants are available as well. Cowen's reasoning can be extended across cultural products and includes not just physical goods and services but also intangibles such as values, ideas, and other informal, complementary institutions. As in the restaurant market, cross-cultural trade has the dual effect of making intangibles more similar and more homogenous in some respects, and more diverse and more heterogeneous in others.

It is important to note that the material gains from exchange and the intangibles produced by cross-cultural trade are not necessarily mutually exclusive. For instance, the economist Benjamin Friedman has recently explored the implications of economic growth or stagnation for the moral character of a country.[18] He concludes, "Economic growth—meaning a rise in standard of living for the clear majority of citizens—more often than not fosters greater opportunity, tolerance of diversity, social mobility, commitment to fairness, and dedication to democracy."[19]

In short, increases in material wealth provide individuals with the ability to pursue other, often intangible, ends and influences other, often non-economic, aspects of society. This lends even more support to the claim in the previous section that there are very sound reasons for the United States to pursue a policy of reducing barriers to trade, even if that policy is unilateral in nature. To reiterate, in addition to providing increases in wealth, free trade also provides subsidiary effects beyond purely economic benefits.

Within this context of cross-cultural trade, consider the recent work by the philosopher Kwame Anthony Appiah, who seeks to revive cosmopolitanism— the notion that individuals are "citizens of the world."[20] The essence of the cosmopolitan ideal is that individuals need to develop habits of coexistence with others at the personal, local, national, and international levels. Appiah emphasizes that cosmopolitanism entails an ongoing conversation with both neighbors *and* strangers. It therefore advances the possibility of achieving mutual understanding between individuals who hold different worldviews and adhere to different moral systems. At the same time, cosmopolitanism recognizes the real possibility that consensus on a single worldview may not be reached. Such a possibility does not necessarily lead to conflict. Instead, it can result in a cooperative decision to "agree to disagree."

A commitment to free trade can be seen as a means of merging cultures and finding a common middle ground. In other words, trade is a means of engaging in an ongoing conversation and pursuing the cosmopolitan ideal. Through cultural trade, individuals in different countries will tend to share, or at a minimum, become aware of, common cultural products.[21]

Recall from the discussion in earlier chapters that in order for formal Western-style institutions to operate, they require certain complementary informal institutions to serve as a foundation. One of the central issues in reconstructing countries via military occupation is that policymakers and occupiers lack the relevant knowledge of how to create these complementary institutions where they do not already exist. However, free trade can be viewed as a means of potentially establishing the complementary institutions that are required for formal Western-style institutions to operate effectively. Societies tend to become more similar, at least in their awareness of others outside their borders, as they become aware of and integrate the ideas, values, organizational forms, and practices of others. Consider for instance that many of the autocracies with which the United States has engaged in large-scale trade (such as Mexico, South Korea, and Taiwan) have moved toward liberal democracy, relative to their starting point, as a result of a larger trade-produced commercial middle class and its demands for political participation. While trade may not lead to countries assuming a mirror image of the West, trade can plant the seeds of tolerance and a willingness to agree to disagree, traits that Appiah notes are central to any notion of global peace.

Benefits of Non-Intervention and Free Trade vs. Military Occupation
Pursuing a commitment to non-intervention and free trade as a strategy to deal with weak, failed, and conflict-torn states will overcome many of the problems that have doomed past reconstruction efforts and that adversely affect the alternatives considered earlier. Again, the knowledge problem of how to construct liberal institutions—both formal and informal—where they do not already exist will no longer pose a problem. By removing itself from the business of attempting to either construct or reconstruct institutions along liberal lines, the United States will no longer need to be concerned with its knowledge deficit in this area.

Yet another major benefit of this approach is the positive impact on the credibility of the United States. As discussed throughout this book, a major issue with U.S. foreign policy is how others throughout the world perceive the underlying motivations for said policies. Even if the motivations of U.S. interventions abroad are in fact benevolent, others often view them as malevolent and respond accordingly. A commitment to non-intervention and free trade would in practice do much to the damaged reputation of the United States by significantly curtailing interventions abroad.

A commitment to non-intervention and free trade would signal that the United States is not an imperial empire that preaches liberalism only to employ illiberal means to accomplish its goals. In stark contrast to the present situation, the United States would lead by example, demonstrating that it is truly committed to liberalism, and not merely in its rhetoric but also in practice. By following such a policy, the United States would demonstrate to others how functional liberal institutions operate at the same time that the economic and cultural benefits discussed above are being realized, benefits that would lend further support to the argument for liberal democratic institutions.

A subsidiary benefit to repairing the credibility of the United States would be a reduction in blowback associated with foreign interventions. Recall that blowback refers to the negative unintended consequence of foreign intervention and occupation. Obviously, to the extent that the United States removed itself from military occupations aimed at exporting liberal democracy, it would also remove the blowback associated with such interventions. To the extent that this strategy and subsequent result is the case, pursuing such a strategy of non-intervention and free trade is a means not only of helping the poorest countries and of exporting U.S. values but of increasing U.S. national security.

A final benefit of the proposed strategy is that it provides a means of proactively dealing with weak and failed states in the face of what John Mueller calls "the Iraq syndrome."[22] Mueller contends that the current effort in Iraq, along with the associated difficulties, will create a "syndrome" whereby much of the American public will be skeptical, and even unsupportive, of similar undertakings in the near future. If Mueller is indeed right, a new strategy will be needed to deal with the threats posed by weak, failed, and conflict-torn states. The strategy proposed here would address these countries while simultaneously removing the United States from the very military engagements that would be met with skepticism by virtue of the Iraq syndrome.

It should be noted that the proposed strategy is different from what historically has been called "isolationism." While the United States would indeed "isolate" itself from long-term military engagements aimed at exporting liberal democracy, it would simultaneously open its economy to as many countries as possible. In doing so, the United States would become increasingly interconnected with the rest of the world instead of more isolated from it.

The strategy outlined here is one means of exercising what the political scientist Joseph Nye has called "soft power." Soft power entails attracting and convincing others to shift their preferences in the desired manner.[23] This approach stands in direct contrast to "hard power," which relies on coercion to achieve the desired end. Within this context, the United States would hardly be isolated, and instead, would use its economic strength to provide other countries with the opportunity for economic development along with the intangibles that are associated with increases in material wealth.

From this viewpoint, the proposed strategy is more likely to generate sustainable change because such change would need to be voluntarily accepted instead of being forced upon others at the point of a gun. Are others more likely to accept and integrate, or at least tolerate, Western institutions and values if they do so voluntarily or if such "acceptance" is forced upon them at gunpoint? The answer seems clear.

It is also important to realize that the proposed strategy does not necessarily preclude the use of military force to protect U.S. citizens from imminent threats or for humanitarian reasons abroad. This strategy does, however, hold that U.S. military forces should not be used as a means for attempting to establish liberal democratic institutions abroad via extended occupations. Further, when considering using military force, either in the case of an imminent threat or a humanitarian crisis, the analysis put forth in this book can assist in informing these decisions.

For instance, this analysis can provide insight regarding how a military intervention, initially motivated by humanitarian ends, can spiral into a full-blown military occupation accompanied by the array of issues inevitably associated with such an occupation. Likewise, if regime change is deemed necessary due to an adjunct moral obligation that also requires a prolonged occupation, the insights of this book can assist in determining if the initial intervention is realistic given the array of constraints associated with military occupations.

The Foundation for Non-Intervention and Free Trade Is in Place

U.S. history, as well as current practice, indicates that the foundations of the strategy proposed herein are in place. Consider for instance that a commitment to free trade and non-intervention can be traced back to several early U.S. leaders. In fact, in his farewell address in 1796, George Washington emphasized that a general rule for U.S. foreign policy should be as follows: "In extending our commercial relations to have with them as little political connection as possible. So far as we have already formed engagements let them be fulfilled with perfect good faith. Here let us stop. . . . It is our true policy to steer clear of permanent alliances with any portion of the foreign world. . . ."[24] While calling for the United States to isolate itself from long-term political entanglements, Washington recognized trade as a basis for interaction with other nations.

Similarly, in his inauguration speech on March 4, 1801, Thomas Jefferson stated as a general principle that the United States would pursue "peace, commerce, and honest friendship with all nations, entangling alliances with none."[25] Finally, on July 4, 1821, Secretary of State John Quincy Adams made clear his view of America's role in the international arena in a speech to the House of Representatives:

> America does not go abroad in search of monsters to destroy. . . . She is the champion and vindicator only of her own. . . . She well knows that by once enlisting under banners other than her own, were they even the banners of foreign independence, she would involve herself beyond the power of extrication, in all the wars of interest and intrigue, of individual avarice, envy, ambition, which assumed the colors and usurped the standards of freedom. The fundamental maxims of her policy would insensibly change from liberty to force.[26]

Of course, the world today is drastically different from the one of these early leaders. Nonetheless, at a minimum, these quotations indicate that the spirit, if not always the practice, of non-intervention and a simultaneous commitment to trade have a long history in the United States. The proposed strategy therefore is not a radical shift from the views of the country's early leaders toward international affairs.

The foundations of a commitment to free trade can also be found in current U.S. international trade practices. Indeed, the creation of free trade zones with countries around the world has long been a key tool used by U.S. policymakers to achieve liberal ends. For instance, during the Cold War, the creation of trade agreements was seen as a central means of containing the spread of communism. More recently, policymakers have made a commitment to establish a U.S.-Middle East free trade area with the realization that free trade is critical for economic development and subsequent social change.

Along these lines, in May 2003, President Bush announced an initiative to establish a free trade area between the United States and Middle East over the next decade. Since then, steps have been taken to meet this goal through the negotiation and signing of free trade agreements (FTAs) with Bahrain and Morocco. Further, negotiations with Oman on an FTA concluded in September 2005. These more recent FTAs follow on the earlier agreements with Jordan, initiated during the Clinton presidency, and with Israel, initiated in 1985 and fully implemented as of 1995.

In their simplest form, FTAs attempt to eliminate barriers to trade—quotas, tariffs, and so on—between parties to the agreement. The specific dynamics of each FTA varies depending on how it is written and what goods, services, and barriers it covers. However, while the specifics vary, FTAs typically phase out barriers to trade while establishing some basic agreement on standards regarding a variety of issues such as labor and the environment.

The main benefit of FTAs is that they create an environment for free trade and the associated benefits described above. Further, because the terms are codified, once signed and implemented, FTAs serve as one binding check against backsliding into the previous situation that included barriers to trade. The main downside of FTAs is that they take a significant time to negotiate and fully implement. Negotiations can take several years, and once approved by the legislative branch in the United States, the terms of the agreement are typically phased in over years or decades. Given that, the full benefits of FTAs will not be realized until well into the future.

To illustrate this point, consider the specifics of the aforementioned United States–Middle East FTAs summarized in Table 8.1. As indicated, the FTAs currently in force in the area—with Jordan, Bahrain, Morocco, and Oman—will not be fully implemented for at least a decade. Negotiations with the United Arab Emirates were initiated, but they have been postponed after the two sides failed to agree on labor and investment laws.

TABLE 8.1 Status of U.S.-Middle East free trade agreements[27]

U.S. Free trade agreement partner	Status	Full implementation date
Israel	In force as of September 1985	Fully implemented as of January 1995
Jordan	In force as of December 2001	To be phased in over ten years
Morocco	In force as of January 2006	To be phased in over eighteen years
Bahrain	In force as of August 2006	To be phased in over ten years
Oman	In force as of September 2006	To be phased in over ten years
United Arab Emirates	Launched negotiations March 2005; postponed as of March 2006	To be determined

Another issue regarding the feasibility of FTAs is that there are a limited number of countries in the Middle East region ready to engage in realistic negotiations with the United States. Many countries in the region are either unwilling or unable to make the necessary policy and legal changes required by the United States. Nevertheless, the citizens of these countries would clearly gain from the benefits associated with free trade. This fundamental problem reaches beyond the Middle East and can be applied to most, if not all, weak and failed states, as well as other relatively poor countries.

Stated differently, the countries whose citizens are most in need of the benefits associated with free trade and access to U.S. markets are typically in the worst position to enter into a free trade agreement. While the fundamental motivation underpinning the United States's willingness to pursue FTAs is positive, the limitations of the FTAs as a mechanism for implementing free trade with those countries most in need of the associated benefits indicates that alternatives must be considered.

To overcome these limitations, I contend that U.S. policymakers should not only continue to pursue FTAs but also unilaterally reduce trade barriers, and not only for countries in the Middle East but also countries around the world. One of the main benefits of unilateral trade barrier reductions is that, in the absence of long negotiations, they allow countries to experience gains from free trade immediately. This strategy would provide a fast solution to the timing problems associated with negotiating and implementing FTAs while allowing poorer countries access to U.S. markets and all the benefits that this access will confer. After relatively poor countries realize the benefits of free trade, they are more likely to be in a position to negotiate an FTA in the future because their economy will be able to incur the costs associated with the minimum standards demanded by the United States.

Similar to the emphasis on free trade through FTAs, unilateral reduction in barriers to U.S. markets also has some precedent. In May 2003, senators Max Baucus and John McCain introduced the Middle East Trade and Engagement Act to create a trade preference program for countries in the Middle East. The proposed bill would have allowed the president to implement unilateral reductions in barriers to U.S. markets for countries in the Middle East that met certain requirements.

While the proposed bill never became law, it again indicates that the strategy for dealing with weak and failed states put forth in this book has some foundation in current practice. Indeed, a broader version of something similar to the proposed Baucus-McCain bill that unilaterally reduces barriers to U.S. markets for countries around the world would overcome many of the previously discussed problems with FTAs while allowing the poorest countries in the world access to U.S. markets.

Similarly, under the Generalized System of Preferences (GSP) program instituted in 1976, the United States provides preferential duty-free treatment for several thousand products from over a hundred designated countries and territories. The underlying logic of the GSP program is that lesser developed countries benefit from free access to U.S. markets as described above. In other words, the GSP program illustrates that policymakers recognize the benefits of free trade with lesser-developed countries. However, basic manufacturing products (for example, leather products, textiles, ceramics, and so on), which are the main exports from developing countries, fail to be covered by the GSP, limiting the effectiveness of the program. The proposed strategy would call for something similar to an expanded version of the GSP program allowing countries to maximize the benefits of free trade while overcoming many of the obstacles associated with FTAs.

One criticism of unilateral trade reductions is that they weaken the incentive for other countries to engage in long-lasting reforms.[28] The logic here is straightforward. If the United States grants free access to its markets with no commitment for reductions or reforms in kind, illiberal countries will not be required to reform and will have little incentive to do so. In other words, by granting access to its markets, the United States can no longer use free trade as a bargaining chip that engenders an incentive to reform. At the extreme, one could argue that unilateral reductions in barriers to U.S. markets could actually result in the counterproductive outcome of slowing reforms and propping up illiberal regimes. Access to U.S. markets would benefit illiberal regimes while preventing, or severely limiting, the gains experienced by citizens of their countries.

While this is a legitimate criticism, I wish to offer a different take on this potential outcome. The alternative to offering all countries unilateral access to U.S. markets is to isolate those countries that do not meet U.S. criteria. Typically, these criteria include a commitment to liberal reforms and support on key foreign policy issues. The central issue then is whether it is better to isolate or integrate countries that do not meet these criteria. It is unclear why we should expect further isolation to be an effective means of generating change toward the desired ends. If illiberal regimes fail to support the ends desired by the United States, they are unlikely to change even with the incentive provided by a potential trade relationship. In contrast to isolation, at least integration through trade provides an opportunity for change over time.

Assuming illiberal regimes can be integrated into U.S. markets, this would have several effects that may very well offset any disincentive to reform. For one, integration into U.S. markets, even if the country in question is run by an illiberal regime, will ultimately raise the cost of engaging in conflict against the United States. Interconnectedness through trade yields benefits, and the potential loss of those benefits raises the cost of engaging in conflict.[29] Given that a key goal of the United States in the larger "war on terror" is to bolster national security, the potential for reducing conflict with illiberal regimes makes this course of action preferable to isolating these nations. Further, to the extent that the benefits of unilateral trade reductions do spill over to citizens in illiberal countries, even if these spillovers are severely limited, they will still provide citizens with some betterment of their position. Finally, unilateral reductions in trade barriers could potentially have the positive effect of ultimately encouraging a response in kind as the benefits from open markets become evident. As mentioned earlier, several of the autocracies that the United States has engaged in large-scale trade have moved closer to liberal democracy relative to their prior position.

One final argument in support of unilateral free trade is the absence of effective alternatives. There is ongoing debate regarding whether economic sanctions that attempt to isolate illiberal countries are effective in generating change, and especially the widespread change desired of weak, failed, and conflict-torn states.[30] Historically, sanctions have done little to transform illiberal regimes while imposing significant costs on the citizens in these countries. Where sanctions have been effective, a specific set of circumstances has existed. For example, in South Africa sanctions were not merely economic but also athletic, artistic, political, and intellectual. As discussed earlier, it is also unclear that monetary aid is able to effectively generate extensive change in these countries. And finally, the core theme of this book is that military occupations aimed at reconstructing countries along liberal democratic lines are more likely to fail than to succeed for a wide array of reasons. In sum, while recognizing that unilateral trade reductions may, in some cases, reduce the incentive for illiberal regimes to engage in reforms, it is unclear that available alternatives will generate a preferable state of affairs on a broad basis.

Of course, while there is a long history of the use of trade by the United States to achieve political ends, both in rhetoric and practice, there is a nearly equally long history of military occupation and reconstruction. For the strategy proposed here to have its full effect, the United States must disengage from current long-term military interventions and refrain from becoming involved in future reconstruction efforts. The continued engagement of military forces in long-term reconstruction efforts will offset many of the benefits associated with a commitment to free trade, including the view of many foreigners that the United States is a hypocritical hegemon that employs illiberal means to achieve asserted liberal ends. Further, such interventions will continue to generate negative unintended consequences, such as further aggressions against the United States.

Summation

In a few words, the strategy of non-intervention and free trade presented here requires (1) disengagement from current military occupations, (2) refraining from subsequent military occupations aimed at establishing liberal democratic institutions, and (3) reductions in trade barriers with the ideal goal of reducing those barriers to zero with as many countries as possible. Of course, given political realities we should not expect the proposed strategy to be implemented immediately. Nonetheless, any movement toward this end should be viewed as preferable to the *status quo*.

To be clear, I am not claiming that markets are a panacea. Indeed, authors such as Benjamin Barber, Amy Chua, and Thomas Friedman, among others, have pointed out some of the significant costs associated with globalization and the spread of markets.[31] Just as we must be careful of the nirvana fallacy when considering reconstruction efforts, so too must we be aware of the same fallacy when considering the alternative proposed here. However, it is precisely because policymakers face a set of imperfect alternatives that non-intervention and free trade must be seriously considered as viable strategies.

The one thing that is clear is that there is no quick and easy fix to the problems caused by weak, failed, and conflict-torn states. Also evident is that, given the array of constraints, reconstruction via military occupation is more likely to fail than succeed. The alternatives that continue to rely on military force in one form or another do not seem to be capable of overcoming these constraints and the associated problems they pose. In contrast, the strategy of non-intervention and free trade does present a viable means to overcome many of these constraints.

In *The Clash of Civilizations and the Remaking of World Order,* Samuel Huntington postulated that world politics had entered a new period.[32] In this new phase, cultural differences are the driving force behind both alliances and antagonisms. This evolving circumstance will require Western leaders to adjust their policies on a wide array of issues. In adapting to this new phase of politics, one major implication for the West is that it must move away from the belief that Western values are universally desired and relevant and therefore can be exported at the point of a gun. Instead, the West should focus, Huntington contends, on protecting the unique Western identity. What better way to preserve that unique identity than to return to the position of America's forefathers—a position of non-intervention and free trade?

Notes

Chapter 1

1. The Inaugural Address is available at www.whitehouse.gov/news/releases/ 2005/01/20050120-1.html. Last accessed December 7, 2006.

2. See Offner 1992, 229–230.

3. On the motivations of the United States behind the intervention in Cuba, see Pérez 1990, Hunt 1987, and LaFeber 1993. The common historical interpretation is that the United States intervened for humanitarian reasons (see, for instance, Offner 1992). LaFeber contends that the United States was motivated not by humanitarian ends but by furthering its own interests and power.

4. For a detailed history of Cuba, see Gott 2004.

5. See Dobbins et al. 2003, 19.

6. For more on Erhard and his role in the reconstruction of Germany, see Mierzejewski 2004.

7. See Dower 1999, 736.

8. Ibid., 226–233.

9. The Northern Alliance, which was the main resistance to the Taliban government prior to U.S. intervention, is a coalition consisting of Tajik, Uzbek, Hazara, and some Pashtun elements.

10. For a narrative of the timeline of events that occurred in Iraq, see Polk 2005, 166–183.

11. For recent documentation of the problems in Iraq, see Baker and Hamilton 2006. For a discussion of some of the problems in Afghanistan, see Rubin 2007.

12. A Pew Research Center for the People & the Press survey conducted November 9–12, 2006, found that approximately 64 percent of those Americans polled believe the war in Iraq is going "Not too Well" or "Not Well at All," while 51 percent of those

polled believe the United States made a mistake sending troops to Iraq. Poll results are available at www.pollingreport.com/iraq.htm. Last accessed December 1, 2006.

13. See, for instance, Fukuyama 2004 and Rotberg 2004a.

14. See Ferguson 2004. Scholars and policymakers often use the terms *weak state* and *failed state* without clarifying what the terms mean. When I utilize these terms, I follow Eizenstat, Porter, and Weinstein (2005, 136), who measure the strength or weakness of states along three margins: security, the provision of basic services, and the protection of essential civil freedoms. Failed states do not provide any of these functions, while weak states are deficient along one or two of these margins.

15. See Heller 1950, Keynes 1980, Mises 2000, and Ohlin 1929.

16. See Brennan and Buchanan 1985.

17. See Greif 2006, 29–53.

18. See, for instance, Diamond 2005, Phillips 2005, and Ricks 2006.

19. Whenever I use the word *institutions,* the reader should interpret this term as incorporating the formal and informal rules governing human behavior and the enforcement of these rules through the internalization of certain norms of behavior, the social pressure exerted on the individual by the group, or the power of third-party enforcers who can use the threat of force on violators of the rules.

20. Regarding the current effort in Iraq, President Bush stated that the goal of U.S. policy is an Iraq that can "govern itself, sustain itself and defend itself" (quoted in Baker and Hamilton 2006, 40). It should be noted that there is a debate regarding the relationship between democracy and economic growth. See, for instance, De Haan and Siermann 1996, Knack and Keefer 1995, and Tavares and Wacziarg 2001. Although an important discussion, it is not my aim to contribute to this debate. There is also a debate regarding what *democracy* actually entails. For a discussion, see Diamond, Linz, and Lipset 1995. These authors point out that *democracy* refers to a political system that is separate from the economic and social realms. While this may be true, it seems clear that the aim of the United States in modern reconstruction efforts is to establish not only a liberal democracy but also liberal market and social institutions as well. See for instance, King (2003), who discusses the plan to implement a liberal market economy in Iraq.

21. For more on "Wilsonianism," see Paris 2004.

22. See Zakaria 2003. The argument that increasing political participation can lead to conflict and instability in states where political institutions are weak was originally made by Huntington (1968). Dahl (1971) and Nordlinger (1971) develop similar arguments.

23. For a discussion of the ethical issues involved with foreign intervention and reconstruction, see Damrosch 1993; Heiberg 1994; Hoffmann, Johansen, Sterba, and Vayrynen 1996; Ignatieff 2003; and Lugo 1996.

24. See Marshall and Jaggers 2003. On the different indices available and why the Polity IV Index is the most reliable and valid, see Munck and Verkuilen 2002.

25. See Marshall and Jaggers 2003, 13–14.

26. Ibid., 14, 36.

27. See Keller 2005 and Rousseau, Gelpi, Reiter, and Huth 1996. Other studies have found that a score of +8 is a more suitable benchmark. See Dahl 1998, Davenport and Armstrong 2004, and O'Loughlin et al. 1998.

28. See Gasiorowski and Power 1998 and Mainwaring 1993.

29. There is debate over which countries are in fact U.S.-led reconstructions. I have tried to consider as broad a list as possible. I have drawn the countries on my list from Lawson and Thacker 2003, Dobbins et al. 2003, Payne 2006a, Pei and Kasper 2003, and Pei 2003. I recognize that there are many cases of U.S. military interventions that are not included in this table.

30. *CIA World Factbook* 2007.

31. The *Freedom of the World* report is available at the Freedom House Website www.freedomhouse.org/template.cfm?page=15&year=2005.

32. For more on how Grenada compares to other reconstruction efforts using the *Freedom of the World* report as a metric, see Lawson and Thacker 2003.

33. For more on the failure of the United States to export democracy to Mexico, Central America, and the Caribbean via military occupation, see Lowenthal 1991.

34. See Bates, Greif, Levi, Rosenthal, and Weingast 1998.

35. Huntington 1991, 38. Also see Shin 1994, 151.

36. The distinction between the know-what and the know-how can be traced back to the philosopher Gilbert Ryle (1949). Hayek (1973, 72) appropriated the distinction to examine the importance of tacit knowledge in the social coordination process. Boettke (2001b: 251–252) also uses the distinction to explore the gap between the wealth of nations.

37. These are only a few of the preconditions for consolidated democracy that have been raised in the literature. For a more complete list, see Huntington 1991, 37–38.

38. See Fish and Brooks 2004.

39. Diamond 2005, 19–20. In earlier work, Diamond, Linz, and Lipset (1995) discuss the factors that contribute to the establishment and consolidation of a democracy.

40. See also Shin (1994, 151), who puts forth several general propositions on the third wave of democratization, which include (1) there are few preconditions for the emergence of democracy, (2) no single factor is sufficient or necessary to the emergence of democracy, (3) the emergence of democracy in a country is the result of a combination of causes, (4) the causes responsible for the emergence of democracy are not the same as those promoting its consolidation, (5) the combination of causes promoting democratic transition and consolidation varies from country to country, and (6) the combination of causes generally responsible for one wave of democratization differs from those responsible for other waves.

41. For troop and aid numbers, see Dobbins et al. 2003, 149–158. Both aggregate and per capita aid numbers are in constant 2001 dollars.

42. See Pejovich 2003.

43. Hayek (1960, 1973), North (1990, 2005), Platteau (2000), and Pejovich (2003) are clear exceptions.

44. See Gellner 1988 and North 1990.

45. North (1990) makes the critical distinction between institutions as the rules of the game and organizations as the players within those rules.

46. Kuran 2004a, 2004b.

47. Fukuyama 1995a, 9.

48. See Diamond 2005, 19–20 and Goldstone and Ulfelder 2004, 10.

49. The importance of culture for the acceptance or rejection of social and economic change is recognized by Boettke (2001b) and North (2005, 48–64).

50. See Demsetz 1969.

51. Owen (2005) extends Mansfield and Snyder's analysis of war between democracies to Iraq.

52. The term *blowback* refers to the unintended consequences of U.S. actions abroad. On the potential blowback generated by the war in Iraq, see Bergen and Reynolds 2005. For a broader analysis of the blowback generated by American foreign policy, see C. Johnson 2000.

53. See Nye 2002, 2004.

54. See Cowen 2002.

Chapter 2

1. See Tocqueville 1835/1839, 277–315.

2. See Schelling 1960.

3. See Boulding 1962.

4. Others using the game theoretic approach to analyze the process of democratization include Acemoglu and Robinson (2006), Colomer (2000), Crescenzi (1999), Gates and Humes (1997), Przeworski (1991), and Sutter (2000).

5. The game theoretic model put forth here was initially developed in Cowen and Coyne 2005.

6. Note that this indicates that $2\alpha > (\gamma + \theta) > 2\beta$, which is to say that mutual cooperation is the socially efficient outcome.

7. The folk theorem was discovered in the 1950s by a number of social scientists simultaneously. It was called the "folk theorem" because it was well known among social scientists, although no one had formally published it. Although he did not discover the folk theorem, Axelrod (1984) is well known for his contributions to the mechanisms for achieving sustained cooperation.

8. For a further discussion of this logic, see Wintrobe 1998. Makiya (1989) provides an analysis of how Saddam Hussein's regime operated in Iraq and serves as an application of this logic.

9. See Diamond 1990.

10. The tipping point model asserts that there is a critical mass stemming from the incremental actions of individuals that will yield collective changes. The model has been applied to a wide range of topics including AIDS, smoking, crime, fashion trends, and education. See Crane 1991, Granovetter 1978, Grodzins 1957, and Schelling 1978.

11. See Hardin 1995 and Mansfield and Snyder 2005.

12. See Coase 1960.

13. See, for instance, Cowen (2004), who applies the Coase theorem to the persistence of the conflict between the Israelis and Palestinians.

14. The mechanisms discussed in the next two chapters draw from previous work by Cowen (2004), Cowen and Coyne (2005), Coyne (2005, 2006a, 2006b), and Boettke and Coyne (2007).

Chapter 3

1. See, for instance, Dobbins et al. 2003, 10, 21.

2. For more on the constabulary force, see Carafano 2002, 75, and Ziemke 1975, 334–341.

3. The constabulary force was officially established in July of 1946. It existed prior to that date but consisted of only the commanding major general and his staff.

4. The troop figure is from Dobbins et al. 2003, 26.

5. For more on the protests in Japan, see Dower 1999, 259–267.

6. See Dobbins et at. 2003, 149–151.

7. The famine, which occurred from late 1991 to 1992, claimed an estimated 240,000 lives. The cause of the famine has been attributed to the armed conflict and plundering that took place during the civil war (Refugee Policy Group 1994, 5).

8. Source of data: Brookings Institute, Iraq Index, available through www.brookings.edu/fp/saban/iraq/index.pdf. Last accessed December 1, 2006.

9. For one example, see Knickmeyer and Brwari 2005.

10. For more on the problems in Iraq, see Baker and Hamilton 2006.

11. See Ibid., 12–26.

12. This section draws on Coyne 2006b.

13. Tocqueville 1835/1839.

14. For Tocqueville's discussion of the role of associations in America, see Ibid., Volume 2, Part II, Chapters 4–9, 509–529.

15. As a point of clarification, in *Democracy in America,* Tocqueville never uses the term *civil society* but instead refers to *associations.*

16. Tocqueville 1835/1839, 528–529.

17. For one example of the debate on how civil society matters, see Encarnación 2003, 715–717.

18. As Fareed Zakaria points out, "In the world of ideas, civil society is hot. It is almost impossible to read an article on foreign or domestic policy without coming across some mention of the concept" (1995,1). Among others, Diamond (2004) and Posner (2004) discuss the importance of civil society in the reconstruction of weak, failed, and post-conflict countries.

19. The Website for the World Bank's social capital initiative is www1.worldbank.org/prem/poverty/scapital.

20. For more on the increase in the percentage of aid being allocated to civil society development programs, see Carothers 1999, Carothers and Ottoway 2000, and Van Rooy 2000.

21. Van Rooy and Robinson 2000, 58–59.

22. Carothers 1999, 50.

23. For an overview of the research in this area, see Portes 1998; Dasgupta and Serageldin 2000; Lin 2001; and Lin, Cook, and Burt 2001.

24. Coleman 1988.

25. For work on social capital in political science, see Putnam 1992 and 2000, Putnam and Feldstein 2002, and Fukuyama 1995b and 1999. For work in the area of economics, see Knack and Keefer 1997; Glaeser, Laibson, and Sacerdote 2000; and Glaeser, Laibson, Scheinkman, and Soutter 2000.

26. For a discussion of the various challenges facing donor agencies, see Howell 2002.

27. In addition to those authors mentioned in the text, also see Huntington 1968 and 1991 and Lipset 1959, 1960, and 1994. On the importance of resolving cultural and ethnic divisions prior to the implementation of democratic institutions, see Rustow 1970.

28. Mill 1848, 82–83.

29. Bellin 2004–2005.

30. Hayek 1979, 107–108.

31. North 1990, 2005.

32. For more on the importance of complementary institutions, see Aoki 2001, 225–229.

33. See North 2005.

34. See Portes and Landolt 1996.

35. See, for instance, Berman 2003 and Iannaccone 2003.

36. On this point, see Encarnación 2003, 714.

37. This section draws on Coyne 2006a.

38. Tsebelis 1991.

39. For more on the relationship and tensions between the various ethnic and religious groups in Iraq, see Anderson and Stansfield 2004.

40. See Baker and Hamilton 2006, 13–19.

41. This skepticism stems beyond Iraq and is characteristic of the entire Middle East; see Telhami 2002.

42. The cited poll consisted of face-to-face interviews with 3,444 adults in all parts of Iraq, both urban and rural. The poll was conducted in Arabic and Kurdish by Iraqi interviewers hired and supervised by the Pan Arab Research Center of Dubai. An online version of the poll results is available at www.cnn.com/2004/WORLD/meast/04/28/iraq.poll/iraq.poll.4.28.pdf. Last accessed September 3, 2005.

43. Quoted in Tyler 2003.

44. Nordlinger 1971, 458.

45. Perhaps the most well-known study in this area is Ryan and Gross's 1943 study

of the diffusion of hybrid corn in Iowa. Other notable diffusion studies include Hagerstrand's 1967 study of the diffusion of TB tests in Sweden and Coleman, Katz, and Menzel's 1966 study of the diffusion of tetracycline among Midwestern doctors.

46. On the al-Sadr factor in the Iraq political process, see Cole 2003 and Allbritton, Ghosh, and Jasim 2005.

47. See Baker and Hamilton 2006, 14–15.

48. See Dower 1999, 330, 363.

49. Friedman 1948.

50. Kydland and Prescott 1977.

51. Boettke 1993, 2001a. For more on the problem of credible commitment see Shepsle 1991 and Weingast 1995.

52. Pons 1995, 347.

53. See Tullock 1985.

54. Cowen 2004, 4, emphasis original.

55. See Axelrod 1984.

56. D. Johnson 2004. Also see Kahneman and Renshon 2007.

57. On the point that individuals tend to think that their own worldview coincides with the interests of others, see Cowen 2005 and Klein 1994.

58. See Akerlof 1989, Cowen 2005, and Rabin and Shrag 1999. For discussions of self-deception from a psychological perspective, see Kruger and Dunning 1999 and Goleman 1985.

59. Diener 1984 and Frank 1989, 1997.

60. On the psychological state of the populace as a context-specific factor that will influence the nature of the reconstruction, see Bellin 2004–2005, 601.

61. For some of the relevant literature on the preconditions for democratization, see Bollen 1983; Burkhart and Lewis-Beck 1994; Doorenspleet 2004; Inglehart 1988; Linz and Stepan 1996; Lipset 1959, 1994; Moore 1966; Przeworski and Limongi 1997; Przeworski, Alvarez, Cheibub, and Limongi 2000; and Rustow 1970. Huntington (1991, 37–38) lists the many precondition variables that have been suggested as contributing to democratization and consolidation. See also Shin (1994), who reviews some of the relevant literature.

62. For some of the relevant literature focusing on the importance of bargaining and the role of political and economic actors in the democratization process, see Kitschelt 1992, O'Donnell and Schmitter 1986, and Przeworski 1991.

Chapter 4

1. Quoted in Dower 1999, 79.

2. Ibid., 205.

3. Two international bodies were created to oversee the U.S. occupation of Japan. These two bodies—the Far Eastern Advisory Commission and the Allied Council for Japan—were composed of eleven countries that had fought against Japan. Their main aim was to ensure that Japan met the terms of its surrender and also to review

the policies of the Supreme Commander for the Allied Powers. However, these bodies were not overly involved in the reconstruction. For one, they were convened only after much of the core policy had been implemented. In addition, MacArthur largely ignored the bodies and pursued his own course of action. For more on these oversight bodies, see Alden 1950.

4. Quoted in Peterson 1977, 67.

5. Ibid., 19.

6. Diamond 2005.

7. Phillips 2005.

8. See Diamond 2005, 27–31.

9. See Pillar 2006.

10. See Tannenhaus 2003.

11. Acemoglu 2003.

12. Luttwak 1994, 1995, and 1996 has developed and offered a defense of the casualty hypothesis. For some criticisms of the casualty hypothesis, see Burk 1999 and Larson 1996.

13. Mueller 1973, 60; 1994, 77; 1996; 2005. For a critique of Mueller's analysis of Iraq and his response, see Gelpi and Mueller 2005.

14. Feaver and Gelpi 2005.

15. The source of campaign contributions, contract value, and contract rank is The Center for the Public Integrity "Windfalls of War" project. The project Website is at www.publicintegrity.org/wow/. Last accessed June 1, 2007.

16. For a detailed analysis of the history of Halliburton's political connections, see Briody 2004.

17. Information on Halliburton's campaign contributions and U.S. government contracts is from Lewis and the Center for Public Integrity 2004, 196–197.

18. Ibid, 205.

19. See the "Windfalls of War" Project, note 15.

20. For a detailed analysis of the history of Bechtel's political connections, see McCartney 1988.

21. Phillips 2005, 71.

22. Dreyfuss 2002, 28.

23. Phillips 2005, 72.

24. See Strobel and Landay 2004.

25. For an account of the investigation and subsequent raids of the INC headquarters, see Bremer 2006, 363–364.

26. The classic studies of bureaucracy in political economy include Mises 1944, Niskanen 1971, and Tullock 1965.

27. Scheuer 2005, 185–192.

28. Ibid., 187.

29. Dreyfuss 2002.

30. Ibid., 26.

31. Pillar 2006.

32. Phillips 2005, 7.

33. Diamond 2005, 28–29.

34. Packer 2005, 113–120.

35. On this point, see Brennan and Buchanan 1985, 76–89.

36. See Davis 2002.

37. See Bilmes and Stiglitz 2006. Wallsten and Kosec (2005) attempt to estimate the direct costs of the war but also the costs that were avoided (that is, the benefit of removing the Hussein regime from power).

38. Bergen and Reynolds 2005.

39. Mises 1929.

40. C. Johnson 2000.

41. See Eizenstat, Porter, and Weinstein 2005, 139, and C. Johnson 2000, xiii–xv.

42. Scheuer 2003, 2005.

43. For a specific list of some of these interventions, see Scheuer 2005, 11–14. For a further discussion of how U.S. policies in the Arab world are a driving factor behind anti-American sentiment, see Gause 2005, 71–74.

44. Nenova 2004 and Nenova and Harford 2004. See also Coyne 2006a and Leeson 2006.

45. For some of the relevant literature on the democratic peace theory, see Brown, Lynn-Jones, and Miller 1996; Gowa 1999; Levy and Razin 2004; Lipson 2003; Oneal and Russett 1999; Ray 1998a and 1998b; Rummel 2003;, Russett, Oneal, and Davis 1998; Weart 2000; and the references therein.

46. Kant 1795.

47. President Bill Clinton, State of the Union Address, January 25, 1994. Available at www.washingtonpost.com/wp-srv/politics/special/states/docs/sou94.htm. Last accessed December 7, 2006.

48. Quote from White House press release, "President and Prime Minister Blair Discussed Iraq, Middle East," November 12, 2004. Available at www.whitehouse.gov/news/releases/2004/11/20041112-5.html. Last accessed December 7, 2006.

49. Mansfield and Snyder 2005.

50. In addition to Mansfield and Snyder, Samuel Huntington (1968) also emphasized the danger of weak political institutions to serve as a check on the increased demand for political participation in democratizing countries.

51. Bergen and Reynolds 2005.

52. Demsetz 1969.

53. See Leeson 2006.

54. Ibid.

55. Quoted in Packer 2005, 113.

56. See Phillips 2005; D. Johnson 2004, 196–213; and Pillar 2006.

57. D. Johnson 2004, 214.

58. See Huntington 2003, 310, and Jarvis 2003, 366.

Chapter 5

1. All postwar estimates are from Dower 1999, 45–47. On the devastation of Japan, see also Allinson 1997, 45–52.

2. See Gordon 2003, especially Chapter 9.

3. Ibid., 96–100.

4. On Japan's industrial development during the Meiji Restoration period, see Gordon 2003, 70–73.

5. Fukuyama 1995b, 165–167.

6. Ibid.

7. Dower 1999, 212.

8. See Gordon 2003, 234.

9. See Dower 1999, 330–339.

10. See Dower 1980.

11. Ibid., 306.

12. For an overview of the reforms undertaken by occupiers, see Allinson 1997, 52–63.

13. On the issue of censorship, see Dower 1999, 405–432.

14. See Bellin 2004–2005, 601.

15. On the exhaustion and despair that characterized the immediate postwar period in Japan, see Dower 1999, 87–120.

16. See Havens 1978, 130.

17. Dower 1999, 121.

18. Ibid., 261.

19. Ibid., 289–296.

20. Ibid., 389. For a discussion of the modifications to the constitution by the Diet, see Bailey 1996, 42–46.

21. Gordon 2003, 233–234.

22. Quoted in von Hippel 2000, 16.

23. Bailey 1996, 37–38, 55.

24. Ibid., 55.

25. Ibid., 35.

26. Peterson 1977, 114. For a firsthand description of the devastation, see Bach 1946, 17–27.

27. For a review of the relevant literature as well as one analysis of the impact of aid in the reconstruction, see Killick 1997. For arguments that are skeptical of the Marshall Plan's contribution to the revival of West Germany, see Cowen 1985 and Milward 1984.

28. Austria, which decided not to join, was the most notable country absent from the Customs Union.

29. Fukuyama 1995b, 209–219.

30. Ibid., 212.

31. See Bellin 2004–2005, 599.

32. See von Hippel 2000, 15.

33. Boehling 1996, 156.
34. Marshall 1989, 191.
35. Boehling 1996, 271.
36. Peterson 1977, 10.
37. Dobbins et al. 2003, 5.
38. See Bach 1946, 87–92.
39. Ibid., 27.
40. Davidson 1959, 48.
41. See Davidson 1959, 13, and Gimbel 1968, 245.
42. Peterson 1977, 138.
43. Ibid., 198.
44. Ibid.
45. Ibid., 20.
46. Ibid., 23–27.
47. Quoted in Peterson 1977, 34.
48. Ibid., 54–113.
49. Ibid., 54.
50. Ibid., 80. Also see Payne 2006b.
51. See Erhard 1958, 14.
52. Quoted in Peterson 1977, 191.
53. For one account of the immediate effect of Erhard's reforms, see Wallich 1955, 71.
54. The tension between the Allied forces can actually be traced to the Potsdam Agreement and its immediate aftermath. See Gimbel 1968, 16–18.
55. Peterson 1977, 70.
56. Ibid., 80.
57. Zingales 2003.
58. Bellin 2004–2005.

Chapter 6

1. See Eizenstat, Porter, and Weinstein 2005, 136.
2. The famine, which occurred from late 1991 to 1992, claimed an estimated 240,000 lives. The cause of the famine is attributed to the armed conflict and plundering that took place during the civil war. Refugee Policy Group 1994, 5.
3. UNSCR 814 indicated that it is critical to establish "transitional government institutions and consensus on basic principles and steps leading to the establishment of representative democratic institutions." Quoted in Dobbins et al. 2003, 67.
4. Dobbins et al. 2003, 58–60.
5. Clarke and Herbst 1996 estimate that 100,000 lives were saved due to the intervention. Also see Menkhaus, 2003.
6. Lewis 1961, 2–4; 1994.

7. *Diya* refers to Islamic blood compensation paid by a person who has committed homicide or wounded another individual.

8. Lewis 1965, 10–12; Adam 1995, 20; Brons 2001, 100–121; Shivakumar 2003, 14–6.

9. Menkhaus 2004, 38.

10. Brons 2001, 164.

11. Marchal 1996; Mubarak 1997, 2028–2029.

12. Somaliland includes the Awdal, Woqooyi Galbeed, Togdheer, Sanaag, and Sool regions.

13. Menkhaus 2004, 17.

14. See Nenova 2004, Nenova and Harford 2004, and Coyne 2006a.

15. For an analysis of the formation of the Somaliland constitution, see Shivakumar 2003.

16. See Leeson 2006.

17. Menkhaus 2004, 18.

18. One estimate of the costs of war approximated that a six-hour battle in Somalia costs the parties involved a total of at least $100,000. See Coke and al-Qaeda 2004.

19. Menkhaus 1996, 43.

20. Dempsey and Fontaine 2001, 45.

21. Ibid.

22. von Hippel 2000, 85.

23. See Buchanan 1975.

24. von Hippel 2000, 85.

25. For an analysis of the perverse effect of foreign aid in Somalia, see Maren 1997.

26. von Hippel 2000, 75.

27. For a list of problems with the UN occupation, see von Hippel 2000, 70–72.

28. Ibid., 75.

29. See von Hippel 2000, 74–78, and Dempsey and Fontaine 2001, 41–42.

30. Clarke and Herbst 1996, 73.

31. For a detailed discussion of these earlier efforts, see Dempsey and Fontaine 2001, 68–74. For an account of the U.S. occupation from 1915 through 1934, see Weinstein and Segal 1984, 22–30.

32. Dobbins et al. 2003, 72–3.

33. Rotberg 2004b, 19.

34. Ferguson 2004, 141.

35. See Heinl and Heinl 1996.

36. See Trouillot 1997, 50.

37. Bailey, Maguire, and Pouliot 1998, 215.

38. Weinstein and Segal 1984, 1–20.

39. Ibid., 2.

40. The estimate of the percentage of elites is from Dempsey and Fontaine 2001, 67.

41. Weinstein and Segal 1984, 3.

42. Ibid., 18.

43. On the array of mechanisms used by the Duvaliers in addition to brute force, see Trouillot 1990.

44. Trouillot 1997, 53.

45. Ibid., 51, 55.

46. See Dempsey and Fontaine 2001, 76–79. The United States invested $97 million in attempting to influence legal reform.

47. Easterly 2006, 147–148.

48. Ibid.

49. See Easterly 2001, 250–251, and 2006, 331.

50. On the improved coordination, see von Hippel 2000, 119.

51. See Coyne 2006a, Leeson 2006, Little 2003, Nenova 2004, and Nenova and Harford 2004.

52. Little 2003, 109.

53. Nenova and Harford 2004, 2, and Nenova 2004, 2–3.

54. Nenova and Harford 2004, 1.

55. Easterly 2001.

56. Easterly 2006.

57. Source of table and data is Easterly 2006, 218.

58. See Clapham 2004 and Herbst 2004. Also see Herbst 2000 for a discussion of the constraints on states to effectively broadcast their power.

Chapter 7

1. Baker and Hamilton 2006, 1.

2. See Rubin 2007.

3. "A Glass Half Full."

4. Ibid., and "Heading South."

5. "Heading South."

6. Ibid., and Rubin 2007.

7. "Afghanistan's Parliamentary Elections: Putting Steel into Karzai."

8. "Bleak Courthouse."

9. "Iraq's Government: Could It Prevail?"

10. Baker and Hamilton 2006.

11. "Murder Is Certain."

12. Ibid.

13. Rubin 2002, x.

14. Goodson 2001, 36.

15. Rubin 2002, 20.

16. Ibid.

17. See Goodson 2001, 19–20, and Rubin 2002, 25–26.

18. See Goodson 2001, 19.

19. Ibid., 101.

20. Ibid., 94.

21. Ibid., 94–95.
22. Military aid figures from Goodson 2001, 99.
23. Ibid., 169.
24. Estimates are from *CIA World Factbook*.
25. Anderson and Stansfield 2004, 16–17.
26. See Polk 2005.
27. ABC News Poll methodology and results available at http://abcnews.go.com/International/PollVault/story?id=1363276. Last accessed December 7, 2006.
28. "Afghanistan's Parliamentary Elections: Putting Steel in Karzai."
29. Telhami 2002, 9.
30. Scheuer 2005, 15.
31. Stephens and Ottaway 2005.
32. United States Government Accountability Office 2005, 4.
33. Ibid.
34. Quoted in Priest 2005.
35. Hearing before the Senate Intelligence Committee, 109th Congress, 1st Session, February 16, 2005.
36. Bergen and Reynolds 2006.
37. Nasr 2006.
38. Ibid., 65.
39. Ibid., 59.
40. Ibid., 60.

Chapter 8

1. Ferguson 2004, 198.
2. Ibid.
3. Marten 2004, 62.
4. Ferguson 2004, 201.
5. Ibid., 293.
6. Marten 2004.
7. Ibid., 158–164.
8. See Eland 2004, 146–147.
9. Ibid., 147.
10. For a study that empirically explores the regional impact of trade versus military occupation, see Leeson and Sobel 2006.
11. On the intellectual history of free trade, see Irwin 1996.
12. Dollar and Kraay 2004, F22. See also Bhagwati 2002.
13. For a concise summary of the connection between trade and growth, see Bhagwati 2004, 60–64.
14. Cline 2004.
15. See Bhagwati 2002, 50.
16. Cowen 2002.

17. Ibid., 16–17.

18. Friedman 2005.

19. Ibid., 4.

20. Appiah 2006.

21. Cowen 2002, 17–18.

22. Mueller 2005.

23. See Nye 2002, 2004.

24. Source of quote: www.liberty1.org/farewell.htm.

25. Source of quote: www.bartleby.com/124/pres16.html.

26. Quoted in Scheuer 2005, 200.

27. Office of the United States Trade Representative, www.ustr.gov/World_ Regions/Europe_Middle_East/Middle_East-North_Africa/Section_Index.html.

28. See, for instance, Özden and Reinhardt 2005.

29. For a classic study exploring the connection between trade and conflict, see Polacheck 1980.

30. On the ongoing debate regarding the effectiveness of economic sanctions, see Bhagwati 2002; Frey 2004, 37–41; Hufbauer, Schott, and Elliot 1990; and Pape 1997.

31. Barber 1995, Chua 2002, and Friedman 2000. For some of the costs and benefits of globalization, see Bhagwati 2004.

32. Huntington 2003.

References

A Glass Half Full. September 17, 2005. *Economist* 376(8444): 66.

Acemoglu, Daron. 2003. Why Not a Political Coase Theorem? Social Conflict, Commitment, and Politics. *Journal of Comparative Economics* 31: 620–652.

Acemoglu, Daron, and James A. Robinson. 2006. *Economic Origins of Dictatorship and Democracy.* New York: Cambridge University Press.

Adam, Hussein M. 1995. Somalia: A Terrible Beauty Being Born? In *Collapsed States: The Disintegration and Restoration of Legitimate Authority,* ed. William Zartman. Boulder, Colo.: Lynne Rienner Publishers.

Afghanistan's Parliamentary Elections: Putting Steel in Karzai. September 24, 2005. *Economist* 376(8445): 17.

Akerlof, George A. 1989. The Economics of Illusion. *Economics and Politics* 1: 1–15.

Alden, Jane M. 1950. Occupation. In *Japan,* ed. Hugh Borton. Ithaca, N.Y.: Cornell University Press.

Allbritton, Christopher, Aparisim Ghosh, and Meitham Jasim. 2005. The Al-Sadr Factor. *Time,* September 12, p. 18.

Allinson, Gary D. 1997. *Japan's Postwar History.* Ithaca, N.Y.: Cornell University Press.

Anderson, Liam, and Gareth Stansfield. 2004. *The Future of Iraq: Dictatorship, Democracy or Division?* New York: Palgrave McMillan.

Aoki, Masahiko. 2001. *Toward a Comparative Institutional Analysis.* Cambridge, Mass.: MIT Press.

Appiah, Kwame Anthony. 2006. *Cosmopolitanism.* New York: W.W. Norton.

Axelrod, Robert. 1984. *The Evolution of Cooperation.* New York: Basic Books.

Bach, Julian. 1946. *America's Germany: An Account of the Occupation.* New York: Random House.

Bailey, Michael, Robert Maguire, and J. O'Neil G. Pouliot. 1998. Haiti Military-Police Partnership for Public Security. In *Policing the New World Disorder: Peace Opera-*

tions and Public Security, eds. Robert Oakley, Michael Dziednic, and Eliot Goldberg. Washington D.C.: National Defense University Press.

Bailey, Paul. 1996. *Postwar Japan: 1945 to Present.* Malden, Mass.: Blackwell.

Baker, James A., and Lee H. Hamilton. 2006. *The Iraq Study Group Report.* New York: Vintage Books.

Barber, Benjamin. 1995. *Jihad vs. McWorld: How the Planet Is Both Falling Apart and Coming Together and What This Means for Democracy.* New York: Times Books.

Bates, Robert H., Avner Greif, Margaret Levi, Jean-Laurent Rosenthal, and Barry R. Weingast. 1998. *Analytic Narratives.* Princeton, N.J.: Princeton University Press.

Bellin, Eva. 2004–2005. The Iraqi Intervention and Democracy in Comparative Perspective. *Political Science Quarterly* 119(4): 595–608.

Bergen, Peter, and Alec Reynolds. 2005. Blowback Revisited: Today's Insurgents Are Tomorrow's Terrorists. *Foreign Affairs* 84(6): 2–6.

Berman, Eli. 2003. Hamas, Taliban and the Jewish Underground: An Economist's View of Radical Religious Militias. *National Bureau of Economic Research Working Paper* No. 10004.

Bhagwati, Jagdish. 2002. *Free Trade Today.* Princeton, N.J.: Princeton University Press.
———. 2004. *In Defense of Globalization.* New York: Oxford University Press.

Bilmes, Linda, and Joseph Stiglitz. 2006. The Economic Costs of the Iraq War: An Appraisal Three Years After the Beginning of the Conflict. *National Bureau of Economic Research Working Paper* No. 12054.

Bleak Courthouse. April 15, 2006. *Economist* 379(8473): 66.

Boehling, Rebecca. 1996. *A Question of Priorities: Democratic Reform and Economic Recovery in Postwar Germany.* Providence, R.I.: Berghahn Books.

Boettke, Peter J. 1993. *Why Perestroika Failed: The Politics and Economics of Socialist Transformation.* New York: Routledge.
———. 2001a. Credibility, Commitment, and Society Economic Reform. In *Calculation and Coordination,* ed. Peter J. Boettke. New York: Routledge.
———. 2001b. Why Culture Matters: Economics, Politics and the Imprint of History. In *Calculation and Coordination,* ed. Peter J. Boettke. New York: Routledge.

Boettke, Peter J., and Christopher J. Coyne. 2007. Liberalism in the Post-9/11 World. *Indian Journal of Business and Economics.* Special Issue: 35–53.

Bollen, Kenneth A. 1983. World System Position, Dependency and Democracy: The Cross National Evidence. *American Sociological Review* 48: 468–479.

Boulding, Kenneth E. 1962. *Conflict and Defense: A General Theory.* New York: Harper & Row.

Bremer, L. Paul III. 2006. *My Year in Iraq.* New York: Simon & Schuster.

Brennan, Geoffrey, and James M. Buchanan. 1985. *The Reason of Rules: Constitutional Political Economy.* Cambridge: Cambridge University Press.

Briody, Dan. 2004. *The Halliburton Agenda.* Hoboken, N. J.: John Wiley & Sons.

Brons, Maria H. 2001. *Society, Security, Sovereignty and the State: Somalia.* Utrecht, Netherlands: International Books.

Brown, Michael E., Sean M. Lynn-Jones, and Steven E. Miller (eds.). 1996. *Debating the Democratic Peace*. Cambridge, Mass.: MIT Press.

Buchanan, James M. 1975. The Samaritan's Dilemma. In *Altruism, Morality, and Economic Theory*, ed. Edmund S. Phelps. New York: Russell Sage Foundation.

Burk, James. 1999. Public Support for Peacekeeping in Lebanon and Somalia: Assessing the Casualties Hypothesis. *Political Science Quarterly* 114(1): 53–78.

Burkhart, Ross E., and Michael S. Lewis-Beck. 1994. Comparative Democracy: The Economic Development Thesis. *American Political Science Review* 88: 903–910.

Carafano, James J. 2002. *Waltzing into the Cold War: The Struggle for Occupied Austria*. College Station: Texas A&M University Press.

Carothers, Thomas. 1999. *Aiding Democracy Abroad: The Learning Curve*. Washington, D.C.: Carnegie Endowment for International Peace.

Carothers, Thomas, and Marina Ottoway. 2000. The Burgeoning World of Civil Society Aid. In *Funding Virtue: Civil Society and Democracy Aid*, eds. Thomas Carothers and Marina Ottoway. Washington, D.C.: Carnegie Endowment for International Peace.

Chua, Amy. 2002. *World on Fire*. New York: Doubleday.

CIA World Factbook. 2007. www.cia.gov/cia/publications/factbook/index.html.

Clapham, Christopher. 2004. The Global-Local Politics of State Decay. In *When States Fail: Causes and Consequences*, ed. Robert I. Rotberg. Princeton, N.J.: Princeton University Press.

Clarke, Walter, and Jeffrey Herbst. 1996. Somalia and the Future of Humanitarian Intervention. *Foreign Affairs* 75(2): 70–85.

Cline, William. 2004. *Trade Policy and Global Poverty*. Washington, D.C.: Institute for International Economics.

Coase, Ronald H. 1960. The Problem of Social Cost. *Journal of Law and Economics* 3: 1–44.

Coke and al-Qaeda. April 3, 2004. *Economist* 371(8369): 58.

Cole, Juan. 2003. The United States and the Shi'ite Religious Factions in Post-Ba'thist Iraq. *The Middle East Journal* 57(4): 543–566.

Coleman, James S. 1988. Social Capital in the Creation of Human Capital. *American Journal of Sociology* 94(supplement): S95–S120.

Coleman, James S., Elihu Katz, and Herbert Menzel. 1966. *Medical Innovation: A Diffusion Study*. New York: Bobbs Merrill.

Colomer, Josep M. 2000. *Strategic Transitions: Game Theory and Democratization*. Baltimore: Johns Hopkins University.

Cowen, Tyler. 1985. The Marshall Plan: Myth and Realities. In *U.S. Aid to the Developing World*, ed. Doug Bandow. Washington, D.C.: Heritage Foundation.

———. 2002. *Creative Destruction*. Princeton, N.J.: Princeton University Press.

———. 2004. A Road Map to Middle Eastern Peace? A Public Choice Perspective. *Public Choice* 118: 1–10.

———. 2005. Self-Deception as the Root of Political Failure. *Public Choice* 124: 437–451.

Cowen, Tyler, and Christopher J. Coyne. 2005. Postwar Reconstruction: Some Insights from Public Choice and Institutional Economics. *Constitutional Political Economy* 16: 31–48.

Coyne, Christopher J. 2005. The Institutional Prerequisites for Post-Conflict Reconstruction. *Review of Austrian Economics* 18(3/4): 325–342.

———. 2006a. Reconstructing Weak and Failed States: Foreign Intervention and the Nirvana Fallacy. *Foreign Policy Analysis* 2: 343–361.

———. 2006b. Reconstructing Weak and Failed States: Insights from Tocqueville. *Journal of Social, Political and Economic Studies* 31(2): 143–162.

Crane, Jonathan. 1991. The Epidemic Theory of Ghettos and Neighborhood Effects on Dropping Out and Teenage Childbearing. *American Journal of Sociology* 96: 1266–1259.

Crescenzi, Mark J. C. 1999. Violence and Uncertainty in Transitions. *Journal of Conflict Resolution* 43: 192–212.

Dahl, Robert A. 1971. *Polyarchy: Participation and Opposition*. New Haven, Conn.: Yale University Press.

———. 1998. *On Democracy*. New Haven, Conn.: Yale University Press.

Damrosch, Lori F. 1993. *Enforcing Restraint: Collective Intervention in Internal Conflicts*. New York: Council on Foreign Relations Press.

Dasgupta, Partha, and Ismail Serageldin. 2000. *Social Capital: A Multifaceted Perspective*. Washington D.C.: World Bank.

Davenport, Christian, and David A. Armstrong. 2004. Democracy and the Violation of Human Rights: A Statistical Analysis from 1976 to 1996. *American Journal of Political Science* 48(3): 538–554.

Davidson, Eugene. 1959. *The Death and Life of Germany*. New York: Alfred A. Knopf.

Davis, Bob. September 16, 2002. Bush Economic Aide Says Cost of Iraq War May Top $100 Billion. *The Wall Street Journal*, 1.

De Haan, Jakob, and Clemens L. J. Siermann. 1996. New Evidence on the Relationship Between Democracy and Economic Growth. *Public Choice* 86(1): 175–98.

Dempsey, Gary T., and Roger W. Fontaine. 2001. *Fool's Errands: America's Recent Encounters with Nation Building*. Washington, D.C.: The Cato Institute.

Demsetz, Harold. 1969. Information and Efficiency: Another Viewpoint. *Journal of Law and Economics* 10: 1–21.

Diamond, Larry. 1990. Three Paradoxes of Democracy. *Journal of Democracy* 1(3): 48–60.

———. 2004. What Went Wrong in Iraq? *Foreign Affairs* 83(5): 34–56.

———. 2005. *Squandered Victory: The American Occupation and the Bungled Effort to Bring Democracy to Iraq*. New York: Times Books.

Diamond, Larry, Juan J. Linz, and Seymor M. Lipset. 1995. Introduction: What Makes for Democracy? In *Politics in Developing Countries: Comparing Experiences with Democracy*, 2nd ed., eds. Larry Diamond, Juan J. Linz, and Seymor M. Lipset. Boulder, Colo.: Lynne Rienner Publishers.

Diener, Edward F. 1984. Subjective Well-Being. *Psychological Bulletin* 95: 542–75.

Dobbins, James, et al. 2003. *America's Role in Nation-Building: From Germany to Iraq.* Santa Monica, Calif.: RAND.

Dollar, David, and Aart Kraay. 2004. Trade, Growth, and Poverty. *The Economic Journal* 114(293): F22–F49.

Doorenspleet, Renske. 2004. The Structural Context of Recent Transitions to Democracy. *European Journal of Political Research* 43(3): 309–335.

Dower, John W. 1980. *Empire and Aftermath: Yoshida Shiqeru and the Japanese Empire, 1878–1954.* Boston: Harvard Council on East Asian Studies.

———. 1999. *Embracing Defeat: Japan in the Wake of World War II.* New York: W.W. Norton.

Dreyfuss, Robert. 2002. The Pentagon Muzzles the CIA. *The American Prospect* 13(22): 26–29.

Easterly, William. 2001. *The Elusive Quest for Growth.* Cambridge, Mass.: The MIT Press.

———. 2006. *The White Man's Burden.* New York: Penguin.

Eizenstat, Stuart, John E. Porter, and Jeremy Weinstein. 2005. Rebuilding Weak States. *Foreign Affairs* 84(1): 134–146.

Eland, Ivan. 2004. *The Empire Has No Clothes.* Oakland, Calif.: The Independent Institute.

Encarnación, Omar G. 2003. Beyond Civil Society: Promoting Democracy After September 11. *Orbis* 47(4): 705–720.

Erhard, Ludwig. 1958. *Prosperity Through Competition.* New York: Praeger.

Feaver, Peter D., and Christopher Gelpi. 2005. *Choosing Your Battles: American Civil Military Relations and the Use of Force.* Princeton, N.J.: Princeton University Press.

Ferguson, Niall. 2004. *Colossus: The Price of America's Empire.* New York: Penguin.

Fish, M. Steven, and Robin S. Brooks. 2004. Does Diversity Hurt Democracy? *Journal of Democracy* 15(1): 154–166.

Frank, Robert H. 1989. Frames of Reference and the Quality of Life. *American Economic Review* 79: 80–85.

———. 1997. The Frame of Reference as a Public Good. *The Economic Journal* 107: 1832–1847.

Frey, Bruno S. 2004. *Dealing with Terrorism—Stick or Carrot?* Cheltenham, United Kingdom: Edward Elgar.

Friedman, Benjamin. 2005. *The Moral Consequences of Economic Growth.* New York: Alfred A. Knopf.

Friedman, Milton. 1948. A Monetary and Fiscal Framework for Economic Stability. *American Economic Review* 38(3): 245–264.

Friedman, Thomas. 2000. *The Lexus and the Olive Tree.* New York: Anchor Books.

Fukuyama, Francis. 1995a. The Primacy of Culture. *Journal of Democracy* 6(1): 7–14.

———. 1995b. *Trust.* New York: Simon & Schuster.

———. 1999. *The Great Disruption.* New York: The Free Press.

———. 2004. *State-Building: Governance and World Order in the 21st Century.* Ithaca, N.Y.: Cornell University Press.

Gasiorowski, Mark J., and Timothy J. Power. 1998. The Structural Determinants of Democratic Consolidation. *Comparative Political Studies* 31: 740–771.

Gates, Scott, and Brian D. Humes. 1997. *Games, Information and Politics.* Ann Arbor, Mich.: University of Michigan Press.

Gause, F. Gregory III. 2005. Can Democracy Stop Terrorism? *Foreign Affairs* 84(5): 62–76.

Gellner, Ernest. 1988. *Plough, Book and Sword.* London: Collins Harvill.

Gelpi, Christopher, and John E. Mueller. 2006. The Cost of War: How Many Casualties Will Americans Tolerate? *Foreign Affairs* 85(1): 139–144.

Gimbel, John. 1968. *The American Occupation of Germany.* Stanford, Calif.: Stanford University Press.

Glaeser, Edward, David Laibson, and Bruce Sacerdote. 2000. The Economic Approach to Social Capital. *National Bureau of Economic Research Working Paper* No. 7728.

Glaeser, Edward, David Laibson, Jose Scheinkman, and Christine Soutter. 2000. Measuring Trust. *Quarterly Journal of Economics* 115: 811–841.

Goldstone, Jack A., and Jay Ulfelder. 2004. How to Construct Stable Democracies. *The Washington Quarterly* 28(1): 9–20.

Goleman, Daniel. 1985. *Vital Lies, Simple Truths: The Psychology of Self-Deception.* New York: Simon & Schuster.

Goodson, Larry P. 2001. *Afghanistan's Endless War.* Seattle: University of Washington Press.

Gordon, Andrew. 2003. *A Modern History of Japan.* New York: Oxford University Press.

Gott, Richard. 2004. *Cuba: A New History.* New Haven, Conn.: Yale University Press.

Gowa, Joanne. 1999. *Ballots and Bullets: The Elusive Democratic Peace.* Princeton, N.J.: Princeton University Press.

Granovetter, Mark. 1978. Threshold Models of Collective Behavior. *American Journal of Sociology.* 83(6): 1420–1443.

Greif, Avner. 2006. *Institutions and the Path to the Modern Economy.* Cambridge, Mass.: Cambridge University Press.

Grodzins, Morton. 1957. Metropolitan Segregation. *Scientific America* 24: 33–41.

Hagerstrand, Torsten. 1967. *Innovation Diffusion as a Spatial Process.* Chicago: University of Chicago Press.

Hardin, Russell. 1995. *One for All: The Logic of Group Conflict.* Princeton, N.J.: Princeton University Press.

Havens, Thomas. 1978. *Valley of Darkness: The Japanese People and World War Two.* New York: Norton.

Hayek, F. A. 1960. *The Constitution of Liberty.* Chicago: The Chicago University Press.

———. 1973. *Law, Legislation and Liberty, Volume I: Rules and Order.* Chicago: The University of Chicago Press.

————. 1979. *Law, Legislation and Liberty, Volume III: The Political Order of a Free People*. Chicago: The University of Chicago Press.

Heading South, February 4, 2006, *Economist* 378(8463): 12.

Heiberg, Marianne (ed.). 1994. *Subduing Sovereignty: Sovereignty and the Right to Intervene*. London: Printer Publishers.

Heinl, Robert Debs, and Nancy Gordon Heinl. 1996. *Written in Blood*. Lanham, Md.: University Press of America.

Heller, Walter W. 1950. The Role of Fiscal-Monetary Policy in German Economic Recovery. *The American Economic Review* 40(2): 531–547

Herbst, Jeffrey. 2000. *States and Power in Africa*. Princeton, N.J.: Princeton University Press.

————. 2004. Let Them Fail: State Failure in Theory and Practic. In *When States Fail: Causes and Consequences*, ed. Robert I. Rotberg. Princeton, N.J.: Princeton University Press.

Hoffmann, Stanley, Robert C. Johansen, James P. Sterba, and Raimo Vayrynen. 1996. *The Ethics and Politics of Humanitarian Intervention*. Notre Dame, Ind.: University of Notre Dame Press.

Howell, Jude. 2002. In Their Own Image: Donor Assistance to Civil Society. *Lusotopie* 1: 117–130.

Hufbauer, Gary Clyde, Jeffrey J. Schott, and Kimberly Ann Elliot. 1990. *Economic Sanctions Reconsidered*, 2nd ed. Washington, D.C.: Institute for International Economics.

Hunt, Michael H. 1987. *Ideology and U.S. Foreign Policy*. New Haven, Conn.: Yale University Press.

Huntington, Samuel P. 1968. *Political Order in Changing Societies*. New Haven, Conn.: Yale University Press.

————. 1991. *The Third Wave: Democratization in the Late Twentieth Century*. Norman: University of Oklahoma Press.

————. 2003. *The Clash of Civilizations and the Remaking of World Order*. New York: Simon & Schuster.

Iannaccone, Laurence R. 2003. The Market for Martyrs. Mimeo. Department of Economics, George Mason University, Fairfax, Virginia.

Ignatieff, Michael. 2003. *Lesser Evil: Political Ethics in an Age of Terror*. Princeton, N.J.: Princeton University Press.

Inglehart, Ronald. 1988. The Renaissance of Political Culture. *American Political Science Review* 82: 1203–1230.

Iraq's Government: Could It Prevail? May 27, 2006. *Economist* 379(8479): 66.

Irwin, Douglas A. 1996. *Against the Tide*. Princeton, N.J.: Princeton University Press.

Jarvis, Robert. 2003. Understanding the Bush Doctrine. *Political Science Quarterly* 118(3): 365–388.

Johnson, Chalmers. 2000. *Blowback: The Costs and Consequences of American Empire*. New York: Henry Holt.

Johnson, Dominic. 2004. *Overconfidence and War: The Havoc and Glory of Positive Illusions.* Boston: Harvard University Press.

Kahneman, Daniel, and Jonathan Renshon. 2007. Why Hawks Win. *Foreign Policy* 158: 34–38.

Kant, Immanuel. 1795 [2003]. *To Perpetual Peace: A Philosophical Sketch.* Trans. Ted Humphrey. Indianapolis: Hackett.

Keller, Jonathan W. 2005. Leadership Style, Regime Type, and Foreign Crisis Behavior: A Contingent Monadic Peace? *International Studies Quarterly* 49(2): 205–231.

Keynes, John Maynard. 1980. *The Collected Writings of John Maynard Keynes: Volume XXV: Activities 1940–44, Shaping the Post-War World: The Clearing Union,* ed. Donald Moggridge. London: Macmillan, for the Royal Economic Society.

Killick, John. 1997. *The United States and European Reconstruction: 1945–1960.* Edinburgh: Keele University Press.

King, Neil Jr. May 1, 2003. Bush Officials Devise a Broad Plan for Free-Market Economy in Iraq. *New York Times: A01.*

Kitschelt, Herbert. 1992. Political Regime Change: Structure and Process-Driven Explanations. *American Political Science Review* 86: 1028–1034.

Klein, Daniel B. 1994. If Government Is So Villainous, How Come Government Officials Don't Seem Like Villains? *Economics and Philosophy* 10: 91–106.

Knack, Stephen, and Philip Keefer. 1995. Institutions and Economic Performance: Cross Country Tests Using Alternative Measures. *Economics and Politics* 7(3): 207–227.

———. 1997. Does Social Capital Have an Economic Pay Off? A Cross-Country Investigation. *Quarterly Journal of Economics* 112: 1251–1288.

Knickmeyer, Ellen, and Dlovan Brwari. August 20, 2005. 3 Sunni Activists Killed in Iraq. *The Washington Post,* A01.

Kruger, Justin, and David Dunning. 1999. Unskilled and Unaware of It: How Difficulties in Recognizing One's Own Incompetence Lead to Inflated Self-Assessments. *Journal of Personality and Social Psychology* 77(6): 1121–1134.

Kuran, Timur. 2004a. Why the Middle East Is Economically Underdeveloped: Historical Mechanisms of Institutional Stagnation. *The Journal of Economic Perspectives* 18(3): 71–90.

———. 2004b. *Islam and Mammon: The Economic Predicaments of Islamism.* Princeton, N.J.: Princeton University Press.

Kydland, Finn E., and Prescott, Edward. 1977. Rules Rather Than Discretion: The Inconsistency of Optimal Plans. *Journal of Political Economy* 85(3): 473–491.

LaFeber, Walter. 1993. *The American Search for Opportunity, 1865–1913.* New York: Cambridge University Press.

Larson, Eric V. 1996. *Casualties and Consensus: The Historical Role of Casualties in Domestic Support for U.S. Wars and Military Operations.* Santa Monica, Calif.: RAND, MR-726-RC.

Lawson, Chappell, and Strom C. Thacker. 2003. Democracy? In Iraq? *Hoover Digest* 3, www.hooverdigest.org/033/lawson.html.

Leeson, Peter T. 2006. Better Off Stateless: Somalia Before and After State Collapse. Mimeo. Department of Economics, George Mason University, Fairfax, Virginia.

Leeson, Peter T., and Russell S. Sobel. 2006. Contagious Capitalism. Mimeo. Department of Economics, West Virginia University, Morgantown, West Virginia.

Levy, Gilat, and Ronny Razin. 2004. It Takes Two: An Explanation for the Democratic Peace. *Journal of the European Economic Association* 2(1): 1–29.

Lewis, Charles, and the Center for Public Integrity. 2004. *The Buying of the President: Who's Really Bankrolling Bush and His Democratic Challengers—And What They Expect in Return.* New York: HarperCollins.

Lewis, I. M. 1961. *A Pastoral Democracy.* New York: Africana.

———. 1965. *The Modern History of Somaliland.* London: Weidenfeld and Nicolson.

———. 1994. *Blood and Bone: The Call of Kinship in Somali Society.* New Jersey: The Red Sea Press.

Lin, Nan. 2001. *Social Capital: A Theory of Social Structure and Action.* Cambridge, U.K.: Cambridge University Press.

Lin, Nan, Karen Cook, and Ronald S. Burt (eds.). 2001. *Social Capital: Theory and Research.* New York: Aldine de Gruyter.

Linz, Juan J., and Alfred Stepan. 1996. *Problems of Democratic Transition and Consolidation.* Baltimore, Md.: The Johns Hopkins University Press.

Lipset, Seymour M. 1959. Some Social Requisites of Democracy: Economic Development and Political Legitimacy. *American Political Science Review* 53: 69–105.

———. 1960. *Political Man: The Social Bases of Politics.* New York: Doubleday.

———. 1994. The Social Requisites of Democracy Revisited. *American Sociological Review* 59: 1–22.

Lipson, Charles. 2003. *Reliable Partners: How Democracies Have Made a Separate Peace.* Princeton, N.J.: Princeton University Press.

Little, Peter D. 2003. *Somalia: Economy Without a State.* Bloomington: Indiana University Press.

Lowenthal, Abraham F. (ed.). 1991. *Exporting Democracy: The United States and Latin America.* Baltimore: Johns Hopkins University Press.

Lugo, Luis E. 1996. *Sovereignty at the Crossroads? Morality and International Politics in the Post–Cold War Era.* Lanham, Md.: Rowman and Littlefield.

Luttwak, Edward N. 1994. Where Are the Great Powers? Home with the Kids. *Foreign Affairs* 73(4): 23–28.

———. 1995. Toward a Post-Heroic Warfare. *Foreign Affairs* 74(3): 109–122.

———. 1996. A Post-Heroic Military Policy. *Foreign Affairs* 75(4): 33–44.

Mainwaring, Scott. 1993. Presidentialism, Multipartyism, and Democracy: The Difficult Equation. *Comparative Political Studies* 26(2): 198–228.

Makiya, Kanan. 1989. *Republic of Fear: The Politics of Modern Iraq.* Berkeley, Calif.: University of California Press.

Mansfield, Edward D., and Jack Snyder. 2005. *Electing to Fight: Why Emerging Democracies Go to War.* Cambridge, Mass.: MIT Press.

Marchal, Roland. 1996. *The Post Civil War Somali Business Class*. Research report for the European Commission Somalia Unit, Nairobi.

Maren, Michael. 1997. *The Road to Hell*. New York: The Free Press.

Marshall, Barbara. 1989. British Democratisation Policy in Germany. In *Reconstruction in Post War Germany*, ed. Ian D. Turner. New York: St Martin's Press.

Marshall, Monty G., and Keith Jaggers. 2003. Polity IV Project: Dataset Users Manual. Center for International Development and Conflict Management, University of Maryland, www.cidcm.umd.edu/inscr/polity.

Marten, Kimberly Zisk. 2004. *Enforcing the Peace*. New York: Columbia University Press.

McCartney, Laton. 1988. *Friends in High Places*. New York: Simon & Schuster.

Menkhaus, Kenneth. 1996. International Peacekeeping and the Dynamics of Local and National Reconciliation in Somalia. *International Peacekeeping* 3(1): 42–67.

———. 2003. State Collapse in Somalia: Second Thoughts. *Review of African Political Economy* 30(96): 405–422.

———. 2004. *Somalia: State Collapse and the Threat of Terrorism*. Washington, D.C.: International Institute for Strategic Studies.

Mierzejewski, Alfred C. 2004. *Ludwig Erhard: A Biography*. Chapel Hill: The University of North Carolina Press.

Mill, John Stuart. 1848. *Principles of Political Economy*. New York: D. Appleton and Company.

Milward, Alan S. 1984. *The Reconstruction of Western Europe, 1945–51*. Berkeley, Calif.: University of California Press.

Mises, Ludwig von. 1929 [1977]. *A Critique of Interventionism: Inquiries into Economic Policy and the Economic Ideology of the Present*, trans. Hans F. Sennholz. New York: Arlington House.

———. 1944 [1983]. *Bureaucracy*. Grove City, Penn.: Libertarian Press.

———. 2000. *The Selected Writings of Ludwig von Mises, Volume 3: The Political Economy of International Reform and Reconstruction*, ed. Richard Ebeling. Indianapolis: Liberty Fund.

Moore, Barrington. 1966. *Social Origins of Dictatorship and Democracy*. London: Penguin.

Mubarak, Jamil A. 1997. The "Hidden Hand" Behind the Resiliance of the Stateless Economy of Somalia. *World Development* 25: 2027–2041.

Mueller, John E. 1973. *War, Presidents and Public Opinion*. New York: John Wiley & Sons.

———. 1994. *Policy and Opinion in the Gulf War*. Chicago: University of Chicago Press.

———. 1996. Policy Principles for Unthreatened Wealth-Seekers. *Foreign Policy* 102: 22–33.

———. 2005. The Iraq Syndrome. *Foreign Affairs* 84(6): 44–54.

Munck, Gerardo L., and Jay Verkuilen. 2002. Conceptualizing and Measuring Democracy: Evaluating Alternative Indices. *Comparative Political Studies* 35(1): 3–34.

Murder Is Certain: Three Years After America Invaded, Iraq Is as Violent as Ever. March 25, 2006. *Economist* 378(8470): 69.

Nasr, Vali. 2006. When the Shiites Rise. *Foreign Affairs* 85(4): 58–74.

National Intelligence Council. 2004. Mapping the Global Future. Available online at www.dni.gov/nic/NIC_globaltrend2020.html. Last accessed June 19, 2006.

Nenova, Tatiana. 2004. Private Sector Response to the Absence of Government Institutions in Somalia. Washington, D.C.: The World Bank.

Nenova, Tatiana, and Tim Harford. 2004. Anarchy and Invention: How Does Somalia Cope Without Government? *Public Policy for the Private Sector.* Washington, D.C.: The World Bank.

Niskanen, William N. 1971. *Bureaucracy and Representative Government.* Chicago: Aldine-Atherton.

Nordlinger, Eric. 1971. Political Development, Time Sequences and Rates of Change. In *Political Development and Social Change*, 2nd ed., eds. Jason L. Finkle and Richard Gable. New York: John Wiley & Sons.

North, Douglass. 1990. *Institutions, Institutional Change and Economic Performance.* Cambridge, Mass.: Cambridge University Press.

———. 2005. *Understanding the Process of Economic Change.* Princeton, N.J.: Princeton University Press.

Nye, Joseph S. Jr. 2002. *The Paradox of American Power.* New York: Oxford University Press.

———. 2004. *Soft Power: The Means to Success in World Politics.* New York: Public Affairs.

Offner, John L. 1992. *An Unwanted War: The Diplomacy of the United States and Spain Over Cuba, 1895–1898.* Chapel Hill: University of North Carolina Press.

O'Donnell, Guillermo, and Phillipe C. Schmitter. 1986. Tentative Conclusions About Uncertain Democracies. In *Transitions from Authoritarian Rule: Prospects for Democracy*, eds. Guillermo O'Donnell, Philippe C. Schmitter, and Laurence Whitehead. Baltimore, Md.: Johns Hopkins University Press.

Ohlin, Bertil. 1929. The Reparation Problem: A Discussion. *Economic Journal* 39: 172–183.

O'Loughlin, John, et al. 1998. The Diffusion of Democracy, 1946–1994. *Annals of the Association of American Geographers* 88: 545–574.

Oneal, John R., and Bruce Russett. 1999. The Kantian Peace: The Pacific Benefits of Democracy, Interdependence, and International Organizations. World Politics 52(1): 1–37.

Owen, John M. IV. 2005. Iraq and the Democratic Peace: Who Says Democracies Don't Fight? *Foreign Affairs* 84(6): 122–127.

Özden, Çaglar, and Eric Reinhardt. 2005. The Perversity of Preferences: GSP and Developing Country Trade Policies, 1976–2000. *Journal of Development Economics* 78: 1–21.

Packer, George. 2005. *The Assassins' Gate.* New York: Farrar, Straus and Giroux.

Pape, Robert A. 1997. Why Economic Sanctions Do Not Work. *International Security* 22(2): 90–136.

Paris, Roland. 2004. *At War's End: Building Peace After Civil Conflict.* Cambridge, U.K.: Cambridge University Press.

Payne, James L. 2006a. Does Nation Building Work? *The Independent Review* X(4): 597–608.

———. 2006b. Did the United States Create Democracy in Germany? *The Independent Review* XI(2): 209–211.

Pei, Minxin. 2003. Lessons from the Past. *Foreign Policy* 137: 52–55.

Pei, Minxin, and Sara Kasper. 2003. Lessons from the Past: The American Record on Nation Building. *Policy Brief 24.* Washington, D.C.: Carnegie Endowment for International Peace.

Pejovich, Svetozar. 2003. Understanding the Transaction Costs of Transition: It's the Culture, Stupid. *The Review of Austrian Economics* 16(4): 341–361.

Pérez, Louis A. Jr. 1990. *Cuba and the United States: Tiers of Singular Intimacy.* Athens: University of Georgia Press.

Peterson, Edward N. 1977. *The American Occupation of Germany: Retreat to Victory.* Detroit: Wayne State University Press.

Phillips, David L. 2005. *Losing Iraq: Inside the Postwar Reconstruction Fiasco.* New York: Basic Books.

Pillar, Paul R. 2006. Intelligence, Policy, and the War in Iraq. *Foreign Affairs* 85(2): 15–28.

Platteau, Jean-Philippe. 2000. *Institutions, Social Norms, and Economic Development.* Amsterdam: Harwood.

Polacheck, Solomon. 1980. Conflict and Trade. *Journal of Conflict Resolution.* 24: 55–78.

Polk, William R. 2005. *Understanding Iraq.* New York: HarperCollins.

Pons, Frank M. 1995. *The Dominican Republic: A National History.* Princeton, N.J.: Mark Wiener Publishers.

Portes, Alejandro. 1998. Social Capital: Its Origins and Applications in Modern Sociology. *Annual Review of Sociology* 24: 1–24.

Portes, Alejandro, and Patricia Landolt. 1996. Unsolved Mysteries. The Tocqueville File II: The Downside of Social Capital. *The American Prospect* 7(26): 18–21.

Posner, Daniel N. 2004. Civil Society and the Reconstruction of Failed States. In *When States Fail: Causes and Consequences,* ed. Robert I. Rotberg. Princeton, N.J.: Princeton University Press.

Priest, Dana. January 4, 2005. Iraq New Terror Breeding Ground. *The Washington Post,* A01.

Przeworski, Adam. 1991. *Democracy and the Market.* New York: Cambridge University Press.

Przeworski, Adam, Michael E. Alvarez, Jose Antonio Cheibub, and Fernando Limongi. 2000. *Democracy and Development.* Cambridge, Mass.: Cambridge University Press.

Przeworski, Adam, and Fernando Limongi. 1997. Modernization: Theories and Facts. *World Politics* 49: 155–183.

Putnam, Robert D. 1992. *Making Democracy Work: Civic Traditions in Modern Italy.* Princeton, N.J.: Princeton University Press.

———. 2000. *Bowling Alone.* New York: Simon & Schuster.

Putnam, Robert D., and Lewis M. Feldstein. 2002. *Better Together.* New York: Simon & Schuster.

Rabin, Matthew, and Joel E. Schrag. 1999. First Impressions Matter: A Model of Confirmatory Bias. *Quarterly Journal of Economics* 114(1): 37–81.

Ray, James Lee. 1998a. Does Democracy Cause Peace? *Annual Review of Political Science* 1: 27–46.

———. 1998b. *Democracy and International Conflict: An Evaluation of the Democratic Peace Proposition.* Columbia: University of South Carolina Press.

Refugee Policy Group. 1994. *Hope Restored? Humanitarian Aid in Somalia 1990–1994.* Washington D.C.: Refugee Policy Group, Center for Policy Analysis and Research on Refugee Issues.

Ricks, Thomas E. 2006. *Fiasco: The American Military Adventure in Iraq.* New York: Penguin.

Rotberg, Robert I. (ed.). 2004a. *When States Fail: Causes and Consequences.* Princeton, N.J.: Princeton University Press.

———. 2004b. The Failure and Collapse of Nation-States. In *When States Fail: Causes and Consequences,* ed. Robert I. Rotberg. Princeton, N.J.: Princeton University Press.

Rousseau, David L., Christopher Gelpi, Dan Reiter, and Paul Huth. 1996. Assessing the Dyadic Nature of the Democratic Peace, 1918–88. *American Political Science Review* 90(3): 512–533.

Rubin, Barnett R. 2002. *The Fragmentation of Afghanistan.* New Haven, Conn.: Yale University Press.

———. 2007. Saving Afghanistan. *Foreign Affairs* 86(1): 57–78.

Rummel, R. J. 2003. *Power Kills: Democracy as a Method of Nonviolence.* New Brunswick, N.J.: Transaction.

Russett, Bruce, John R. Oneal, and David R. Davis. 1998. The Third Leg of the Kantian Tripod for Peace: International Organizations and Militarized Disputes, 1950–85. *International Organization* 52(3): 441–467.

Rustow, Dankwart A. 1970. Transitions to Democracy: Towards a Dynamic Model. *Comparative Politics* 3(2): 337–364.

Ryan, Bruce, and Neal C. Gross. 1943. The Diffusion of Hybrid Seed Corn in Two Iowa Communities. *Rural Sociology* 8: 15–24.

Ryle, Gilbert. 1949. *The Concept of Mind.* London: Hutchinson.

Sanctions: History Lessons. October 21, 2006. *Economist* 381(8500): 80.

Schelling, Thomas C. 1960. *The Strategy of Conflict.* New York: Oxford University Press.

———. 1978. *Micromotives and Macrobehavior.* New York: W.W. Norton.

Scheuer, Michael. 2003. *Through Our Enemies' Eyes: Osama Bin Laden, Radical Islam & the Future of America.* Washington, D.C.: Potamic Books.

———. 2005. *Imperial Hubris: Why the West Is Losing the War on Terror.* Washington, D.C.: Potomac Books.

Shepsle, Kenneth A. 1991. Discretion, Institutions and the Problem of Government Commitment. In *Social Theory for a Changing Society,* eds. Pierre Bourdieu and James S. Coleman. Boulder, Colo.: Westview Press.

Shin, Doh Chull. 1994. On the Third Wave of Democratization: A Synthesis and Evaluation of Recent Theory and Research. *World Politics* 47: 135–170.

Shivakumar, Sujai J. 2003. The Place of Indigenous Institutions in Constitutional Order. *Constitutional Political Economy* 14: 3–21.

Stephens, Joe, and David B. Ottaway. November 20, 2005. A Rebuilding Plan Full of Cracks. *The Washington Post,* A01.

Strobel, Warren P., and Jonathan S. Landay. 2004. Iraqi Exile Group May Have Violated Rules Barring It from Lobbying. *Knight Ridder Newspapers.* Available at www.realcities.com/mld/krwashington/news/special_packages/iraq/intelligence/11866148.htm.

Sutter, Daniel. 2000. The Transition from Authoritarian Rule: A Game Theoretic Approach. *Journal of Theoretical Politics* 12: 67–89.

Tannenhaus, Sam. May 9, 2003. Deputy Secretary Wolfowitz Interview with Sam Tannenhaus, *Vanity Fair.* Available at www.defenselink.mil/transcripts/2003/tr20030509-depsecdef0223.html.

Tavares, Jose, and Romain Wacziarg. 2001. How Democracy Affects Growth? *European Economic Review* 45: 1341–1378.

Telhami, Shibley. 2002. Understanding the Challenge. *The Middle East Journal* 56(1): 9–18.

Tocqueville, Alexis de. 1835/1839 [1969]. *Democracy in America,* Vols. 1 and 2, ed. J. P. Mayer, trans. George Lawrence. New York: Doubleday.

Trouillot, Michel-Rolph. 1990. *Haiti: State Against the Nation.* New York: Monthly Review Press.

———. 1997. A Social Contract for Whom? Haitian History and Haiti's Future. In *Haiti Renewed: Political and Economic Prospects,* ed. Robert I. Rotberg. Washington, D.C.: Brookings Institution Press.

Tsebelis, George. 1991. *Nested Games: Rational Choice in Comparative Politics.* Berkeley, Calif.: University of California Press.

Tullock, Gordon. 1965. *The Politics of Bureaucracy.* Washington, D.C.: Public Affairs Press.

———. 1985. Adam Smith and the Prisoners' Dilemma. *The Quarterly Journal of Economics* 100(5): 1073–1081.

Tyler, Patrick E. October 5, 2003. Three Wars Over Iraq: Staying the Course May Be the Hardest Battle. *New York Times,* Section 4, Column 1, Week in Review Desk, Pg. 1.

United States Government Accountability Office. July 2005. *Afghanistan Reconstruction: Despite Some Progress Deteroriating Security and Other Obstacles Continue*

to Threaten Achievement of U.S. Goals. Available at www.gao.gov/new.items/
d05742.pdf.

Van Rooy, Alison (ed.). 2000. *Civil Society and the Aid Industry.* London: Earthscan.

Van Rooy, Alison, and Mark Robinson. 2000. Out of the Ivory Tower: Civil Society
and the Aid System. In *Civil Society and the Aid Industry,* ed. Alison Van Rooy.
London: Earthscan.

von Hippel, Karin. 2000. *Democracy by Force.* Cambridge, Mass.: Cambridge University Press.

Wallich, Henry C. 1955. *Mainsprings of the German Revival.* New Haven, Conn.: Yale
University Press.

Wallsten, Scott, and Katrina Kosec. 2005. The Economic Costs of the Iraq War. *AEI
Brookings Working Paper 05-19.*

Weart, Spencer R. 2000. *Never at War: Why Democracies Will Not Fight One Another.*
New Haven, Conn.: Yale University Press.

Weingast, Barry. 1995. The Economic Role of Political Institutions: Market-Preserving
Federalism and Economic Development. *Journal of Law, Economics and Organization* 11(1): 1–31.

Weinstein, Brian, and Aaron Segal. 1984. *Haiti: Political Failures, Cultural Successes.*
New York: Praeger.

Wintrobe, Ronald. 1998. *The Political Economy of Dictatorship.* New York: Cambridge
University Press.

Zakaria, Fareed. August 13, 1995. Bigger Than the Family and Smaller Than the State: Are
Voluntary Groups What Makes Countries Work? *New York Times Book Review,* 1.

———. 2003. *The Future of Freedom: Illiberal Democracy at Home and Abroad.* New
York: W.W. Norton.

Ziemke, Earl F. 1975. *The U.S. Army in the Occupation of Germany 1944–1946.* Washington, D.C.: Center of Military History.

Zingales, Luigi. November 9, 2003. For Iraq, A Plan Worthy of Zambia, *The Washington Post,* B02.

INDEX

Acemoglu, Daron, 83–84, 198n4
Adams, John Quincy: on foreign policy, 188
Afghanistan, 3, 12, 15, 16, 20, 25, 31, 112, 136; art of association and nested games in, 161–64; and Bonn Agreement, 5, 159; constitution of, 5, 159; constraints on reconstruction in, 24, 50, 52, 65, 72, 159–60, 161–64, 165–67, 168–70; elections in, 24, 159, 166, 169; ethnic groups in, 164, 195n9; expectations in, 165–67; geography of, 164; insurgency in, 6, 158, 159–60; vs. Iraq, 5–6, 8, 10, 24, 28, 50, 52, 65, 98–100, 108–9, 158–59, 160, 165, 168–69, 170, 172; vs. Japan, 6, 10, 24, 117, 164; Karzai government, 159, 166–67; kinship ties in, 162; monetary aid to, 22, 24, 156, 168–70; national identity in, 65; negative unintended consequences in, 25, 105, 108–9, 111, 170; Northern Alliance in, 5, 195n9; opium production in, 160, 163, 166; problem of credible commitment in, 165–67; Shi'a Muslims in, 164; Soviet invasion of, 25, 105, 109, 111, 163–64; special interests regarding, 91; Sunni Muslims in, 164; Taliban

government of, 5, 13, 105, 159, 164, 166, 195n9; tribes qawms) in, 162–63; and war on terror, 98–99, 158, 170; vs. West Germany, 6, 24, 117, 164
Allawi, Ayad, 81
Allied Council for Japan, 201n3
al-Qaeda. See Qaeda, al-
alternatives to military occupation, 20, 70, 78, 113, 117; brute force, 173–78; free trade and commitment to non-intervention, 8, 28–29, 181–94, 208n10; peacekeeping, 178–81; Somalia's private governance, 107, 110, 153–54; state collapse, 156–57
Amanullah Khan, 162
analytic narrative method, 19–20
Anderson, Liam, 165
Anglo-Afghan wars, 161
Angola: monetary aid to, 156
Appiah, Kwame Anthony, 184–85
Aristide, Jean-Bertrand, 147, 152
Army Corp of Engineers, 97
art of association, 51–56; in Afghanistan, 161–64; in Haiti, 147–50; in Japan, 119–22, 125, 133; and nested games, 54–56, 62–64, 77, 119–22, 125, 127–29, 133, 138–43, 147–50, 161–65, 176–77, 178; and reconstruction, 54–56,

paying groups in, 138–39, 206n7; expectations in, 143–45; failure of reconstruction in, 14, 20, 22, 25, 28, 41, 46–47, 52, 55, 65, 69, 106–7, 111, 136–46, 151–54, 179, 180; famine in, 46, 137, 199n7, 205nn2,5; vs. Haiti, 117, 151–53, 155, 156–57; *heer* in, 139; vs. Japan, 10, 46–47, 55, 117, 144; mission creep in, 10, 137–38, 145–46, 179, 180; Mogadishu, 46, 137, 141, 145; monetary aid to, 144–45, 151, 155, 156; national identity in, 143; Polity IV scores for, 15, 17; private means of governance in, 107, 110, 153–54; and public choice theory, 145–46; Siad Barre regime, 25, 46, 137, 140–41, 142, 144–45; telecommunications industry in, 154; troop levels in, 22, 46; and United Nations, 137–38, 141, 142, 145–46, 153, 205n3

Somali National Movement (SNM), 141

Somali Patriotic Movement (SPM), 141

Somali Salvation Democratic Front (SSDF), 141

South Africa: sanctions against, 192

South Korea: American occupation of, 15, 17, 18; Polity IV scores for, 15, 17, 18; trade with United States, 185

South Vietnam: Polity IV scores for, 15, 17

Soviet Union, 162; and East Germany, 36, 37–38, 41, 80, 126, 132, 133, 205n54; invasion of Afghanistan, 25, 105, 109, 111, 163–64; reformers in, 67

Spanish-American War and Cuba, 1–3

special interest groups, 86, 89–96, 97, 103; domestic interest groups, 90–94, 126; foreign interest groups, 90–91, 94–96; and Iraq, 91–96

Stalin, Joseph, 36, 37–38, 41

Stansfield, Gareth, 165

Stephens, Joe, 168–69

successful reconstruction: in Austria, 18, 40; defined, 10–11; in Grenada, 16; and institutions, 8–9, 34–35; likelihood of, 16–17, 18–19, 26–27, 117, 192; in Panama, 14, 16, 18; and

Polity IV Index, 12–19, 41; as rapid, 40; relationship to art of association, 54–56, 77, 78, 119–22, 125, 127–29, 133; role of coordination around good conjectures in, 35–39, 40, 41–42, 44, 45–46, 47, 58, 62–65, 71–72; role of expectations in, 20, 73–76, 113–15, 122–23, 129; role of goals in, 31–32; role of incentives in, 8–9, 30, 31–32, 34–39, 40, 44, 83, 84; role of indigenous troops in, 70; role of monetary aid in, 22, 24; role of pre-existing conditions in, 32, 54–56, 64, 65, 77, 119–22, 123, 127–30, 133–35, 144, 201n61; role of troop levels in, 22, 24; and rules of the games, 8–9. *See also* Japan; West Germany

Sudan: monetary aid to, 156

Sutter, Daniel, 198n4

Syria, 13, 14, 172

Taiwan and trade with United States, 185

Telhami, Shibley, 168, 200n41

Teller Amendment, 2

Thacker, Strom C., 197n29

Tocqueville, Alexis de: on art of association, 51–52, 54–55, 62; *Democracy in America*, 32, 51–52, 199n15; on selfinterest, 51

transaction costs: and Coase theorem, 42–44, 48–50; and reconstruction, 42–44, 48–50, 53, 59–60, 61, 64, 82–83, 112, 120, 121, 132–33, 139–40, 143, 144, 150, 153–54, 167–68

troop levels, 12, 22, 24, 46, 48, 54, 78, 82, 88, 95, 176

Trouillot, Michel-Rolph, 151

Trujillo, Rafael Leónidas, 106

Truman, Harry S., 125

Tullock, Gordon, 202n26

unintended consequences, negative, 25–27, 83, 84, 117, 193; in Afghanistan, 25, 105, 108–9, 111, 170; as blowback, 26, 109, 171, 186, 198n52; and dynamics of intervention, 103–12; as external, 25–26, 107–9; as internal, 25, 106–7,